REDINGTON FIELD GUIDES

TO
BIOLOGICAL
INTERACTIONS

PLANTS IN WETLANDS

CHARLES B. REDINGTON, Ph.D.
SPRINGFIELD COLLEGE

DRAWINGS BY
PAMELA H. SEE

KENDALL/HUNT PUBLISHING COMPANY
4050 Westmark Drive   Dubuque, Iowa 52002

This edition has been printed on recycled paper.

For my wife Carolyn Snow-Redington
and my children Charles B., II and Laurel Hunt,
who share my love of the natural world.

Whatever befalls the earth befalls the sons and daughters of the earth. We did not weave the web of life; we are merely strands in it. Whatever humanity does to the web, it does to itself. Earth is precious to God, and to harm the earth is to heap contempt on its Creator.

- Attributed to Chief Seattle of the Duamish tribe

TABLE OF CONTENTS

PART 2. The BIOLOGICAL INTERACTIONS

Forward 1.

Many years ago a philosopher said, "All Nature is one." As all fields of science have continued their extraordinary development, particularly during the past century, the truth of this statement has become more and more prophetic. We now have so much interrelationship between scientific fields that many terms indicative of their closeness are commonplace in technical language: biogeochemistry, ethnobotany, astrophysics, and many others.

Although relationships between animals and plants have been observed undoubtedly since the periods of primitive human development, it has been through the centuries almost always treated as a curiosity or as an interesting aspect casually noted by zoologists and botanists in their writings.

There have, however, been notable exceptions. One need cite only the highly complex relationships between ants and plants and the example of certain insects anatomically structured to be able to fertilize only certain species of orchids through pseudocopulation with flowers.

This book is in many ways rather unique, by the mere fact there is no other one like it available. First, it is a field guide written and designed to consider biological interactions between plants and the full range of animal groups in wetlands generally east of the Mississippi River, mammals, plants, birds, reptiles, amphibians, insects, spiders, fish, and the community interactions of which they are a part. Secondly, at this time wetlands are occupying a very significant place in our growing preoccupation with environmental conservation and preservation of ecological niches. It shows in most cases the interdependency of living systems without which the individual members might not survive. As can be appreciated from the uses by man, which are mentioned for many species in the text, there is a type of interrelationship between some plants and mankind. Thirdly, the approach is biosystematic, concentrating on community dynamics, making it possible to include a surprising amount of information in an easy-to-use format. Fourthly, by including invertebrates and not only birds and mammals, the book deals with those organisms that constitute the vast majority of life on earth, and many of which who play important, often recondite, roles in the ecosystem.

All of these characteristics and others tend to make this volume of interest and estimable to a wide variety of users: laymen interested in nature; students in a number of fields of the natural sciences; teachers and professors; individuals in sundry occupations such as foresters, rangers, agriculturists, and especially environmental consultants.

"As a botanist who has devoted his professional life to work in the Amazon rain forests, I applaud the author of this book, realizing that while the flora and fauna of the north temperate region is much more limited in species of living organisms than the tropics, we often know less about the natural phenomena close to our homes than those in far off regions that often seem to be more glamorous. I predict that this book will have a long and useful life and will be appreciated by a wide audience."

Richard Evans Schultes, Ph.D., F.M.L.S.

Jeffrey Professor of Biology and Director, Harvard Botanical Museum(Emeritus)

Forward 2.

Dr. Redington's guide is elegant in its style and simple to use in its design. A great deal of information is packed into the pages without taking up more space than is needed.

It is the interactions between organisms and their environment that interests most of us, as it should, since we too interact every breathing minute with the same environment shared by all living things on the planet. By examining the interactions of plants and animals in ecological communities, we must necessarily ask ourselves what impact we have in the same places. The conclusions, thanks to Dr. Redington's book, is that we have a great impact on the planet and we should act more responsibly towards it.

Wetlands may be among the most endangered of all biological communities in America and nowhere more than in areas east of the Mississippi River where many fresh and saltwater marshes, kettle hole ponds, shrub swamps, vernal pools, brooks, streams, and rivers have been altered, piped, paved over, or otherwise rendered incapable of functioning. Saving what is left and restoring those that can be is an important endeavor for all citizens and the first step to doing this is understanding some of the complex interactions that occur in those species of plants and animals that make wetlands their home. Dr. Redington's book will help students, homeowners, conservationists, developers, and others better understand what is really at stake in these marvelous worlds.

Since life on this planet is dominated by insects, it is refreshing to see a natural history and conservation book that is not too heavily weighed in mammals and birds. Important as these vertebrates are, they are simply a part of a very complex set of interactions between them, other animals, plants, and the physical environment. Dr. Redington helps us to see the other inhabitants of ecosystems without judging who is more important- in fact subtly indicating that all species have an equal right to exist and interact with other members of their communities.

Thomas F. Tyning

Master Naturalist, Massachusetts Audubon Society

Preface

This is a field guide which in scope is unlike any other presently on the market. Most field guide are only on a particular group of organisms, such as for flowers, birds, insects, etc., which cover their identification, comments on range, and possibly something of their life history. This *Field Guide to Biological Interactions* will clearly, simply, and precisely communicate how a specific or "Keystone" plant interacts within its overall environment. It will show how each species reaches out in many directions to act upon or in turn to be acted upon by its community of mammals, other plants, birds, reptiles, amphibians, insects spiders, fish. There are also comments as to the overall community role and human/ economic importance of this plant. This volume is a field guide to biological interactions - PLANTS IN WETLANDS. A hypermedia version of this guide will be available in the near future and should serve as a powerful educational tool in class, lab, or field.

The book is organized into a very easily used format with two parts. Part 1 includes a "How to Use" section, keys to wetland communities (bogs, fresh marshes, salt marshes, wet meadows, shrub swamps, and tree swamps), and a brief narrative on each of these communities. An additional and unique aspect of this field guide in Part 1 which I feel makes it valuable is that it can involve the user, becoming "Interactive." In that there is so much more to learn, the "Interactive" concept creates a "Need to Know" which means that a person can help collect information on the Field Data Forms (found for each plant at the end of the guide) in the field for plants included in the guide but for which there may be little known. The user can then send their information to the author with proper documentation with possible inclusion of this information and personal recognition in subsequent editions. For those interested in using this field guide as a teaching tool, Part 1 also includes methods for determining "Habitat Value" and for delineating "Wetland Boundaries." However, the largest, most unique, and valuable aspect of this field guide is found in Part 2 entitled BIOLOGICAL INTERACTIONS. In this part, the user will find a simple and clear line drawing of a "Keystone" plant on the left facing page with the accompanying "Biological Interactions" on the right facing page organized in an approximate evolutionary sequence and labeled as shown. Here you will find a treasure trove of many details of how the plant relates to the world in which it lives. This book is actually three in one, a field guide, lab/field manual, and desk top reference.

With the current national interest in wetlands, I feel the guide is an invaluable repository of important information and concepts presented in a manner appealing to a very wide ranging audience. This book should be useful to grade, high, prep, college, and university level students, to teachers and professors (those who have the important job of exciting the urge to learn more about our natural world), researchers, environmental consultants working on wildlife habitat evaluations and environmental impact statements, conservation commission members charged with permit issuing, and those lay people with little or no formal training in ecology but who want to learn more of its mysteries.

I am honored and humbled that world renowned botanist and conservationist Dr. Richard Evans Schultes of Harvard University wrote a forward for this field guide. I am also grateful to Tom Tyning for his support and contributions throughout, including writing a forward.

I hope you enjoy using this with the same enthusiasm I had for writing it.

Acknowledgments

This field guide was written after nearly twenty-five years of teaching experience and nearly twenty years as an environmental consultant. The idea for the unique format of this guide came as a result of my fascination with the diversity of God's natural world. When I decided to consider writing this guide, I went to Dr. Richard Evans Schultes of Harvard University and Tom Tyning of Massachusetts Audubon for their reaction to the idea. Dr. Schultes honored me with his support and encouragement throughout my research and writing. Mr Tyning's infectious enthusiastic and constant support included several detailed reviews and edits of the manuscript and major contributions to the amphibian and reptile portion of this guide. My wife Carolyn gave great moral support as well as a gift of a computer to speed me along my journey. I valued the computer graphics input and research of Mr. Robert Speare of Audubon's Laughing Brook Education Center and Wildlife Sanctuary. Bob's computer artistry helped with the unique format of the INTERACTIONS section of this guide. Dr. John Burk of Smith College shared his knowledge, made the college herbarium available to the artist and reviewed some of the plant drawings. Special credit goes to Mrs. Ruth Segien and Mr. Richard Segien who beautifully prepared the camera ready interaction tables. Others I wish to thank who have contributed in various ways to this guide include Dr. David E. Fairbrothers of Rutgers University, Ms. Klara Dienes of the Smith College Young Science Library, Paul Goldstein of the University of Connecticut, Mr. Rusty Walton of Chilmark on Martha's Vineyard, Dr. Carlos Carranza and Randy Christensen of Baystate Environmental Consultants, Ms. Alice Mohrman and Mr. Gus Ben David of Felix Neck Wildlife Sanctuary on Martha's Vineyard, Mr Scott Jackson of Mass. Audubon and the University of Massachusetts, Mr. Bill Wilcox of the University of Massachusetts Extension Service, Mr. Ted Watt and Mr. Tom Chase of the Trustees of the Reservation, my doctoral mentor Dr. Joseph L. Peterson of Rutgers University, my colleagues Dr. Frank Torre and Dr. Joseph Berger of Springfield College for their encouragement and computer instruction, Dr. Robert C. Barkman of Springfield College for his support and "need to know," Mr. Bob Kudley of the Springfield College library, the staff at the Harvard libraries, The Massachusetts Audubon Laughing Brook Education Center and Wildlife Sanctuary, Chris Leahy, Director, Center for Biological Conservation of Massachusetts Audubon, the staff of the Wakeman Center of Martha's Vineyard, Joanne C. Norton of Hingham, MA, and Dr. Norman Vincent Peale who feels "enthusiasm makes the difference."

I would like to give a very special thanks to Smith College graduate, Ms. Pamela See of Northampton MA, for the excellent plant drawings which added immeasurably to this guide.

The final product is my responsibility. I ask you to consider the following:

"If you have remarked errors in me, your superior wisdom must pardon them. Who errs not while perambulating the domain of nature? Who can observe everything with accuracy? Correct me as a friend, and I as a friend will requite with kindness." -*Linnaeus*

Introduction

The Mercedes came to a stop on the sandplain grassland, a vegetative association many consider to be the rarest ecosystem in New England. The tires of the car rested heavily upon several Bird's-foot violets (*Viola pedata*), a Bearberry (*Arctostaphylos Uva-ursi*), and on several Sickle-leaved Golden Aster (*Chrysopsis falcata*), while its hot muffler scorched the flower of the Butterfly Weed (*Asclepias tuberosa*). As the land developers and their lawyers stepped out of the car, one kicked with disdain at some of the plants under foot and commented, "You want to save these weeds? They have no value!" It is clear, I thought to myself, that things gain value only by weight of peer authority. When I asked, they agreed that Picasso's works have value, that the gold of the Atocha shipwreck has value, and that their Mercedes had value, all of which are assigned worth by various peers including art curators, governments, and by owners of fancy cars. I explained that these various plants of the sandplain grassland have value too, as judged by such peers as Massachusetts Audubon, Harvard, Yale, Springfield College, and the Massachusetts Natural Heritage and Endangered Species Program. I proceeded to inform them and the jury visiting the site that the plants just kicked, crushed, and otherwise scorched were part of a unique assemblage of organisms without which there would be no sandplain grassland community. Quite simply for example, one of these plants, the Bird's-Foot violet, is the larval host or food plant of the state-listed threatened Regal Fritillary Butterfly, while the previously mentioned aster and butterfly weed serve as nectar sources for the adult stage. Without these and closely related plants, we have no butterfly and without the butterfly, the flowers have one less pollinator around to assure its reproductive success. I also pointed out that the destruction of the Bearberry would result in the loss of the primary hiding place of the Sandplain Tiger Beetle as it lies in wait for its prey to pass. This network of interdependency is quite important to the very survival of life on the sandplain grassland. From their behavior and commentary, it was quite clear to me that it is not often that someone looks at a plant in terms of its interrelationships to the scene (plant association) of which it is a part. Just as no one is an island, so is no plant an island - it gives and it takes from its environmental association.

As it is in the sandplain grassland, so it is in all vegetative communities including a wetland. For example, when a person visits a marsh and looks at a cattail, there is so very much to know about how this plant interacts with other organisms in its environment. The interactions may be the result of food, shelter, over-wintering sites, breeding areas, ecotonal edge, or migratory pathways to a variety of animal life. This, then, is my purpose: to show in a direct and simple manner how a given plant reaches out in many directions to interact within its wetland community of mammals, plants, birds, reptiles, amphibians, insects, spiders, fish, and humans and to comment on its economic and ecological importance.

For nearly twenty five years I have been teaching the biological and ecological sciences at the college level with this very approach- trying to show the interrelatedness of life. To me it was not enough simply to learn a plant or animal name. Rather, I had to look at it in the larger picture as to how it fit into the scheme of life. I also found students much more interested and receptive to learning if they knew, for instance, that a Cattail was not just a marsh plant but it was a food plant to the American Natives. It is also where the Cattail Moth spends its entire life cycle and is home not only to the Red-winged Blackbird but to the Swamp Sparrow and many other birds. The Cattail, in addition, is useful and necessary to a host of other animals including certain mammals, amphibians, reptiles, insects, and fish.

I have complemented my teaching with over 20 years as an environmental consultant, working with land developers, lawyers, conservation commissions, lay people, engineers, farmers, and non-profit organizations. Through these practical experiences, it became clear to me that our ENVIRONMENT IS AT RISK and that a responsible approach of balancing economic and ecological needs is paramount. In order to do this, everyone involved must have as much information at hand as possible when making decisions impacting upon our natural ecosystems. For example, we know that a proposed development which fragments a salt marsh into less than a 200 acre parcel will perhaps end up creating a resource area too small to support a nesting pair of Short-eared owls (*Asio flammeus*). This points out " the need to know" for informed decision making so that there is no further loss of this habitat.

This field guide is intended to serve the needs of anyone interested in better understanding the environment and looking at isolated elements of the land in a more holistic, interrelated way. Such people include teachers, who have the primary role in injecting a love of our natural systems in the young, researchers, environmental consultants, and those with little or no formal training in ecology but who just love natural associations and want them not to disappear.

A book of this type exposes the author's interests, limitations, impressions, and experiences. These are reflected in the types of vegetative communities chosen for study and the specific "Keystone" or common plants covered in the interactions. I have attempted to select vegetative associations hopefully well known to most, even to those who may have never taken a formal field course but might recognize them if they were standing in a swamp, bog, or forest. The plants selected, called KEYSTONE PLANTS, were those I considered to be among the most COMMONLY SEEN and most often associated with a particular wetland community. The major interactions of organisms are organized into those groups familiar to nearly everyone namely, mammals, higher plants, birds, reptiles, amphibians, insects, spiders, and fishes. The animals recorded herein are mostly those from my field experiences. There may be nesting sites other than those I observed or other beetles that eat a certain plant that someone else knows of, or another berry eaten by a mammal that does not appear on my list. This is by no means an exhaustive guide, and as such does not include all that can be seen by any stretch of the imagination. This guide is but a starter that reflects the experiences of myself and those of several other colleagues and acquaintances who have generously shared their secrets with me, for which I am thankful. I would further add that some of the animals such as moths and butterflies are what might be termed "facultative", that is, they are found in wetlands only because their hostplant is there and thus might be expected in any environment that such suitable plants exist. It is also to be noted that while some species of insects are species-specific in their host utilization, others are genus-specific (e.g. many herbivores associated with the genus *Carex* or *Salix)*. This latter condition is good in that it allows for you, the observer, to anticipate a great deal of interaction associated with some plants. It is also true that many of the animals noted herein are habitat specific, meaning they are generally expected to be found in wetlands and possibly associated with one or more of the KEYSTONE plant species. While this is a field guide and as such I have selected as many of the more common plants and animals to address, no attempt is made to eliminate the more obscure species, but rather to cover whatever was available to me. The fact remains that many so-called uncommon species are probably uncommon because we have been preoccupied with the obvious when the not-so-obvious may be the very brick and mortar of life.

To save species we must protect their habitat and understand their roles or interactions in it. The UNIQUE FEATURE OF THIS GUIDE, found in no other such volume, is that it brings together into one treatment key pieces of information on the INTERACTIONS of a given plant within its community of organisms. A tree guide, for instance, describes and identifies the tree and perhaps mentions something of its life history and use. Some guides may comment primarily upon the plant value as wildlife food or its economic importance. This is the first field guide which explores the MANIFOLD INTERRELATIONSHIPS of life forms. In this regard, as soon as a plant is identified, one can instantly determine many of its roles in the community setting based upon the information supplied in the BIOLOGICAL INTERACTION BOXES accompanying each.

GENERAL FORMAT OF THE FIELD GUIDE

This field guide series is organized around a key factor: the INTERACTIONS of KEYSTONE plants with other organisms within a given habitat. It is important to realize that the common plants found in this field guide tend to live in vegetative associations (habitats) best suited to their growing requirements. Furthermore, since habitats often merge one into another, there are cases where the same plant is listed in more than one of the communities covered in this book.

Part 1 of the book is devoted to;

(1) A QUICK START to the Interactions in Part 2.

(2) The use of the HABITAT KEY.

(3) HOW YOU CAN CONTRIBUTE to this field guide.

(4) How you can learn to EVALUATE A HABITAT.

(5) How to set approximate WETLAND BOUNDARIES.

(6) A brief NARRATIVE of the important elements of each wetland type.

It also includes a list of the KEYSTONE species commonly associated with each. In Part II, the reader finds the unique feature of this guide, a comprehensive explanation of the KEYSTONE plant and its INTERACTIONS within its community. Distributed throughout this part the reader will find short essays on a variety of topics relating to wetlands.

WHAT ARE BIOLOGICAL INTERACTIONS?

Webster's dictionary defines INTERACTIONS as "acting one upon the other; a mutual or reciprocal influence or action." Interactions, then, imply that there are "interactors" or participants in the action of interactions. In biological systems, it implies that one interactor (organism # l) is acted upon by another interactor (organism #2) in such a way that organism #2 is influenced by organism #1 and vice-versa. It is this process of INTERACTION which is the network of living systems, the connective tissue, so to speak, which holds life in ecological communities. An interaction might include a given species providing food, shelter, cover, or a breeding area for another species. As you read the interactions in Part 2 you will learn so many more. You may look at your world differently when you begin using this field guide and in the process hopefully learn how a given plant relates to the wetland world.

WHAT IS AN ECOLOGICAL COMMUNITY?

An ecological community can be considered an assemblage of plant and animal populations living and interacting together in their environment. Communities may be as small as a square meter-sized vernal pool, or as large as a thousand acre salt marsh.

WHAT ARE WETLANDS?

There is no specifically agreed upon definition of wetlands. However, most professionals working in this area would generally agree that wetlands are areas where water is the primary factor in determining the kinds of soils, plants, and animals to be found in them. Wetlands are characterized by one or more of the following four indicators: vegetation, topography, hydrology, and soils. Although vegetation is the primary emphasis of this guide, the brief explanation outlined below may be useful in understanding each of these indicators and their role in wetland determination.

l. VEGETATION - Wetland indicator plants are those species adapted to a watery regime including standing water and saturated soils. The U.S. Department of the Interior's Fish and Wildlife Service recognizes the following categories of wetland indicator plants based upon their relative frequency of being found in wetlands as indicated by their Wetland Indicator Status (WIS) - (Region 1 was used in this guide):

OBLIGATE (OBL) - Found in wetlands 99% of the time

FACULTATIVE WET (FACW) - Found in wetlands 67-99% of the time

FACULTATIVE (FAC) - Found in wetlands 34-66% of the time

FACULTATIVE UPLAND (FACU) - Found in wetlands 1-33% of the time

UPLAND (UP) - Found in wetlands less than 1% of the time

2. TOPOGRAPHY - (a term referring to the surface shape of the land) Wetlands usually lie in lowlands or depressions where the water table is at or near the surface; a variable criteria since some wetlands can be sloping.

3. HYDROLOGY - Wetlands are often characterized by noticeable water at or near the surface.

4. SOILS - Look for highly organic soils that appear mucky, peaty, and of varying dark colors. Such soils may also be clayey, sticky, and can be rolled in the hand; they are often gray in color and impermeable to water; such soils may have the smell of hydrogen sulfide.

When trying to locate wetland habitats to explore, you may want to obtain a map from one of the following sources:

U.S. Geological Survey Topographic Maps (scale 1:24,000); which are available at selected bookstores and other places such as sporting goods shops that show general wetland locations.

U.S. Fish and Wildlife Service National Wetland Inventory Maps (scale 1:24,000 and 1:25,000); available at the University of Massachusetts/Amherst Cartographic Information Research Service (phone 413-545-0359).

Town Wetland Maps which may be available from the conservation commissions or various state departments of Environmental Protection

Since the elements of soil, vegetation, and hydrology are common in the definition of wetlands in general, the wetland HABITAT KEY in this guide correlates with the U.S. Fish and Wildlife Service *Classification of Wetlands and Deep Water Habitats of the United States* (Cowardin et al, 1979) (see Appendix A). This correlation includes only that part of the Palustrine and Estuarine systems which deals with vegetated wetlands.

RANGE of USE

This field guide covers wetlands found generally east of the Mississippi River from the southern states to those on the northern border with Canada.

PART I

How To Use This Guide

How to Use This Guide in the Field

A. QUICK START TO INTERACTIONS FOUND IN PART II

1. Turn to Part II beginning on page 37. Leaf through the pages and simply compare the plant you are looking at to those diagrammed in the book . You will note that this section is divided into three (3) major plant life forms including TREES, SHRUBS, and HERBS, arranged alphabetically by common names.

2. If your plant is one of the KEYSTONE species and you find it in Part II, you are now ready to carry out your detective work with the help of this guide. On the right facing page (page opposite the line drawing) you will find a series of boxes labeled with one or more of the following: COMMUNITY INTERAC-TIONS, MAMMALS, PLANTS, BIRDS, REPTILES, AMPHIBIANS, SPIDERS, INSECTS, FISH, and HUMAN/ ECONOMIC USE. These boxes contain key information indicating how this plant interacts with species in each of these groups of organisms. These are interactions which may be readily "observed" or "expected to be observed." This latter comment, "expected to be observed," relates to the fact that on a given day you may actually observe the interactions noted if the correct seasonal conditions exist and if you are fortunate enough to be in the right place at the right time. However, if you do not actually observe the interactions noted, it means that you can still expect them to be observed at some other time when conditions are just right.

3. Now you can carefully begin to inspect the plant and its community, look-ing with the anticipation and excitement of a treasure hunter for a Mammal, Plant, Bird, Reptile, Amphibian, Insect, Spider, or Fish noted in the boxes. You will also learn interesting facts as to its value to humans and what role(s) it plays in the environment as well as facts about its life cycle and habit of growth. You may go back to the plant many times over many years and each time find one of the interactions not previously seen or to even discover a NEW one. In the end, it is my hope that you will come away from a field trip with a greater recognition and appreciation for the intricacies of community dynamics and that no plant or animal, including you, stands alone in the environment. I also hope you will be more sensitive to the potential impact of human intervention on these delicate biological interactions which, once disturbed, may be difficult to recreate if they do not perish forever.

B. KEY TO WETLAND COMMUNITIES (Habitats)

If you are interested in learning more about the habitat where you found the plant(s), this key will help.

This part of the guide organizes wetlands into discrete, commonly used categories including BOGS, SALT MARSHES, FRESH MARSHES, WET MEADOWS, SHRUB SWAMPS, and TREE SWAMPS.

This key will assist you in;

(1) Determining what wetland community your are in.

(2) Refer you to a page where you will find a brief chapter describing the community structure and function, and a list of the KEYSTONE plants covered in Part 2 (Biological Interactions).

You will note that the following key is DICHOTOMOUS, meaning that you have to make choices in each couplet (set of two). Looking at the key for example, the first number one (1) indicates Coastal/Seashore Lowlands found on page19, whereas the second number one (1) indicates Inland Lowlands. If you choose the second number one (1), you are in Inland Wetlands, and you now move to the couplet number two (2) in the key. If you choose the first number two(2), the area you are in or near is Treeless, possibly with short shrubs and sometimes near open water. Your next move is to choose between the first and second number three (3) of that couplet. If you decide upon the first number three (3), you have determined that this wetland is a BOG, characterized by a possible quaking moss-covered mat. Upon looking to the right side of the page opposite the word BOG, you are directed to a page. Here you will find a picture and a description of a bog from the standpoint of structure, function, ecology, and a list of KEYSTONE plants characteristic of this community. Simply look up in Part II the KEYSTONE plants listed under BOG and compare to your specimen. Upon proper identification, proceed with your investigation of the Biological Interactions indicated in the boxes in the manner explained in the "Quick Start" section above.

The Key to Wetland Communities

I. COASTAL/SEASHORE LOWLANDS   **Saltmarsh** pg.19
   Area directly affected by salt water and is intertidal

1. INLAND LOWLANDS
   Area affected by fresh water

   2. Treeless/possible short shrubs;area sometimes
       adjacent to open water

      3. Moss covered, possibly floating/quaking mat   **Bog** pg.11
          and could have low shrub cover

      3. Not moss covered floating/quaking mat

         4. Area flooded or at least covered by   **Fresh Marsh** pg.15
             at least 6"of water during the growing
             season and commonly dominated by
             cattails or other persistent herb

         4. Area not flooded or covered by 6" of   **Wet Meadow** pg.23
             water during growing season; soil
             saturated to surface or up to several
             inches of water during growing season;
             dominate plants are herbs

   2. Trees and Shrubs; area sometimes adjacent
       to open water

      5. Not tree-dominated, rather is shrub   **Shrub Swamp** pg. 27
          dominated possibly with saplings and
          may be flooded to a foot of water during
          growing season

      5. Tree-dominated, which are flooded by   **Tree Swamp** pg. 31
          up to a foot of water or saturated soil
          during growing season

5

C. YOU CAN CONTRIBUTE TO THIS FIELD GUIDE AND GAIN RECOGNITION

(AN INTERACTIVE APPROACH)

In designing this field guide series, I have used the concept that LIVING THINGS INTERACT AND AFFECT EACH OTHER. Through this I hope to create in the user of this guide a NEED TO KNOW and a desire to help find some answers to interactions where not much is presently known. This field guide will tell you a fair amount, but it will also let you know "what we don't know but more about what we need," I once assisted a professor at Rutgers University who came to lecture one day and said he was going to lecture on the things we DON'T know about photosynthesis. This approach had quite an impact on me at the time. I had accepted books and lectures at face value as the last word on a particular subject. It is obvious that this is not the case, and actually the more we know of a subject, the more we learn we do not know.

With these thoughts in mind, I would like to invite the user of this field guide to play an active role in helping to accumulate knowledge and to make a contribution to natural history and in turn be rewarded for it. This approach can serve to promote natural curiosity and incite the learning process of all who use this guide. Throughout the field guide you will find a " NEED TO KNOW" Interaction space with a given plant. This is where you might want to become involved. It is my hope you will want to adopt a plant (or plants) and start making observations, and as a naturalist would do, record all you observe. If you document a certain spider, insect, bird, mammal, reptile, or other animal associated with your plant, record what you learn in the manner suggested on the form entitled Field Data Form for this plant found at the back of the guide. Any properly documented information will be included in the next edition and will cite your name as the source of the information. Send your observations to the author, in care of the Bio/Chem Department, Springfield College, Springfield, MA 01109.

It is hoped that in this way we can develop a natural awareness of the intricacies of community dynamics by having people like yourself actually take on a custodial role of our environment in a very direct manner using this as an environmental education tool. You can learn natural history by being a naturalist in the great tradition of Muir, Linnaeus, and Thoreau. We know that there are many more important interactions - CAN YOU HELP DISCOVER THEM?

D. LEARN HOW TO EVALUATE THE IMPORTANCE OF WILDLIFE HABITAT

A potentially interesting and productive activity for anyone is to learn how to determine if a given environment is a valuable wildlife habitat. This activity can be carried out as a lab/field activity or even by you and your family on your next outing. Carefully read the following steps and follow them as explained in conducting your WILDLIFE HABITAT EVALUATION.

1. It is well established that habitat loss leads to wildlife loss.

2. We must be able to recognize good habitat and in turn work to preserve it so we can preserve wildlife.

3. This exercise is designed to help you gain a greater appreciation of what constitutes valuable wildlife habitat. By knowing what questions to raise you can predict the value of a given habitat and possibly work towards its preservation armed with the information you have assembled.

4. In evaluating habitats, I have selected several "resources" or "factors" which are considered by most to be characteristic of valuable habitat. Each "resource" is defined and assigned an "EcoValue" in the table (Habitat Evaluation Table) accompanying this activity. The total "EcoValue" can be calculated for several habitats and the scores compared. The one with the higher "Ecovalue" can be checked against the "Rating Key" at the bottom of the table to determine its overall relative value as wildlife habitat.

5. The "Resources"

I. STRUCTURAL "Resources"
(those that create physical structure in the environment)

A. VEGETATIVE LAYERS - typically there are four of these including GROUND COVER, SHRUBS, SUBCANOPY, AND CANOPY. Each layer provides habitat or "living" space for organisms. The more layers there are, the more diverse the habitat which in turn allows for a greater diversity of wildlife.

B. ECOTONES - Picture an area where there is a woodland at the edge of an open field. Ecotones are basically the transitional areas between two kinds of vegetative communities, in this case, forest and field. Because such areas are a mixture of vegetation from both vegetative communities, this increased habitat diversity leads to increased wildlife diversity in such areas. How many different ecotones can you spot in your study area?

C. WATER - Water is required by all forms of life. Its actual presence on a site enhances the habitat value by providing drinking water and water for breeding, egg laying, and rearing of young.

II. FUNCTIONAL "Resources" (those that are action oriented for wildlife)

    A. FOOD SOURCE
    B. SHELTER
    C. BREEDING/NESTING
    D. OVERWINTERING SITE
    E. MIGRATORY CORRIDOR

III. PROCEDURES (use the following Habitat Evaluation Table)

    A. Under the "Resource" column circle those structural and functional values observed in your habitat.

    B. Under the "Notes"column jot down anything noteworthy regarding each resource circled, e.g., of the kinds plants found, etc.

    C. Under the "EcoValue" column, enter "25 points" on the line opposite each item you circled.

    D. Add up all points for each habitat and calculate the percent for each (your total divided by the total possible number of points which is 350).

    E. Look at the "Rating Key" to determine the relative value of each habitat. Is it worth preserving?

HABITAT EVALUATION TABLE

Date: _____ Place: _____ Observer: _____

RESOURCE (circle)	NOTES	EcoValue(25 pts)*
I Structural Value		
A. Layers		
1. Ground Cover		_____
2. Shrub Layer		_____
3. Subcanopy		_____
4. Canopy		_____
B. Ecotones (circle a 1 for each seen)		
1. 1		_____
2. 1		_____
3. 1		_____
4. 1		_____
C. Water		
1. 1		_____
II. Functional Value (circle each one noted)		
A. Food		_____
B. Shelter		_____
C. Breeding/Nesting		_____
D. Overwintering		_____
E. Migratory		_____
	Total Score =	_____
	% (Total/350) =	

Rating Key: O=Outstanding= 90-100% H=High= 80-89% M=Moderate= 70-79% L=Low=60-69%
* "EcoValues" are arbitrary linear numbers

E. WETLAND DELINEATION
(where is the wetland boundary?)

The following "vegetative inventory" method is a very reliable yet simple way to decide if a wetland boundary has been properly established in the field, usually denoted by colored flags tied to vegetation:

1. Stand at the "flagged" boundary and look uphill and away from the wetland

2. Now move 10' away from the flags into the upland portion (outside the flagged area), establish a center or reference point and then record the following:

   a.) Tree types in a 30' radius from the center of your observation point

   b.) Shrub types in a 15' radius from the center of your observation point

   c.) Herb types in a 3' radius from the center of your observation point

3. Separate plants (trees, shrubs, herbs) into wetland and upland types and then calculate the percentage of wetland plants (number of wetland plants divided by the total number of plants found = percent wetland plants).

4. If the average percentage value for the area is less than 50% of the species, the flags were more than likely properly placed. In many states the generally accepted rule is that if more than 50% of the plants are wetland types, it is a wetland. This does not correspond, however, to the Army Corps of Engineers method which requires wet vegetation, wet soil types, and a wet hydrology together, nor to states like Connecticut which use soils as the criterion for delineation. This method is approximate but will allow you to be reasonably confident in your observations.

CHAPTER 1

BOGS

My introduction to bogs started one evening in 1963 at the University of Michigan Biological Station. At dinner a discussion ensued regarding our field trip next day. As we talked, my mind began conjuring up images of fog shrouded moors right out of Bronte's *Wuthering Heights*. What is more, I had heard that people mysteriously disappear in such places and where the fully preserved remains of Iron Age humans, some over 2000 years old, had been found by people digging out the peat moss for fuel. The well-preserved specimens are possible because the very acid conditions of such wetlands do not support growth of decomposer bacteria to any extent. Needless to say, when we arrived at the bog the next morning, it was with some trepidation that I stepped out onto the carpet of sphagnum moss. As I slowly walked on the mat with my feet sinking deeply into the soggy moss, I felt for sure that I might break through and vanish only to be discovered thousands of years later preserved complete with unshaven face. I began to notice that the sphagnum mat would quiver with each step taken which sent ripples out across the mat as waves on water. I soon learned that this was a "quaking" bog which consisted of a mat of sphagnum moss literally floating over the water. I was eventually put at ease by our professor when told that although not all bogs are floating, this quaking mat where we walked was perhaps 20-30 feet thick and not at all likely to swallow me whole. The class proceeded to explore the unusual plant and animal life of the bog, ever mindful of the quaking, shuddering, floating mat upon which we so gingerly treaded. To this day, as I take students onto the bogs, they too proceed with a tinge of excitement for the images created in their minds through stories told them.

STRUCTURE, FUNCTION, and GENERAL ECOLOGY of BOGS

A bog, as defined in this guide, is easily recognized as an isolated, usually round to oval area most likely covered by sphagnum moss that is saturated because of the high water table. *The Classification of Wetlands and Deepwater Habitats of the United States* (Cowardin et al, United States Fish and Wildlife Service) identifies bogs as part of the Palustrine System of the Moss-Lichen Wetland Class and the Moss Subclass with sphagnum moss as the dominance class. In the northeast, bogs are typically found in a basin or "kettle hole" left behind by the retreating glaciers of the pleistocene. Huge chunks of ice eventually melted to become the first source of water for the immediate area. These basins or kettle holes are often characterized by having no obvious channels leading into them and thus lack any appreciable surface inflow or outflow of water. Bogs generally obtain their water and nutrients through precipitation and groundwater and are therefore called OMBROTROPHIC (rain-feeding). Bogs typically prevail in areas where precipitation exceeds evaporation. They are primarily found in the glaciated areas of northern states, in the Great Lakes region, New England, and Canada. In New England, some of the more northerly bogs are forested , characterized by a well developed growth of Black Spruce on or around the mat. In southern and coastal areas, Atlantic White-cedar may invade the bogs and be interspersed with the Black Spruce and Red Maple. Often the granitic bedrock of a region imparts to a bog a very nutrient deficient environment. The low nutrient conditions are reflective of a community of plants and animals specially adapted to such harsh conditions. Nitrogen, phosphorous, and potassium are key minerals for successful plant growth that are in low supply in the bog. Many bog plants have evolved strategies to persist in such nutrient-poor environments.The Ice Age Cotton-grass solved the low nutrient problem by requiring very low amounts of mineral for its growth and development. Others like sundews and bladderworts have become carnivorous to a degree by trapping insects and through partial digestion recovering minerals vital for growth. Still others, such as Sweet Gale, supplement their supply of nitrogen through nitrogen fixation, whereby gaseous nitrogen is converted into a mineral form by bacteria residing in nodules on their roots. Because of the overall low nutrient supplies, bogs are not high producers of energy by plants. The low productivity of energy and the relatively low diversity of plant life has led to a generally low diversity of animal life in bogs. Furthermore, since their is little or no surface flow, there is no aeration, resulting in low oxygen levels in the bog water. The lack of oxygen slows decomposition that leads to a build up of organic matter (peat moss) with much of the nutrients still trapped in the dead tissues. These partially decomposed materials act as organic acids contributing to the acid nature of bog waters. In addition, the physiology of the bog plants creates hydrogen ions which further acidifies the bog waters. Bogs are interesting because they are rare , have some of the most unusual plants known adapted to acidic and nutrient poor substrate conditions, and do function as wetlands with values worthy of protection.

As you begin to study the plants of the bogs and their biological interactions, it will be clear that they have important wildlife value. In times of extremely high precipitation, bogs can function to control flooding and protect against storm water damage, especially if they are near any streams, ponds, and lakes which overflow their banks. Bog acidity and low nutrient status do not make them ideal candidates for the eventual invasion by upland species less tolerant of these conditions. In fact, bogs are fairly stable ecosystems resistant to change even under conditions of extreme wetness or dryness. Under drier circumstances, the mat supports more of a forested bog community, whereas when water levels increase, they return to a more open or slightly shrubby community. The mere fact that many bogs still exist as remnants of the last Ice Age that ended here about 12,000 years ago, serve as testimony to their stability.

KEYSTONE (Common) Bog Plants

TREES

Atlantic White Cedar	*Chamaecyparis thyoides* (L.) BSP
Larch or Tamarack	*Larix laricina* (Duroi) K. Koch
Black Spruce	*Picea mariana* (Miller) BSP
Red Maple	*Acer rubrum* L.

SHRUBS

Leatherleaf	*Chamaedaphne calyculata* L.
Sheep Laurel	*Kalmia angustifolia* L.
Sweet Gale	*Myrica gale* L.
American Cranberry	*Vaccinium macrocarpon* Aiton
Bog Rosemary	*Andromeda glaucophylla* Link
Labrador Tea	*Ledum groenlandicum* Oeder
Bog Laurel	*Kalmia polifolia* Wangenh

HERBS

Sphagnum Moss	*Sphagnum palustre* and *S. rubrum*
Pitcher Plant	*Sarracenia purpurea* L.
Sundew	*Drosera rotundifolia* L.
Rose Pogonia	*Pogonia ophioglossoides* (L.) Ker Gawler
Swamp-pink	*Arethusa bulbosa* L.
Cotton-grass	*Eriophorum virginicum* L.
Bladderwort	*Utricularia vulgaris* L.

13

Other Plants of Bogs

There are other plants that may be encountered in Bogs, such as those listed below, and that may or may not be covered in the interactions section.

TREES

Tupelo   *Nyssa sylvatica* Marshall

SHRUBS

Highbush Blueberry   *Vaccinium corymbosum* L.

Poison Sumac   *Rhus vernix* (L.) Kuntze

White Swamp Azalea   *Rhododendron viscosum* (L.) Torr.

Water Willow   *Decodon verticillatus* (L.) Elliott

Rhodora Azalea   *Rhododendron canadense* (L.) Torr.

HERBS

Cinnamon Fern   *Osmunda cinnamomea* L.

Jack-in-the-pulpit   *Arisaema triphyllum* (L.) Schott

CHAPTER 2

FRESH MARSH

One of my fondest remembrances of fresh water marshes takes me back to my Aquatic Vascular Plant course with Dr. Edward Voss of the University of Michigan Biological Station. There we were four row boats with Dr. Voss in the lead as we slowly made our way through a patch of water-lilies so thick it seemed one could walk upon them. Dr. Voss had the habit of standing at the front of the boat scanning the waters ahead for our next plant treasure. Suddenly I heard a yell, "There it is," followed by a loud splash. To my utter amazement, Dr. Voss had gotten so excited with his find (probably a pondweed, plants of which he seemed especially fond) that he could not wait for his rowing crew to get there. Instead, he had leapt out of the boat into the water and had begun half swimming, half walking towards the plant. The only right thing to do at the time seemed to be to join him. With that thought in mind, I found myself jumping out of the boat. As I touched bottom, the soft muck gave way under foot and I began to sink. The thought crossed my mind that I might disappear forever. Eventually I did stop sinking and started to move my feet in the direction of Dr. Voss. I have never forgotten how I got so totally "immersed" in the subject of marshes and expect my students to follow me into the wetlands with selfsame dedication and enthusiasm.

STRUCTURE, FUNCTION, and GENERAL
ECOLOGY of FRESH MARSHES

Marshes are recognized as the wettest vegetated wetlands that are typically dominated by soft-stemmed (herbaceous) plants. Marshes are generally formed

15

in a depression that is capable of holding water long enough to favor the establishment of hydrophytic (water-loving) vegetation. Usually these depressions are lined with soft highly organic muck or clay that helps retain the water. The water regime of a marsh is usually an open system, whereby streams of varying size bring water in and let it out. This system works best when the flooded area is large and the inflow/outflow is small. Other sources of water for a marsh include run-off from nearby slopes, rain, snow, and ground water. Marshes can form along streams, ponds, and lakes where there might be a depression. The water depth may vary from several inches to 5-6 feet that could result in shallow and deep marshes respectively. Shallow marshes are characterized by a water depth which normally does not exceed a foot during the growing season. A shallow marsh is dominated by emergents, which are plants with their roots and lower stems submerged and with their upper portions out of the water. Examples of these types of plants include cattails, sedges, arrowheads, and rushes. Deep marshes are those that have water levels reaching 5-6 feet during the growing season and unlike many shallow marshes, tend to remain permanently flooded. Deep marshes may be characterized by open water which is interspersed with floating vegetation, such as pondweeds and water-lilies along with many totally submerged plants. Deep marshes frequently have the same emergents along their shallow edges as those found in shallow marshes. *The Classification of Wetlands and Deepwater Habitats of the United States* (Cowardin, et al) recognizes many marshes as the Palustrine System of the Emergent Class and of the Persistent (emergent) Subclass with a possible cattail Dominance Type or Nonpersistent with a wild rice or arrowhead Dominance Type.

In that marshes are hydrologically open systems, inflowing water laden with nitrogen, phosphorous, and oxygen result in enrichment of the marsh basin. The high oxygen levels of such waters hasten the breakdown of organics, a condition preventing the accumulation of organic acids which create the acid conditions typical of bog waters. As a result of the high nutrient levels, marshes are among the highest energy producing ecosystems on earth. This claim is supported by the vast numbers of waterfowl that depend upon marshes for food and cover. There are literally tens of millions of migrating birds that find life support in the marshes along their flyways. Marshes are also characterized by some of the greatest plant diversity of all wetland systems. This vegetative diversity leads to tremendous animal diversity, as we shall see in the interactions section of the guide.

Marshes are extremely valuable wetland communities and as such are worthy of our understanding, protection, and preservation. Overall, marshes function in one or more of the following ways: they are potential sources of public or private water supply, many serve as sources for ground water recharging, they can prevent pollution through water filtration, some act as catch basins to control flooding and in turn reduce storm damage, and many serve as extremely valuable wildlife habitat.

KEYSTONE (Common) Fresh Marsh Plants

SHRUBS

Swamp Loosestrife	*Decodon verticillatus* (L.) Elliott
Buttonbush	*Cephalanthus occidentalis* L.
Leatherleaf	*Chamaedaphne calyculata* L.
Sweet Gale	*Myrica gale* L.
Meadowsweet	*Spirea alba* var. *latifolia* (Aiton) Dippel

HERBS

Common Cattail	*Typha latifolia* L.
Bur-reed	*Sparganium americanum* Nutt.
Arrowhead	*Sagittaria latifolia* Willd.
Pickerelweed	*Pontederia cordata* L.
Tussock Sedge	*Carex stricta* Lam.
Wool-grass	*Scirpus cyperinus* (L.) Kunth
Soft Rush	*Juncus effusus* L.
Spatterdock	*Nuphar variegatum* Durand
Water or Pond Lily	*Nymphaea odorata* Aiton
Wild Rice	*Zizania aquatica* L.
Common Reed Grass	*Phragmites australis* (Cav.)Trin.
Purple Loosestrife	*Lythrum salicaria* L.
Duckweed	*Lemna sp.* L.
Bulrush	*Scirpus atrovirens* Willd.
Umbrella Sedge	*Cyperus strigosus* L.
Water Smartweed	*Polygonum punctatum* Elliott
Marsh Marigold	*Caltha palustris* L.
Rose Mallow	*Hibiscus moscheutos* L.
Water Hemlock	*Cicuta maculata* L.
Blue Vervain	*Verbena hastata* L.
Narrow-leaved Cattail	*Typha angustifolia* L.
Watercress	*Rorippa nasturtium-aquaticum* (L.) Hayek
Sweet Flag	*Acorus calamus* L.
Swamp Candles	*Lysimachia terrestris* (L.) BSP
Rice-Cutgrass	*Leersia oryzoides* (L.) Swartz

Other Plants of the Fresh Marsh

There are other plants that may be encountered in Fresh Marshes, such as those listed below, and which may or may not be covered in the interactions section.

HERBS

Reed-canary Grass	*Phalaris arundinacea* L.
Arrow-arum	*Peltandra virginica* (L.) Schott & Endl.
Blue Flag	*Iris versicolor* L.
Purple Joe-pye-weed	*Eupatorium purpureum* L.
Boneset	*Eupatorium perfoliatum* L.
Jewelweed	*Impatiens capensis* Meerb.
Soft-stem Bulrush	*Scirpus validus* Vahl.
Spike-rush	*Eleocharis obtusa* Willd.
Three-square Bulrush	*Scirpus americanus* Pers.
Three-way Sedge	*Dulichium arundinaceum* (L.)Britton.
Sensitive Fern	*Onoclea sensibilis* L.
Marsh Fern	*Dryopteris thelypteris* (L.) Gray
Water-plantain	*Alisma subcordatum* Raf.
Steeplebush Spirea	*Spirea tomentosa* L.
Grass-leaved Goldenrod	*Euthamia graminifolia* (L.) Nutt.
Skunk Cabbage	*Symplocarpus foetidus* (L.) Nutt.
Wild Calla	*Calla palustris* L.
Freshwater Cord Grass	*Spartina pectinata* Link
Arrow-leaved Tearthumb	*Polygonum saggitatum* L.

CHAPTER 3

SALT MARSH

I grew up near Lake Erie in Ohio. Having explored the wetlands around this as well as Lakes Michigan, Ontario, and the greatest of all, Superior, I felt little else could compare. During this time of my life I recall my fascination with an alluring song quite popular about old Cape Cod Bay. I think this song began to awaken my more primitive side drawing me towards the sea of the origin of life on earth. I did not get to the sea until 1964 while driving south out of New York City towards Rutgers University in New Brunswick, New Jersey, where I was to enroll as a graduate student. On this drive my eyes fell upon broad expanses of meadows which at first made me a little homesick for the corn and wheat fields of Ohio. I soon learned that these were salt marshes. I was impressed with the rather uniform and neat appearance of these marshes. Little did I realize at the time that this seeming monotony would, upon closer examination, turn out to be a dynamic pattern of vegetative zones, animal life, and nutrient cycling that could result in one of the most productive communities on earth. More than 2/3 of the fin fish and shell fish (oysters, crabs, and shrimp) spend part of their lives in salt marshes. They are also home to phytoplankton, including diatoms, dinoflagellates, other algae, and the larval stages of barnacles.

On August 19, 1991, Hurricane Bob crashed into the New England coast. I watched the 10-12 foot waves tear up a road, crack a sea wall, and rip trees out of the ground. As the energy of these large waves dissipated, the flood waters moved out over the salt marsh near where I was watching the storm. This marsh went to work absorbing great quantities of water which saved the nearby uplands from the damage of flooding. Within hours of the storm the salt marsh had released its flood waters with the outgoing tide, the sea ducks and swans had returned to the narrow channels and open water, and its grasses continued to wave in the breezes. I was indeed impressed with the resiliency of this salt marsh and how it had served to calm the onslaught of a hurricane. I still jog by Farm Pond and this salt marsh and consider a sunset across its domaine one of the most beautiful of experiences.

STRUCTURE, FUNCTION, AND ECOLOGY of SALT MARSHES

Salt marshes are open systems , in which water moves in and out with the tides. They fill in at a rate of about 1 inch per year due to the fine sediments brought in by these tides that settles out in the cord grasses. They are delicate systems to the extent that direct wave action can destroy them. For this reason, salt marshes do not develop along exposed high energy shores but rather in lagoons and bays behind the protection of a barrier beach. These are areas where the water is shallow enough and the land flat enough to allow for the build up of sediments brought in by the tides or from rivers and streams which end in bays. Salt marshes are not found as often in more northerly regions (e.g., Maine). This is attributable in large part to the hard crystalline rock and steep topography asso- ciated with a drowned Ria coast. Further contributing to a poor environment for salt marsh development in these areas is the fact that the rocks do not weath- er readily to form the required fine nutrient-rich sediments and mud required for the marsh substrate. Salt marshes are in a constant state of change. They can be destroyed by being buried in the sand carried by waves from an ocean storm (i.e., hurricanes) or sediments carried downstream after storm erosion. Salt marshes can disappear if coastal processes from wind, waves, and storm activity result in their being submerged too long in seawater. Salt marshes can even become fresh water marshes and swamps if the hydrology upstream is changed, a condition resulting in increased dilution of the salt content of the water below that required for salt marsh plant and animal life.

Exploring such a marsh is quite difficult on foot because one gets easily mired down in the mud substrate so typical of these communities. For this reason, a salt marsh is best viewed at a distance with binoculars so as to avoid this prob- lem and to not disturb the resident life. The more serious student of these envi- rons may study marsh life from a canoe or other small nonpowered boat by qui- etly moving up and down the channels. This makes for the best exploring of the salt marsh because you can often get quite close to animals without disturbing their tranquility. Whether on foot or in a boat, if you begin near the back edge of a salt marsh and look towards the sea, distinct zones of vegetation prevail. Up to 7 feet tall, *Spartina alterniflora* (Saltmarsh Cordgrass) is farthest from you and closest to the water. This plant is tolerant of twice per day (diurnal) flooding and can also withstand total inundation for short periods. Behind this (and closer to you) in a slightly higher and drier portion of the salt marsh you find *S. patens* (Saltmeadow Cordgrass) which is shorter than *S. alterniflora* and less tolerant of tidal flooding. A third zone emerges at the back edge of the marsh where the terrain is even higher and where a variety of other plants begin to appear, including *Solidago sempervirens* (Seaside Goldenrod) and *Iva frutescens* (Marsh Elder). The plants of this region are tolerant of the very high levels of salt which often concentrate here because of the constant evaporation of surface water and the resultant build up of residual salt.

The Classification of Wetlands and Deepwater Habitats of the U.S. (Cowardin, et al) recognizes salt marshes as the Estuarine System of the Intertidal Subsystem of the Emergent Class and Persistent Subclass with a *Spartina* dominance type. Salt marshes are among the world's most productive communities, and exceed all others including agricultural systems and second perhaps only to the tropical rainforests in their yield of food energy. This high productivity, which can approach over 200 pounds of fats, carbohydrates, and proteins per acre per day, is the result of a fascinating array of three food producing units which include the marsh grasses, the algae within the mud, and the phytoplankton found in the tidal creeks. The eventual decomposition of the cordgrasses nourishes the waters of the estuaries and bays and in turn the entire food chain from decomposer bacteria and algae to invertebrates, shellfish, fish, birds, and mammals (including you). To the casual observer, these things tend to go unnoticed because they occur out of sight in mud, underwater, and involve microscopic creatures. It is interesting to note that the characteristic rotten egg smell usually emanating from a salt marsh especially at low tide is a combination of sulfur and methane gases. These gases are by-products of anaerobic (without air) nitrogen-reducing bacteria, methane-generating bacteria, and sulfur-reducing bacteria, all of which are working to decompose the dead plant and animal life of the marsh.

In addition to food production, salt marshes perform many other important wetland functions including but not limited to the following: protection of shellfish and fisheries, flood control, storm damage prevention, wildlife habitat where they provide cover, nesting sites, food, as well as recreation, and education. Human activity including bulldozing and dredging can destroy a salt marsh in a matter of weeks which is estimated to take a thousand or more years to produce. It is quite evident that salt marshes are valuable ecosystems and deserve our utmost stewardship and understanding.

KEYSTONE (Common) Salt Marsh Plants

SHRUBS

Sweet Gale	*Myrica gale* L.
Marsh Elder	*Iva frutescens* L.
Rugosa Rose	*Rosa rugosa* Thunb.
Poison Ivy	*Toxicodendron radicans* (L.) Kuntze

HERBS

Saltmarsh Cordgrass	*Spartina alterniflora* Loisel
Saltmeadow Cordgrass	*Spartina patens* (Aiton) Muhl.
Seaside Goldenrod	*Solidago sempervirens* L.
Common Glasswort	*Salicornia europaea* L.
Common Reed Grass	*Phragmites australis* (Cav.) Trin.
Salt Marsh Bulrush	*Scirpus robustus* Pursh
Purple Loosestrife	*Lythrum salicaria* L.
Rose Mallow	*Hibiscus moscheutos* L.
Blue Flag	*Iris versicolor* L.
Narrow-leaved Cattail	*Typha angustifolia* L.
Sea Lavender	*Limonium carolinianum* (Walter) Britton

Other Plants of Salt Marshes

There are other plants that may be encountered in salt marshes, such as those listed below, and that may or may not be covered in the interactions section.

SHRUBS

Grounsel Tree	*Baccharis halimifolia* L.

HERBS

Bog Cordgrass	*Spartina cynosuroides* (L.) Roth
Sea Lavender	*Limonium carolinianum* (Walter) Britton
Saltmarsh Spike	*RushEleocharis albida* Torr.
Saltmarsh Sedge	*Carex paleacea* Wahlenb.
Saltmarsh Aster	*Aster tenuifolius* L.
Beaked Spike Rush	*Eleocharis rostellata* (Torr.) Torr.
Great Soft-stemmed Bulrush	*Scirpus validus* Vahl.
Marsh Mallow	*Althea officinalis* L.
Switchgrass	*Panicum virgatum* L.
Goosefoot	*Chenopodium album* L.
Japanese Fleece Flower	*Polygonum cuspidata* Sieb.& Zucc.
Curled Dock	*Rumex crispus* L
Salt-marsh Fleabane	*Pluchea purpurascens* (Swartz) DC.
Spike Grass	*Distichlis spicata* (L.)Greene
Black Grass	*Juncus gerardi* Loisel
Orach	*Atriplex patula* L.

CHAPTER 4
WET MEADOW

A great place to find a wet meadow is on a farm in a low lying field often near a pond or stream. At first glance, it probably looks like any country meadow, resplendent with grasses and wildflowers nodding in the breeze. Most people have difficulty believing that a given meadow might actually be a wetland . Yet, when armed with a modest amount of information about the types of plants associated with these areas,you soon are aware that indeed there are such wetlands. I remember a most vivid and interesting situation, one I often refer to as the case of the "now you see it, now you don't and then again it's back" wetlands. I was asked to investigate a piece of land and render such an opinion. When I first observed it from the car window it looked like an overgrown field. In fact, another environmentalist with me commented that he felt it was obviously not a wetland. However, as soon as I stepped onto this land my boots sunk several inches through the surface into the soggy wet soil. There we stood, amidst a mixture of cosmopolitan field herbs, such as wild carrot, purple vetch, various clovers, chicory, and others not strongly associated with wetlands. My companion, notwithstanding the soggy soils , was quick to suggest that these plants supported his contention that this was an upland vegetative community. However, a closer look revealed a more complex vegetative mix that included such wetland indicator species as irises, water loving grasses, some small cattails, and a number of rushes and sedges. After an analysis of the entire vegetative community, I concluded that this was indeed a wet meadow. It is not always a very popular decision when one locates a wetland where to many there is not supposed to be one. If someone is interested in developing such wetlands, these wetlands often seem to disappear beneath the blades of a dozer or at the edge of a plow. In the present instance, plans were made to construct a building on the the site the following spring. Quite illegally and unknown to me at the time, the land was cleared. It laid devoid of life through the fall and winter as construction plans were drawn up. Nature had other plans however, and as spring approached the land flushed out in a carpet of small green seedlings. Within weeks the plants had begun to mature making their identity clear. They were the same wetland plants I had recognized a year before. The wetland had returned because apparently the correct soil water conditions prevailed for the seeds, rhizomes, and rootstocks of water loving plants. Fortunately, the conservation commission became aware of the wetland in time to save it from the intended development.

STRUCTURE, FUNCTION, AND ECOLOGY of WET MEADOWS

Herbaceous,wet meadows are primarily considered dry marshes because, unlike marshes that have standing water, their surface is dry in summer. Like marshes, wet meadows have an open system, getting a constant supply of water from springs, high ground water, and run-off from adjacent slopes. Such conditions keep the water at or near the surface for only a portion of the growing season. These circumstances also result in drier soils with higher oxygen levels than those found in a marsh. Generally, the soils of wet meadows are not as acid as those of a marsh which results in greater nutrient availability, a higher microbial population, and nitrogen fixation. All of these conditions favor higher soil fertility, more rapid nutrient cycling, and ultimately a different plant community than that found in the marsh. While it is true that some wet meadows remain as such for years, others lose their sun-loving plants to the encroachment of woody shrubs. For this reason, wet meadows are commonly thought of as transitional vegetative communities between marsh and swamp.

The Classification of Wetlands and Deepwater Habitats of the U.S. (Cowardin, et al) classifies wet meadows as the Palustrine System of the Emergent Class with a Non-persistent Subclass and with grasses and broad-leaved plants as the dominance types. Wet meadows are important wetlands and are worthy of our protection and understanding. Some wet meadows may function as a source of groundwater recharge for public and private water supplies and, in addition, may serve to control flooding, filter pollutants, and provide high quality wildlife habitat.

KEYSTONE (Common) Wet Meadow Plants

SHRUBS

Meadowsweet	*Spirea alba var. latifolia* (Aiton) Dippel

HERBS

Soft Rush	*Juncus effusus* L.
Sensitive Fern	*Onoclea sensibilis* L.
Marsh Fern	*Dryopteris thelypteris* (L.) Gray
Blue Vervain	*Verbena hastata* L.
Blue Flag	*Iris versicolor* L.
Reed-canary Grass	*Phalaris arundinacea* L.
Spotted Joe-pye-weed	*Eupatorium maculatum* L.
Boneset	*Eupatorium perfoliatum* L.
Fowl-meadow Grass	*Poa palustris* L.
Tussock Sedge	*Carex stricta* Lam.
Wool-grass	*Scirpus cyperinus* (L.) Kunth
Wild Rice	*Zizania aquatica* L.
Water-hemlock	*Cicuta maculata* L.
Stick-tight	*Bidens connata* Muhl.
Purple Loosestrife	*Lythrum salicaria* L.
Turtlehead	*Chelone glabra* L.
Grass-leaved Goldenrod	*Euthamia graminifolia* (L.) Nutt.
Curled Dock	*Rumex crispus* L.
Cleavers Bedstraw	*Galium palustre* L.
Northern White Violet	*Viola macloskeyi* F. Lloyd var. *pallens* (Banks) C.L. Hitchc.
Panic-grass	*Panicum rigidulum* Nees.

Other Plants of Wet Meadows

There are other plants that may be encountered in Wet Meadows, such as those listed below, and that may or may not be covered in the interactions section.

SHRUBS

Swamp Loosestrife	*Decodon verticillatus* (L.) Elliott
Poison Ivy	*Toxicodendron radicans* (L.) Kuntze

Continued next page

SHRUBS *(continued)*

Swamp Rose	*Rosa palustris* Marshall
Buttonbush	*Cephalanthus occidentalis* L.
Winterberry	*Ilex verticillatus* (L.) A. Gray
Highbush Blueberry	*Vaccinium corymbosum* L.
Swamp Azalea	*Rhododendron viscosum* (L.) Torr.
Steeplebush	*Spiraea tomentosa* L.

HERBS

Freshwater Cord Grass	*Spartina pectinata* Link
Cinnamon Fern	*Osmunda cinnamomea* L.
Blue-joint Grass	*Calamagrostis canadensis* (Michx). P. Beauv.
Mint	*Mentha arvensis* L.
Cardinal Flower	*Lobelia cardinalis* L.
Jewelweed	*Impatiens capensis* Meerb.
Sphagnum Moss	*Sphagnum palustre*
Meadow Rue	*Thalictrum polygamum* Pursh
Marsh Marigold	*Caltha palustris* L.
Arrow-leaved Tearthumb	*Polygonum sagittatum* L.
Sweet Flag	*Acorus calamus* L.
Rose Pogonia	*Pogonia ophioglossoides* (L.) Ker Gawler
Swamp-pink	*Arethusa bulbosa* L.

CHAPTER 5

SHRUB SWAMP

Frequently my work involves assessing damage and recommending restoration procedures to wetlands carelessly destroyed by individuals who have little regard for them. These people either are ignorant of local, state, and federal laws and regulations guiding the use and protection of wetlands or simply choose to overlook them. As a result, these offenders may find themselves under "cease and desist" orders often resulting in legal and environmental consulting costs and in some cases expensive fines. Late in the summer of 1987 I was supervising a wetland restoration in an alder-willow shrub swamp which had been partially destroyed during a construction project. This shrub swamp bordered a wet meadow. I was fortunate in having with me one the finest landscapers in our area whose stock in trade was using local, indigenous vegetation in his work. Whenever I work in such natural sites I proceed in a quiet manner in order not to disturb the indigenous wildlife. As a result, I have been rewarded more than once. For example, I had the good fortune of chancing upon a mother black bear as she watched her two cubs playfully wrestling on a hillside adjacent to a stream. In the present case, as my friend and I went quietly about our work, I suddenly sensed something nearby. Keeping the rest of my body still, I slowly turned my head to look over my left shoulder. There standing no more than 50 feet from us between two alders was one of the most exciting and unexpected natural wonders I have observed. With its head facing in my direction, I saw the dark cheeked face of a mountain lion (*Felis concolor*) with its yellowish top coat, white undersides, and very obvious black-tipped tail. After a furtive glance, it quickly moved along in the direction it was heading. Of course in my excitement I yelled in uncharacteristic fashion to my friend to look at this beauty which he too spotted. Although sightings in southern New England are rare, if the favored deer prey is abundant and the area is relatively undisturbed and somewhat isolated, the chance of such a sighting is there. I did call our local census officer and a naturalist friend, both of whom agreed with my description and commented that there had been a few other sightings in the general area. Therefore, wetlands are more than what meets the eye and often serve as excellent habitat for many animals including such magnificent creatures as the mountain lion.

STRUCTURE, FUNCTION, AND ECOLOGY of SHRUB SWAMPS

Shrub swamps are often considered to be transitional communities between the wet meadow and wooded tree swamp. In fact, it is not unusual to find an interspersion of wet meadow and tree swamp plants along the ecotonal edges of the shrub swamp. Commonly, deciduous shrub swamps get started in wet meadows, shallow marsh edges, or in the soggy soil of water course edges. Establishment is most successful where human intervention has not resulted in burning, grazing, and mowing of the vegetative community. The water regime of a shrub swamp is an open one so that water from run-off, streams, and rivers moves in and out during the course of a year. This results in conditions where the ground water is near the surface to 1″ deep seasonally. In general these swamps are drier than wet meadows or marshes. Part of this is attributable to the build up of the soil thickness as a result of the decomposition over the years of the marsh or wet meadow vegetation. One can often observe high spots or hummocks above the standing water in these swamps. It is usually on these hummocks where you will find the shrubs and tree saplings growing because they are generally intolerant of the low oxygen levels which accompany prolonged root soaking. The shrubs and young trees typically found in this kind of shrub swamp include alders, azaleas, willows, arrowoods, American elm, red maple, and others. It is interesting to note that alders can fix nitrogen into the soil and are thus very important pioneer plants assuring an adequate supply of this vital element for other plants moving into the community. It is generally conceded that such soils are fairly fertile due in great part to the open water regime of the system which carries in nutrient rich sediments. Also contributing to the high nutrient status of the soils is the rapid decomposition of dead organic plant and animal materials.

The Classification of Wetlands and Deepwater Habitats of the U.S. (Cowardin et al) places shrub swamps in the Palustrine System of the Scrub-shrub Class and the broad-leaved deciduous Subclass with various shrub dominance types including alder and willow with a considerable overlap in species along the ecototonal edge, as previously noted. Shrub swamps are very important wetlands worthy of our understanding and protection. Some of the key functional roles of these plant communities include being sources of ground water recharge, serving as water filters and thus pollution attenuators, reducing storm damage through flood control, and providing superior wildlife habitat.

KEYSTONE (Common) Shrub Swamp Plants

TREES
Red Maple	*Acer rubrum* L.

SHRUBS
Speckled Alder	*Alnus incana* var. *americana* Regel
Swamp Azalea	*Rhododendron viscosum* (L.) Torr.
Buttonbush	*Cephalanthus occidentalis* L.
Pussy Willow	*Salix discolor* Muhl.
Silky Dogwood	*Cornus amomum* Miller
Highbush Blueberry	*Vaccinium corymbosum* L.
Spicebush	*Lindera benzoin* (L.) Blume
Sweet Pepperbush	*Clethra alnifolia* L.
Poison Sumac	*Toxicodendron vernix* (L.) Kuntze
Winterberry	*Ilex verticillata* (L.) A. Gray
Common Elderberry	*Sambucus canadensis* L.
Sweet Gale	*Myrica gale* L.
N. Arrowwood	*Viburnum dentatum* var. *lucidum* Aiton
Maleberry	*Lyonia ligustrina* (L.) DC.
Alder Buckthorn	*Rhamnus frangula* L.
Swamp Rose	*Rosa palustris* Marshall
Trailing Swamp Blackberry	*Rubus hispidus* L.

HERBS
Swamp Milkweed	*Asclepias incarnata* L.
Skunk Cabbage	*Symplocarpus foetidus* (L.) Nutt.
Cinnamon Fern	*Osmunda cinnamomea* L.
Jewelweed	*Impatiens capensis* Meerb.
Sensitive Fern	*Onoclea sensibilis* L.
Water-hemlock	*Cicuta maculata* L.
Cardinal Flower	*Lobelia cardinalis* L.
Jack-in-the-pulpit	*Arisaema triphyllum* (L.) Schott
Mint	*Mentha arvensis* L.
Marsh Marigold	*Caltha palustris* L.

Other plants of Shrub Swamps

There are other plants that may may be encountered in Shrub Swamps, such as those listed below, and that may or may not be covered in the interactions section.

SHRUBS

Red-osier	*DogwoodCornus stolonifera* L.
Steeplebush	*Spirea tomentosa* L.
Meadow-sweet	*Spirea alba* var. *latifolia* (Aiton) Dippel
Shadbush	*Amelanchier canadensis* (L.) Medikus
Leatherleaf	*Chamaedaphne calyculata* L.
Sheep Laurel	*Kalmia angustifolia* L.
Wild Raisin	*Viburnum nudum* var.*cassinoides* (L.) T. & G.
Swamp Loosestrife	*Decodon verticillatus* (L.) Elliott
Greenbrier	*Smilax rotundifolia* L.

HERBS

Goldthread	*Coptis trifolia* var. *groenlandica* (Oeder) Fassett
Royal Fern	*Osmunda regalis* L.
Meadow-rue	*Thalictrum polygamum* Pursh
Sphagnum Moss	*Sphagnum palustre*
Mint	*Mentha arvensis* L.
Blackberry	*Rubus allegheniensis* T.C.Porter

CHAPTER 6
TREE SWAMP

I had seen many wooded swamps by 1987. This one, however, turned out to be a little different than the rest. The reason is that it involved a plane flight to document that a forested wetland was being destroyed by a developer who was building a road through the area. These people did not obtain the proper approvals because in their opinion these were not wetlands. Furthermore, they would not allow anyone on the site to verify their claims, alleging that the dynamiting they were doing was too dangerous for us to be near. Our next course of action was to fly over the area and to get close enough with a video camera to be able to get film to allow for identification of the trees and shrubs and the locations of any watercourses. I had flown many times before, including trips into the Serengeti and Masai Mara in Africa aboard the venerable DC-3 with its ever present and unnerving oil- spewing engines, but at least this plane and the others had wings. I must admit that up to this particular mission on what turned out to be aboard a Jet Bell Ranger helicopter with a former Vietnam veteran pilot, I was the proverbial white knuckle flier. If you have a fear of flying, it is somehow magnified exponentially by the thoughts of doing it in a plane without wings. I like to call helicopters "flying tadpoles," they are not supposed to fly! Of course I had to check out the pilot's credentials and experience. I learned during this "interview" that he had flown 454 missions in Vietnam and had been downed twice. Knowing he had been through so much and had great faith in his craft was very reassuring to me. We boarded the chopper and soon were skimming over mountain tops and arriving safely at our destination. We developed our so-called game plan and began our mission. At one point, for the benefit of

31

my needs to get some close up footage, the pilot put the plane into some dives and tips which made me think he was back in Vietnam. When he pulled out of one such dive, I found myself so frightened that I broke out into an instant sweat drenching my shirt and slacks to such an extent it looked as though I had stood in a shower. Furthermore, my heart was racing at least 3 miles a minute. When the plane finally leveled out, a certain peace and calm fell over me. I can't explain it totally, but my confidence level rose and since that time I have actually come to enjoy flying. This particular flight turned out to be quite valuable in that we indeed documented activities impacting on wetlands which justified an on-site investigation. The eventual on-site reconnaissance showed that parts of the wooded tree swamp were being destroyed. We also documented that in the process they were threatening the existence of some rare and endangered wetland plant species. The result of this was the stopping of construction until the proper permits were obtained. Furthermore, certain fines had to be paid, and the plants of concern had to be saved.

STRUCTURE, FUNCTION, AND ECOLOGY of TREE SWAMPS

Tree swamps generally occur in poorly drained depressions often characterized by wet and mucky soils and temporary spring flooding. While there are no absolutes as to what vegetation one will find in the tree swamp (deciduous forested wetland), it is usually dominated by red maple, the most ubiquitous tree east of the Mississippi river. These wetlands often succeed the shrub swamp communities. Tree swamps are hydrologically open systems characterized by a high ground water similar to that of the shrub swamp where the ground water ranges from just below the surface to l-inch standing water for a significant part of the growing season. These wetlands are very often contiguous with rivers, streams, and lakes which play an important role in supplying the spring flood waters needed for their survival. Quite frequently the hummocky nature of the forest floor creates temporary water-filled or vernal pools which serve as extremely important breeding grounds for a vast array of amphibians and reptiles. It should be noted that such forests can tolerate flooding for only 3-4 months of the year. Any more than this usually results in forest decline. Often when a road is built, natural drainage channels are blocked which in turn cause water to back up and thus create ponds and small lakes. This changed hydrology soon suffocates the swamp forest community a condition which leaves behind the standing tree hulks and creates an eerie and stark dead wood swamp.

In addition to red maple, this tree-dominated community is characterized by such trees as the American elm, yellow birch, and green ash. Because most of the trees cannot tolerate permanent standing water that contains 30-40 times lower oxygen levels than a comparable volume of air, they are most frequently found growing on the raised mounds or hummocks so that the root systems do not remain submerged. These trees are further characterized by shallow fibrous root systems which not only serve to knit adjacent tree roots together for stability so the trees do not fall over in the slightest wind, but also to assure adequate exposure to the oxygen vital to root metabolism. For these reasons, any human impact which may alter the hydrology, the result of which there is excessively prolonged flooding or raising of the ground water, will have a killing effect on these swamps. While shrubs do exist in tree swamps, the much lower light intensities have the distinct effect of reducing the numbers and types compared to those in a shrub swamp. The same is true for the herbal layer which is lower in numbers and types because of the very shaded conditions on the forest floor. The dynamic nature of these forest communities is such that through the build-up of litter, the soil depth and fertility increases to such an extent as to bring about an overall drying of the soil and the ultimate displacement of this wetland by an upland mixed hardwood forest.

The Classification of Wetlands and Deepwater Habitats of the U.S. (Cowardin et al) places tree swamps in the Palustrine System of the Forested Wetland Class and a broad-leaved deciduous Subclass with a variety of dominance types including Red Maple and Tupelo. Tree swamps are extremely important wetlands which perform many valuable functions and as such deserve our protection and care. Such swamps are often ground water recharge areas that serve to control flooding and thus lower storm damage. Some are major water filtration systems that remove pollutants, and many provide valuable wildlife habitat.

KEYSTONE (Common) Tree Swamp Plants

TREES

Red Maple	*Acer rubrum* L.
American Elm	*Ulmus americana* L.
Atlantic White Cedar	*Chamaecyparis thyoides* (L.) BSP
Green Ash	*Fraxinus pennsylvanica* Marshall
Tupelo	*Nyssa sylvatica* Marshall
Swamp White Oak	*Quercus bicolor* Willd.
Yellow Birch	*Betula lutea* Britton
Hemlock	*Tsuga canadensis* (L.) Carriere
Black Spruce	*Picea mariana* (Miller) BSP
Larch	*Larix laricina* (Duroi) K. Koch
Ironwood	*Carpinus caroliniana* Walter
Pin Oak	*Quercus palustris* Muench.

SHRUBS

Highbush Blueberry	*Vaccinium corymbosum* L.
Sweet Pepperbush	*Clethra alnifolia* L.

Continued

SHRUBS *(continued)*

Spicebush	*Lindera benzoin* (L.) Blume
Swamp Azalea	*Rhododendron viscosum* (L.) Torr.
Sheep Laurel	*Kalmia angustifolia L.*
N. Arrowwood	*Viburnum dentatum* var. *lucidum* Aiton
Shadbush	*Amelanchier canadensis* (L.) Medikus
Poison Ivy	*Toxicodendron radicans* (L.) Kuntze

HERBS

Skunk Cabbage	*Symplocarpus foetidus* (L.) Nutt.
Cinnamon Fern	*Osmunda cinnamomea* L.
Sensitive Fern	*Onoclea sensibilis* L.
Sphagnum Moss	*Sphagnum palustre*
Goldthread	*Coptis trifolia* var. *groenlandica* (Oeder) Fassett
Jack-in-the-pulpit	*Arisaema triphyllum* (L.) Schott
Tussock Sedge	*Carex stricta* Lam.
Jewelweed	*Impatiens capensis* Meerb.
Indian Poke	*Veratrum viride* Aiton

Other Plants of Tree Swamps

There are other plants that may be encountered in Tree Swamps, such as those listed below, and that may or may not be covered in the interactions section.

TREES

Black Ash	*Fraxinus nigra* Marshall
White Pine	*Pinus strobus* L.
Sweet Gum	*Liquidambar styraciflua* L.
Eastern Cottonwood	*Populus deltoides* Marshall

SHRUBS

Poison Sumac	*Toxicodendron vernix* (L.) Kuntze
Common Elderberry	*Sambucus canadensis* L.
Wild Raisin	*Viburnum nudum* var. *cassinoides* (L.) T.&G.
Canada Yew	*Taxus canadensis* Marshall

SHRUBS *(continued)*

Dewberry/Trailing Swamp Blackberry	*Rubus hispidus* L.
Maleberry	*Lyonia ligustrina* (L.) DC.
Mountain Holly	*Nemopanthus mucronatus* (L.) Trel.

HERBS

Ostrich Fern	*Matteuccia struthiopteris* (L.)Todaro
Lady Fern	*Athyrium Filix-femina* (L.) Roth
Marsh Fern	*Thelypteris palustris* Schott

PART II
The Interactions

Key to Icons

 = Community Interactions

 = Mammals

 = Plants

 = Birds

 = Reptiles

 = Amphibians

 = Insects

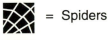 = Fish

= Spiders

= Human/Economic Use

TREES

American Elm *Ulmus americana* L.

ULMACEAE (Elm Family)

General Description -
Native tree formerly reaching 100 feet in height, but usually observed as a poorly growing scruffy thin understory tree barely reaching 25 feet because of the devastation by the Dutch Elm disease.

Stem; although they can grow to 6 feet in diameter, more commonly are 1-6 inches with grayish, furrowed bark, reddish-brown drooping twigs, and oval hairy end buds.

Leaves; alternate and stalked, oval, doubly toothed, with left and right sides of leaf blade uneven and with a rough upper surface.

Flower; wind pollinated, individually stalked, brown and in drooping clusters.

Habitat; wooded swamps, wet bottomlands, and stream channels.

WIS; FACW-

American Elm Interactions

Community Interaction; although large trees are rare, many small saplings may be found as understory creating vertical habitat stratification; provide food for wildlife through a fairly copious crop of wind borne seeds; occasionally serve as nesting sites for birds, but generally offer very limited cover for wildlife.

Mammals; you may observe Red and Gray Squirrels eating seeds, buds, and twigs while the Whitetail Deer browse on leaves and twigs.

Birds; seeds are eaten by the Mourning Warbler (although primarily an insectivore), Purple Finch, American Goldfinch, Rose-breasted Grosbeak, and the Ring-necked Pheasant; Baltimore Orioles favor this and the willow as nesting sites; tree provides both cover and nesting areas for the Purple Finch and the Hairy Woodpecker.

Reptiles; Wood Turtles feed on grapes and fruits of other plants that often grow on dead elm trees; N. Brown Snake, Ringneck, Redbelly, and young water Snakes will use Elm bark as refuge sites.

Amphibians; Gray Treefrogs perch on brances and commonly take refuge under loose bark; Peepers may use saplings as perching and calling sites; Four-toed and Redback Salamanders often use the fallen bark as refuge.

Insects; without a doubt, insects love this plant as witnessed by the list of those that have this as their larval food plant such as the following: many moths including Elm Sphinx, Franck's Sphinx, Twin-spotted Sphinx, Blinded Sphinx, Imperial, Cecropia, Large Tolype, Bella, Yellow-haired Dagger, Dotted Graylet, Double-toothed Prominent,and Elm Spanworm; several butterflies use this as their larval food plant including the Question Mark, Hop Merchant, and the Mourning Cloak; this is the larval and adult food plant for the Smaller European Elm Bark Beetle *Scolytus multistriatus* or Native Elm Bark Beetle *Hylurgopinus rufipes*, a vector of the Dutch Elm disease fungus; if you locate galleries or grooves on the wood surface under the bark, you may also find larvae and adults of the Dubious Checkered Flower Beetle *Thanasimus dubius*, which is a predator of the Elm Bark Beetle larvae.

Spiders; Two-spotted Spider Mites *Tetranychus urticae* suck juice from leaves and lay eggs on buds; although rather inconspicuous, the Crab Spider *Philodromus washita* may be seen on the trunks.

(continued)

American Elm Interactions

Human/Economic Interactions; American Natives and early settlers used a bark infusion to treat dysentery; tonic made from inner bark scrapping was used as a diuretic; is implicated as an allergin in sensitive individuals because of the primary component 'asafoetida' (an oleoresin) in the wind borne pollen; the bark of this tree has been used in folk medicine as a poultice to reduce inflammations and skin discolorations such as from bruises; the Mohegan made a bark tea for coughs; the very existence of these trees is in jeopardy because of the Dutch Elm Disease; old elm wood piles and diseased trees is where the eggs of the Elm Bark Beetle, the primary vector of the disease causing fungus, are laid; these vector breeding grounds must be destroyed, preferably by fire.

Need To Know about interactions involving other plants.

Importance of Wetlands in Nitrate Removal

Plants and animals require nitrogen to build body proteins. Nitrogen is available to plants and animals in several forms, such as nitrates. Nitrates are applied to crops and lawns as fertilizers. Those which are not absorbed by plants may make their way to wetlands and ultimately our drinking water through run off or percolation through the soil into the ground water. Naturally occurring bacteria in the human gut can convert the nitrates in drinking water into harmful nitrites and nitrosamines. Nitrites can reduce hemoglobin levels, a process that reduces vital oxygen transport to cells. Nitrosamines are known carcinogens. Nitrate removal from drinking water is, then, quite important to our health. Wetland soils contain anaerobic (do not require oxygen for life) nitrate removing (denitrification) bacteria. These bacteria break down the nitrates and return them as a gas to the atmosphere. Wetlands are our allies in purifying drinking water through nitrate removal. It appears wetlands will perform this function best if left intact, therefore, their preservation is important to all.

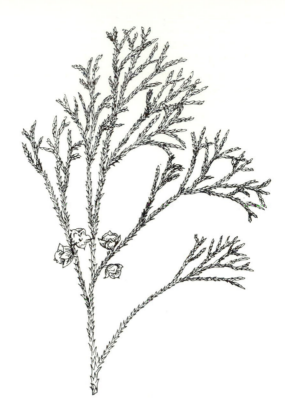

A. White Cedar *Chamaecyparis thyoides* (L.) BSP

PINACEAE (Pine Family)

General Description -
Native evergreen conifer tree growing to 60 feet in height.

Stem; diameter to 2 feet and tapering towards the top, characterized by shredding reddish brown-bark and short side branches in horizontal flat sprays.

Leaves; minute, scale-like and overlapping to cover twigs and with a small gland on back, aromatic and pale green.

Reproductive; separate spherical short-scaled male and female cones appearing in April, with female persisting for year or more.

Habitat; primarily, it is in more southern coastal bogs and swamps, in an acid environment where the pH of the substrate ranges from 3 - 5.5.

WIS; OBL

Atlantic White Cedar Interactions

Community Interactions; wind important in pollination and seed dispersal; deep shade intolerant, very slow growing and known to live to 1000 years or more; adaptation to wet soils seen in being shallow rooted thus closer to ambient oxygen supplies; roots often intertwined into a mat with those of other nearby trees which creates stability against wind and possible uprooting; grow in such dense stands as to make human passage quite difficult while affording excellent cover for breeding, nesting, and overwintering for wildlife; known as a pioneer or early successional species, it is often the first to become established after forest clearing through cutting or fire; as long as the seeds are not submerged, they can germinate on open Sphagnum mats.

Mammals; in swamps where this dominates it is often the preferred habitat of the Marten where it "roosts" or dens in the rotted stumps; mice, deer, and rabbits may feed on the bark or on young saplings.

Plants; out compete Black Spruce yet dies out when the more shade tolerant hemlocks, oaks, and birches grow over top of them creating too much shade.

Birds; in White Cedar swamps, trees are often nesting sites for the Snowy Egret, Cattle Egret, and Common Grackle; along with other trees, this one is often included in the habitat of the Barred Owl and the Parula Warbler.

Reptiles; Painted Turtles can be seen in the open waters of swamps dominated by these trees; in parts of the New Jersey Pine Barrens, Timber rattlesnakes commonly overwinter under the root systems of this tree.

Amphibians; the Northern Red Salamander breeds and lives adjacent to these wetlands while the Spring Peepers breed and feed here and may be found living in the crowns.

Insects; this is the larval food plant for Hessel's Hairstreak butterfly which is found almost exclusively in bogs; also serves as a larval food plant for the Porcelain Gray moth.

Human/Economic Use; a fragrant and strong close grained wood used for shingles in the construction of homes, as fence posts, for interior finish, in landscaping, and as railway ties; various American Native tribes used the wood for canoe framing while the Ojibwa steamed it as an herbal to reduce muscle pain.

Need To Know about interactions involving spiders.

Black Spruce *Picea mariana* (Miller) BSP

PINACEAE (Pine Family)

General Description -
Native evergreen conifer tree growing to 25 feet in height.

Stem; trunk diameter growing to 8", with grayish-brown, thin-scaled bark; side branches more or less horizontal and upturned at ends.

Leaves; blunt-tipped, four sided, dark blue-green, stalked, borne singly and whorled around twig.

Reproductive; male cones are small, borne at tips of last year's growth whereas female cones are larger and borne along branches, cones appearing in April.

Habitat; bogs, but also swamps, pond and lake margins.

WIS; FACW-

Black Spruce Interactions

Community Interactions; wind important in pollination and seed dispersal; generally a more northerly bog resident which is often seen invading their margins and thereby increasing the ecotonal edge diversity of the habitat; also known to move to southerly extent of its range in advance of other members of its northern community; will root from the lower or reclining stems thus capable of readily establishing pure stands; can also produce adventitious roots from stems in response to a rising water table thus assuring its survival by replacement of any drowned roots.

Mammals; cones and seeds eaten by Eastern Gray Squirrel, Red Squirrel, Porcupine, and Eastern Chipmunk while Eastern Cottontail and Snowshoe Hare, Porcupine, and Whitetail Deer can be observed consuming needles, bark, and twigs.

Plants; Black Spruce seedlings do not grow well where there is an established understory of Sheep Laurel which may release allelopathic (poisons) materials into the ground.

Birds; one may observe the Spruce Grouse foraging for needles and ground nesting here in its favored environment; Blackburnian Warblers can be found nesting high amongst needles in a flat spray of branches.

Reptiles; Redbelly and the S. Green Snakes are found in cool boggy areas where this tree grows.

Amphibians; Mink Frog and Four-toed Salamanders are most likely found in association with this tree.

Insects; larval food plant for a number of moths which one might observe or expect to observe, including White Triangle Tortix, a major pest the Spruce Budworm, Pale-Marked Angle, Large Purplish Gray, Porcelain Gray, and the Gray Spruce Looper; it is also the larval food plant for the Bog Elfin butterfly most typically when this plant is in the Black Spruce-Tamarack-Sphagnum bog association; the Woolly Larch Aphid *Adelges strobilobius* moves here from the Larch to complete its life cycle by forming galls; the very injurious Spruce Coneworm *Dioryctria reniculelloides* along with the Spruce Cone Axis midge of the genus *Dasineura (rachiphage)* and Spruce Cone Maggot *Lasiomma (anthraacinum)* depend upon this tree for their food; ; this may fall victim to the Spruce Gall Louse *Adelges abietis* where it creates swellings at the base of the needles; see Hemlock for the Pine Webworm whose larvae use the leaves for protection and eat them as adults.

(continued)

Black Spruce Interactions

 Spiders; the Comb-footed spider *Theridula emertoni* has been found on this tree.

 Human/Economic; although it is soft and not very strong, this tree finds manifold uses, finding its way into the construction of house interiors, barrels, musical instruments, and turpentine; it is also used as pulp in the paper industry and its pitch (resins) in chewing gum; the boiled bark extract can be made into a drink called Spruce Beer or a remedy for curing stomachache, kidney stones, and arthritic pain; Native Americans used the pitch as a waterproofing material for canoes and used the cones as a source of yellow dye; the Algonquin chewed the gum to stimulate bowel activity.

Wetland Value - Groundwater recharge

Groundwater reserves, often called aquifers, are a major source of public drinking water. The standing water often seen in wetlands is the source for groundwater recharge. It is important to realize that the hydrologic (water) cycle is tied directly into our wetlands which serve as temporary surface storage areas. This standing water comes from a variety of sources including annual spring flooding and storm water run off. What this means is that the surface water may percolate down through the soil to the aquifer or ground water supply thus serving to maintain an adequate water table and in turn water for human consumption.

Green Ash *Fraxinus pennsylvanica* Marshall

OLEACEAE (Olive Family)

General Description -
Native tree growing to 60 feet in height.

Stem; bark of older stem is gray with ridges and furrows, whereas young twigs are gray, thin, hairless, and oppositely branched.

Leaves; opposite, pinnately compound with 7 leaflets which are shiny green on top and occasionally hairy on bottom and with saw toothed to smooth margins; becoming bright yellow in fall.

Flower; small cluster of wind pollinated, greenish, petal-free, stalked flowers with male and female on separate trees; appearing in April.

Habitat; wooded swamp, in floodplain, or along a streambank.

WIS; FACW

Green Ash Interactions

Community Interactions; one of the most widely distributed ashes, it is a rugged and fast growing shade tolerant tree often forming a dense subcanopy which provides breeding and nesting sites for birds; in the year following a season of above average rainfall or significant flooding event, I have noticed that while many other woody species seedlings appeared destroyed, seedlings of this tree survive, indicating their tolerance to such conditions; its branching well developed root system stabilizes banks; the flowers are a major producer of wind borne seeds and thus serve as a significant food source for wildlife.

Mammals; the wood and seeds are used as food by several familiar mammals including Porcupine, Beaver, Black Bear, White-footed Mice and White-tailed Deer.

Plants; this is a canopy tree very often found growing with Red Maple and Swamp Oak.

Birds; seeds are a favored food for Cardinal, Wood Duck, Evening Grosbeak, Purple Finch, and the Red-winged Blackbird; the Mourning Dove, Evening Grosbeak and possibly the Rose-breasted Grosbeak may find cover and nesting sites here.

Reptiles; fallen logs are basking sites for Eastern Painted Turtles and occasionally Snapping Turtles; N. Water Snakes also will use this for basking.

Amphibians; Green frogs will use fallen ash logs for resting and scouting sites; Peepers and Gray Treefrogs will climb lower branches and vocalize during the breeding season.

Insects; this is a plant which plays a very important role as the larval food plant for many moths including the Ash Sphinx, Waved Sphinx, Great Ash Sphinx, Polyphemus, Spicebush Silkmoth, Cecropia, Large Tolype, Spotted Apatelodes, Grote's Sallow, and the Ash Tip Borer which bores into the base of the stems and then eventually exits the stem to pupate in the ground; several butterflies, including the Hickory Hairstreak and the Tiger Swallowtail, have been known to use this as their larval food plant; the flowers and seeds are fed upon by a Squash Bug *Anasa spp.*

Spiders; see Appendix D.

(continued)

Green Ash Interactions

Human/Economic Use; implicated as an allergin to sensitive individuals, the pollen is characterized by the presence of the oleo-resin 'asafoetida'; the bark is the source of an infusion used in folk medicine to reduce hemorrhoidal swelling and itching; a favored bow wood for N.E. Native Americans.

Need To Know about interactions involving spiders.

Leopard Frog.

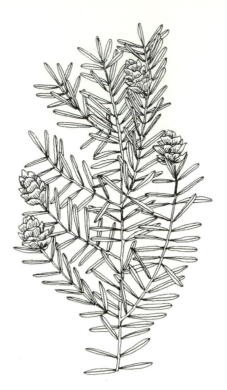

Hemlock *Tsuga canadensis* (L.) **Carriere**

PINACEAE (Pine Family)

General Description -
Native evergreen tree growing to 80 feet in height.

Stem; straight trunk with light brown, deeply fissured bark; branches with thin yellow twigs are more or less horizontal and becoming shorter towards the top which results in a pyramidal silhouette.

Leaves; short stalked paired needles which are flat and dark green on top with two white stripes on bottom and with rounded tips.

Reproduction; wind pollinated, with male cones being small ephemeral structures in clusters in leaf axils, whereas female cones have brown scales, are at twig ends and persist.

Habitat; wooded swamps, near bogs, in ravines, and on the cool, shady, moist north slopes.

WIS; FACU

Hemlock Interactions

Community Interaction; more tolerant of ozone than many other trees; decaying leaves are an important source of nitrogen to soils; shade tolerant; characterized by shallow extensive roots which are quite important in stabilizing slopes; smaller trees create a dense understory which affords a year around source of cover for breeding, nesting, and overwintering, in addition to which they are a major food source for wildlife; known to grow on hummocks in bottom-lands; produce large numbers of seeds of which approximately 30% are viable (will germinate).

Mammals; Porcupine, which eat the seeds, may also strip the bark to get at the fresh sapwood and cambium, their favorite food; Beaver will occasionally eat the seeds, wood and bark; White-footed Mice use the leaves and seeds for food as do Deer Mice, Southern Red-backed Vole and Red and Gray Squirrels; twigs are eaten by the Eastern Cottontail; the Silver-Haired Bat will occasionally roost here, especially if its along a water course.

Plants; often grows interspersed amongst deciduous trees including Red Maple and Yellow Birch.

Birds; the Ruffed Grouse, Black-capped Chickadee, and Pine Siskin will eat the seeds; the Sharp-shinned and Red-shouldered Hawk, along with the Northern Saw-whet Owl, find this a favored nesting tree, as does the Veery, especially when growing along an edge or ecotone, since this bird tends to avoid dense forests.

Reptiles; cool-adapted species are found in wetlands with Hemlocks: these include Spotted Turtle, Wood Turtle, Blanding's Turtle, Northern Redbelly Snake, C. Garter Snake, N. Ribbon Snake, and the Smooth Green Snake.

Amphibians; you might expect to uncover Northern and Mountain Dusky Salamander adults under the bark of fallen Hemlocks along stream edges; N. Spring Salamanders and Two-lined Salamanders are common in cold brooks that are edged by Hemlocks.

Insects; this plant plays host as the larval food plant to several moths including the Bicolored, Northern Variable Dart, Pale-marked Angle, Hemlock Angle, Porcelain Gray, Gray Spruce Looper, and the northerly Jocose Sallow; a Hemlock Borer Beetle *Melanophila fulvoguttata* may be found attacking weakened trees and a Metallic Wood-boring Beetle *Dicera spp.* breeds here and eats the leaves; this serves as the larval food plant for the Spruce Budworm

(continued)

Hemlock Interactions

Insects (continued); *Choristoneura fumiferana*; the larvae of the Pine Webworm *Acantholyda erythrocephala* roll up the leaves into a protective housing and later when they mature into adults, eat the leaves.

Spiders; an orb weaver *Uloborus americanus* and the Triangle Spider *Hyptiotes cavatus* may place their webs between branches of trees, especially in those growing in cool shady places;the Comb-foot Spider *Theridula emertoni* has been found here and on Black Spruce.

Human/Economic Use; the Cherokee and other Native Americans chewed or made an infusion of the bark and leaves to treat diarrhea; the bark is also a source of tannins once used in tanning leather and a source of high quality brown dye; a bark poultice was made by the Chippewa for use as an hemostat to stop bleeding; tea from the leaves is high in Vitamin C; the soft wood has a high usage in the construction field; the leaves were used by various tribes including the Delaware and Iroquois to reduce swelling associated with boils and bruises.

How much of U.S. is wetland?

It is quite difficult to estimate how many acres of wetlands exist in the lower 48 states. The primary reason for this is that the definition of what a wetland is falls subject to a variety of interpretations. However, in 1983 the U.S. Fish and Wildlife Service commissioned the National Wetland Trends Study (NWTS). This study utilized the most widely accepted wetland definition and delineation techniques in effect at the time. The results indicated that there were approximately 108 million acres of wetlands in the lower U.S. in 1954, only half of what may have been present in the 1600's in pre-settlement times. The study further showed that by 1974, the 1954 levels had decreased to 98 million acres, showing a loss of nearly 10 million acres in just 20 years. Current estimates indicate that since 1974 the overall annual rate of wetland loss approaches 5 percent a year- an area equal to nearly half the size of Rhode Island. These losses are the result of human activities including draining, clearing, and filling for development. When one realizes that nearly three quarters of existing wetlands are considered prime wildlife habitat by the U.S. Fish and Wildlife Service, we can begin to appreciate the impacts of such destruction. Such losses are further critical when we consider the other functional values of wetlands including flood control, public and private water supply, pollution attenuation, fisheries, and recreation. From this information, it is obvious that such trends of wetland losses must be brought under control.

Ironwood *Carpinus caroliniana* **Walter**

BETULACEAE (Birch Family)

General Description -
Small native tree occasionally growing to 30 feet in height.

Stem; gray bark with a fluted, wavy (muscular) appearance.

Leaves; alternate and oblong, with a pointed tip, rounded base and having doubly toothed margins.

Flower; very small male and female flowers in separate spikes with the male drooping from last year's stem whereas female is borne singly from current growth; both appearing April-May.

Habitat; wooded swamps, stream borders, damp forest ravines and into uplands.

WIS; FAC

Ironwood Interactions

Community Interactions; frequently, this small tree grows in thick stands along the edge of a swamp providing some food and cover for breeding, nesting, and overwintering; it may also grow in clumps as woody understory in swamps resulting in verticle stratification and increased habitat diversity; generally produces a large seed crop which is a great food source for wildlife.

Mammals; Gray and Red Squirrels are known to eat the buds, seeds, bark, and gnaw on the wood; Whitetail Deer browse on twigs and foliage.

Birds; if growing at the forest edge, you may see Ring-necked Pheasant, Ruffed Grouse, and the Mourning Warbler taking the seeds.

Reptiles; Wood and Box Turtles forage at the base of the tree.

Insects; this is a larval food plant for the Red-spotted Purple Butterfly and for several moths including the Mustard Sallow, Sleeping Baileya, Slug Caterpillar *Apoda y- inversum*, and the Casebearer, whose reddish brown flat cases can be seen in winter attached to branches and bark ; an adult Metallic Wood-boring Beetle *Dicerca (divaricata)* may be found feeding on the branches and possibly eating the foliage; a small very inconspicuous two-winged fly *Cecidomyia pudibunda* lays its eggs in the leaf tissue resulting in a swelling usually along a vein; the living beech borer *Goes pulverulentus* lives in the younger branches of this tree.

Human/Economic Use; pollen has been implicated as an allergin (Hayfever Plant); the wood is for tool handles and burned as fuel; Delaware Indians combined these roots and bark with the bark of cherry to make a tea to treat debility.

Need To Know about interactions involving other plants, amphibians, and spiders.

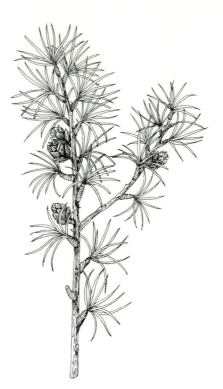

Larch *Larix laricina* (Duroi) K. Koch

PINACEA (Pine Family)

General Description -
Native deciduous conifer tree growing to 70 feet in height.

Stem; trunk diameter to 2 feet, reddish-brown bark with round scales, and with horizontal to slightly drooping side branches which have short spurs.

Leaves; short (1 inch), occurring singly along stem or in tight clusters of 15-20 on a spur and turning yellow and dropping off in fall.

Reproductive; separate male and female cones with females, in contrast to the males, being reddish to brown scaled, erect, and borne singly on short spur.

Habitat; bogs, but also pond margins and swamps.

WIS; FACW

Larch Interactions

Community Interactions; wind pollinated; will grow in both acid or limestone soils, in wet or drier sites and although preferring full sun, they will grow in partially shaded forest settings; tree is salt tolerant and thus potentially useful as a roadside planting where salting may occur and in landscaping near the sea; they are more common than Black Spruce in southerly bogs; Larch are intolerant of high nitrogen dioxide levels of air pollution; as an adaption to high soil water, they have a shallow and wide spreading root system where they are closer to ambient oxygen; such root systems also serve to stabilize soils against erosion and their stems from windthrow; there is some evidence that younger trees have higher levels of a defense chemical (possibly an amino acid) than older ones and as such are less susceptible to defoliation by larch moths; Larch function as nesting and breeding sites, and supply seeds, leaves, and bark as food for wildlife.

Mammals; needles, twigs, and inner bark serve as food for Whitetail Deer, Porcupine, Snowshoe Hare, and the Red Squirrel.

Birds; Purple Finch, Spruce and Ruffed Grouse, Red Crossbill, and Pheasant eat seeds; the Spruce Grouse will roost on limbs and often nests on ground under these while Blue Jays, Robins, and Golden-crowned Kinglets have been observed finding cover and nesting sites here; the Yellow-bellied Sapsucker may eat the seeds and feed on beetles and other insects attracted to the sap oozing out of the holes these birds create.

Reptiles; Wood, Spotted, and Bog Turtles live in Larch wetlands; the Northern Water Snake, Ribbon, and Redbelly Snakes bask on logs or hide in rotting wood.

Amphibians; Green Frogs, Mink Frogs, Bullfrogs, Four-toed Salamanders, Spotted and Jefferson's Salamanders breed and live here.

Insects; this is a larval food plant for a variety of moths including the Bicolored, Brown-spotted Zale, Gypsy, Pale-marked Angle, Hollow-spotted Angle,Large Purplish Gray, Porcelain Gray, Pine Sphinx, Apple Sphinx, White Triangle Tortrix, and the Eastern Panthea; the Larch Casebearer Moth *Coleophora laricella* mines the leaves and overwinters in an elongate case attached to the buds; although they are capable of defoliating this tree, there is some evidence that plants resistant to Larch Sawfly have a resin called isopimaric acid which serves as a larval feeding deterrent- may suggest a biological control; this is the principle host tree for Eastern Larch

(continued)

Larch Interactions

Insects (continued); Beetle *Denroctonus simplex* which overwinters as an adult beneath bark and emerges in spring to attack healthy trees and lay eggs; trees which produce more resins are more resistant to beetle attack-perhaps the resins flood the larval galleries forcing them out; adult Click Beetles *Ampedus (pedalis)* feed on the reproductive buds, Metalic Wood-boring Beetles *Anthaxia (quercata)* and Flathead Borers *Chrysobothris (dentipes)* feed on leaves, and the adult Long-horned Beetle *Phymatodes dimidiatus* breeds here and eats the leaves, buds, and pollen; also see Hemlock for the Pine Webworm which uses this plant also.

Spiders; Branch-tip Spiders *Dictyna sublata* are occasionally observed on these branches.

Human/Economic Uses; a very hard and disease resistant wood is used in the construction of buildings near water, boat docks, and for telephone poles; tea from bark extracts is used as a laxative and diuretic and reportedly by early settlers as an effective treatment for jaundice, various skin disorders, rheumatism, as a throat gargle, and cure for stomachaches; the Chippewa would prepare a poultice from the inner bark to place on burns and the Abenaki would make a bark infusion to treat coughs; the bark contains 'pyrone'(maltol (3-hydroxy-2-methyl-4-pyrone), an FDA approved taste-modifying sugar substitute for cakes, cookies, candies, etc.

Need To Know about interactions involving other plants.

Red-spotted Purple Butterfly.

Pin Oak *Quercus palustris* Muench.

FAGACEAE (Beech Family)

General Description -
Native tree growing to 70 feet in height.

Stem; bark dark gray and smooth, eventually developing furrows and ridges; upper branches ascend, middle are horizontal and lower point downward, with all branches having short shoots or "pins" along their length.

Leaves; alternate, shiny light green with hairs at vein junctions on lower surface, growing towards ends of branches and having deep and wide sinuses which nearly reach to the midvein, and with bristle-tipped lobes or teeth.

Flower; wind pollinated, the male borne in a long (4 inches) drooping spike with female borne singly or in small clusters and appearing May-June.

Habitat; wooded swamp, floodplain, riverbanks, and some damp upland sites.

WIS; FACW

Pin Oak Interactions

Community Interaction; although it has no serious disease problems, they are intolerant of fire; they are one of the more important food sources for wildlife, providing acorns, and bark; Voles, squirrels, and various birds including Blue Jays help these plant spread by burying the acorns in food caches; occasionally these grow in dense dwarf thickets, providing good wildlife cover; their shallow and fibrous root systems help stabilize bottomland soils subject to flooding.

Mammals; although you may add many more to this list, Whitetail Deer browse on the branches and foliage, Black Bears eat acorns and may use the fallen trees as den sites, and Red and Gray Squirrels, White-footed Mice, and Chipmunks eat the acorns as well.

Plants; generally intolerant in the shade of other species.

Birds; Ruffed Grouse are known to use thickets for moulting and escape cover and Wild Turkey, Wood Ducks, and Mallards will eat the acorns.

Amphibians; Redback Salamanders are found in the drier portions of these woodlands.

Reptiles; Eastern Box Turtles and Wood Turtles are likely inhabitants, as they forage for food.

Insects; Gypsy Moths use this as a larval food plant and are major defoliators of the tree; also a larval food plant for the Tephra Tussock Moth; a frequent visitor to this oak is the Common Walking Stick *Diapheromera femorata*, which is occasionally an important factor in defoliation; a gall-wasp *Callirhytis palustris* oviposits on the leaves of this plant causing the Succulent Oak Gall.

Spiders; See Appendix D.

Human/Economic Use; very similar to the Swamp White Oak in these regards; the "pins" or short shoots are quite strong and stiff and are used as "tendons" to hold boards together.

Need To Know about interactions involving spiders.

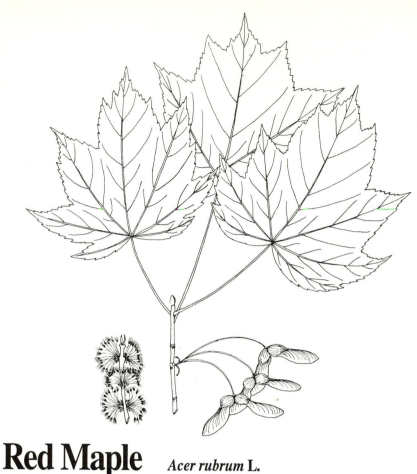

Red Maple   *Acer rubrum* L.

Aceraceae (Maple Family)

General Description -

Native tree growing to 60 feet in height (some part of plant is red in every season -see stem, leaves, flower below).

Stem; young stem has smooth, gray bark becoming cracked and rough as it ages; opposite branching pattern with reddish end buds visible winter and early spring.

Leaves; opposite, usually 3-lobed (sometimes 5), toothed margins with reddish leaf stalk (petiole), blades frequently turning red in fall.

Flower; wind and insect pollinated, with male and female in separate flowers on same or different trees; female is red while male is red with bright yellow anthers, both appearing in spring.

Habitat; wooded swamps, and as sapling in shrub swamps; this tree is also found in uplands (actually the most widely distrubuted tree east of the Mississippi River).

WIS; FAC

Red Maple Interactions

Community Interactions; although primarily wind pollinated, honey bees use pollen in early spring possibly facilitating pollination; wind and some animals play primary roles in seed dispersal; survival against hungry spring seed predators is enhanced through its characteristic delayed seed development; reproduces not only from seeds but can reforest an area by means of stump sprouting from recently cut stems which may also serve as deer browse; because their seedlings are relatively quick growing, Red Maple is often an early invader of recently cleared areas; appears intolerant of fuel oil spills reaching wetlands, saplings often dying off following such accidents.

Mammals; although Chipmunks and Red and Gray Squirrels eat seeds, these animals are also important in seed dispersal by 'planting' (storing) seeds in caches where some germinate and grow into trees; Black Bear may den under fallen trees as will Opossum; saplings, twigs, and bark, which are eaten by Beaver and Porcupine, also serve as important browse and pre-rut rubbing sites for Whitetail Deer.

Plants; Poison ivy grows more profusely in direct association with Red Maple than if separated; Red Maple seeds do not germinate well under Atlantic White Cedar, although the latter succeeds well under Red Maple; since this tree is usually one of the most abundant members of the canopy layer in swamps, it will be found growing with a vast diversity of other trees, shrubs, and ground cover as noted in the shrub swamp and tree swamp habitat keystone plant lists.

Birds; used for nesting and cover by Robin, Goldfinch, Great Egret, Red-tailed Hawk, Eastern Hairy Woodpecker, Northern Downy Woodpecker, Yellow-bellied Sapsucker and as rookery sites for the Great Blue Heron; the Eastern Screech Owl uses Red Maple swamps frequently in winter for roosting and hunting; seeds and buds eaten by Cardinal, Bobwhite, Rose-breasted Grosbeak, and Wild Turkey.

Reptiles; very suitable breeding habitat tree cover type for the Five-lined Skink, Eastern Ribbon Snake, and Northern Ringneck Snake; Red Maple swamps are excellent Wood Turtle habitat; one may observe the Bog Turtle basking on Sphagnum or other herbs of those bogs with Red Maple canopy; Northern Water Snakes and Redbelly Snakes forage in and around Red Maple wetlands.

Amphibians; preferred type of tree swamp vernal pool habitat for breeding by Marbled, Jefferson, Spotted, Mountain Dusky, Four-toed, and Northern Spring salamanders; also Wood Frogs, Northern

(continued)

Red Maple Interactions

Amphibians (continued); Leopard Frogs, and Northern Spring Peepers are common breeding inhabitants of these swamps.

Insects; the larval food plant for a large number of moths including Maple Spanworm, Imperial, Io, Polyphemus, Spicebush Silkmoth, Cecropia, Spotted Apatelodes, Woolly Bear Tiger, Yellow Bear Tiger, Retarded Dagger, Maple Looper, and Definite Tussock; often see Oystershell scale insects on branches; although not a favored food, the Japanese Beetle begrudgingly will eat this, and just about any other plant if needed; both the Rove Beetle *Anthobium hornii* and False Darkling Beetle *Anaspis rufa* may be found in the flowers as well as the Squash Bug *Anasa tristis*, which feeds on both flowers and seeds; on branches, one can find the Forest Tent Caterpillar *Malacosoma disstria*, a pest which is in turn fed upon by salamanders and wasps; larvae of Stag Beetle (the well known Pinching Bug, *Pseudolucanus capreolus)* feed on plant juices; the Potato Leafhopper *Empoasca fabae* feeds on maple leaves as does the Lace Bug *Corythuca* spp.; cankers associated with oviposition of the Snowy Tree Cricket *Oecanthus fultoni* are often located where a maple pathogenic fungus *Cryptosporiopsis* spp. is found, implicating the cricket as a vector for this disease.

Spiders: see Appendix D.

Human/Economic Value; a close-grained and curly wood which has found use as "curly Maple" for framing in cabinets and furniture; although sugar level is low, it has been tapped for maple syrup; Cherokees boiled twigs and made a syrup which they used as an eye wash; the pollen may be an allergin, causing hayfever in many.

Legal Protection of Wetlands

Historically, wetland protection has been the province of state and federal agencies. In recent years more states have taken the initiative to control impacts to wetlands. While some states such as Massachusetts, Florida, Connecticut, New Hampshire, Vermont, Maine, and New York have very strict wetland protections regulations, others such as Georgia, Delaware, and Arizona have just begun to look at the problem. Section 404 of the Federal Pollution Control Act (FWPCA Amendments of 1972, PL92-500) and the 1977 Clean Water Act Amendments have given the Army Corps of Engineers authority over "waters of the United States", which includes both coastal and inland wetland areas. Section 404 of the FWPCA gives the Army Corps of Engineers the right to establish a permitting system to regulate any activities which may involve dredging or filling of wetlands. The Clean Water Act of 1977 broadened the scope to include regulating any activity in or near wetlands which might alter negatively the quality of the water associated with those wetlands. ACOE authority over federal wetlands can be superseded by the U.S. Environmental Protection Agency if issues of national interest (significance) are involved. Federal 404 reviews also include advisory participation by the U.S. Fish and Wildlife Service, the Coast Guard, and others. The act further authorized the U.S. Fish and Wildlife Service to create an inventory of all wetlands of the United States. Other federal involvement in wetland protection includes the Coastal Zone Management Act of 1972 which provides financial incentives to states which develop wetland protection regulations as part of a coastal management plan and consistency review. The Flood Disaster Protection Act of 1973(77) offers flood insurance to states which prohibit development in the floodplain. The management and preservation of wetlands requires the continued modification and evolution of regulatory guidelines. Although the federal government has set the initial tone for the guidelines, there is evidence that states must and hopefully will take on a greater role in wetland protection and management.

Swamp White Oak *Quercus bicolor* Willd.

FAGACEAE (Beech Family)

General Description -
Native tree growing to 70 feet in height.

Stem; light grayish-brown bark which develops a plate-like appearance; lower branches are drooping and scraggly with young twigs yellowish.

Leaves; alternate, light green on top with white hairs on bottom, obovate, with a wedge shaped base, blunt tips and wavy edges (margins), lacking the deep sinuses characterisitc of Pin Oak.

Flower; wind pollinated with males typically in long (3 inches), drooping spikes of very small flowers whereas the females are borne singly or in very small clusters that give rise in April to small light brown acorns covered more than 1/2 by a cap.

Habitat; wooded swamps, floodplains, and streambanks.

WIS; FACW+

Swamp White Oak Interactions

Community Interactions; this along with Maple and Hemlock are more tolerant of ozone than most other trees; the high tannic acid content of the leaves contributes appreciably to acidification of swamp soils and waters; usually it produces a large crop of acorns every 2-3 years that is a major food source for wildlife; usually can withstand 1 or 2 successive defoliations by Gypsy Moths with, however, a third defoliation normally proving fatal in over 80% of the cases; among the largest and oldest trees of the swamp and characterized by a deep tap roots accompanied by a highly branching surface root system that serve to place them near ambient oxygen, to further stabilize the trees from falling over, and to help prevent surface soil erosion; easily transplanted.

Mammals; the high energy level of the acorns makes them an important food source to many mammals including Whitetail Deer, Black Bear, Red Fox, Muskrat, New England Cottontail, Beaver, Red and Gray Squirrel, White-footed Mouse, Raccoons, and Chipmunk; squirrrels are scatter-horders of acorns and are thus important in seed dispersal and planting.

Plants; since this is a late seeder, usually doing so after the spring floods, it has a lower mortality rate than earlier seeding species; thus this plant out competes flood sensitive species at the seed germination phase but it will not outcompete established maples that are much more flood tolerant.

Birds; cavities of old large trees are favored nesting and roosting sites for the Barred Owl; Blue Jays transport and bury acorns up to 3 miles from point of origin and are thus important dispersal agents and tree planters since they don't often retrieve the nuts they've buried; acorns are eaten by many birds including Mallard, Blue Jay, Wild Turkey, Cardinal, Wren, Starling, Wood Duck, Ruffed Grouse, White-breasted Nuthatch, Yellow-throated Warbler, Red-bellied Woodpecker, and in more open woodlands where the Red-headed Woodpecker will eat them; such trees are occasionally nesting sites for the Northern Red-Shouldered and Red-tailed Hawk.

Reptiles; Spotted Turtles, Box Turtles, Wood Turtles, Eastern Ribbon Snakes, Redbelly Snakes and Northern Ringneck Snakes all feed and take refuge in these areas.

Amphibians; Gray Treefrogs, Spring Peepers, and Northern Cricket Frogs forage and breed in swamp oak wetlands.

(continued)

71

Swamp White Oak Interactions

Insects; the vast array of moths that use this is rather convincing as to the oak's importance to them; normally, the Polyphemus Moth will not release her sex attractant pheromone for mating unless she's in the presence of oak; this is a food plant to such moths as the Blinded Sphinx, Spiny Oakworm, Io, Slug Caterpillar, Polyphemus, Large Tolype, Dot-lined White, Lappet, Spotted Apatelodes, Scalloped Sackbearer, Clymene, Large Looper, Tephra Tussock, Casebearer, and the Gypsy; the Cynipid Gall Wasp *Amphibolips confluenta* creates "spongy oak apple galls" that are in turn fed upon by the Filbertworm Moth ; Periodical Cicadas (e.g. the 13 and 17 year species) feed on the roots and if in sufficient numbers, are known to reduce wood growth of young trees; the well known Pinch Bug (Stag Beetle) *Pseudolucanus capreolus* feeds on plant juices while the Checkered Beetle *Cymatodera* spp. can be expected to lay eggs near galls containing the wasp eggs the beetle larvae eventually invade to feed upon.

Spiders; see Appendix D.

Human/Economic Use; this is a very strong and long lasting wood used for furniture, interior panels, flooring, barrels for aging whisky, a source of tannin once used in leather tanning, and medicinally as an alkaloidal precipitant in the treatment of drug overdoses e.g. for cocaine; several tribes including the Cherokee and Delaware used bark preparations for the treatment of many disorders including fever, asthma, coughs, cancer, and rheumatism.

Need To Know about interactions involving spiders.

Fishing Spider under water.

Tupelo *Nyssa sylvatica* Marshall

CORNACEAE (Dogwood family)

General Description -
Tree growing to 40 feet in height.

Stem; straight trunk giving rise to distinctly horizontal crooked branches which having a chambered pith and many spur-like brownish twigs; bark is grayish-brown with a rough exterior of furrows and ridges.

Leaves; alternate, dark, shiny, egg-shaped, and clustered toward twig ends with generally smooth (entire) margins, leaves turning brilliant red in the fall.

Flowers; bee pollinated, greenish, and not too densely clustered with the stalked male and female flowers generally on separate trees; appearing April-May.

Habitat; wooded swamps, lowlands (floodplains), pond and marsh borders.

WIS; FACW-

Tupelo Interactions

Community Interactions; one of the few tree that can withstand decades of permanent flooding resulting from altered hydrology; it is adapted to a wide range of light conditions, thriving in shade or full sun, often becoming subcanopy in mature Red Maple forests; tree is fire resistant but can not tolerate high winds.

Mammals; the fruits may be eaten by Gray Squirrel and Opossum, and if reachable, by Black Bear and Whitetail Deer.

Plants; if this tree is present, it is most commonly associated with Red Maple.

Birds; the fruits are eaten by many birds with some of the heaviest feeders being Mallard, Wood Duck, Wild Turkey, Robin, Mockingbird, Catbird, Yellow-shafted Flicker, Eastern Bluebird, Crow, Red-bellied Woodpecker, Starling, Ruffed Grouse, Purple Finch, Red-eyed Vireo, and the Wood and Swainson's Thrush; it is quite probable that many of these birds are important in spreading the seeds through fecal droppings.

Reptiles; the fallen trunks often become basking sites for Eastern Painted Turtles, Spotted Turtles, and the Northern Water Snakes.

Amphibians; certainly black gum swamps are alive with Northern Spring Peepers and other amphibians during their breeding season; Gray Treefrogs, Green frogs, and Bullfrogs are known to inhabit these swamps.

Insects; this tree has very few insect pest and I've observed very few insect visitors except bees that help with pollination and the Shield Bearer Moth using this as a larval food plant.

Spiders; See Appendix D.

Human/Economic Use; the soft yet strong and light wood has found many uses in American industry including as yokes and rollers in glass factories for veneers, crates, pulp, gun stocks, and wheel hubs; the name 'beetlebung' is associated with a special clump of these trees in Chilmark on Martha's Vineyard; "beetlebung" are called such after the practice of using the wood to make 'beetles' or mallots used to pound in 'bungs' or plugs to close barrels of whale oil; fruits can be used to make jams and jellies; this water resistant wood is often used in warf pilings; the Cherokee prepared bark teas for use in controlling diarrhea and intestinal worms.

Yellow Birch *Betula lutea* Britton

BETULACEAE (Birch Family)

General Description -
Native tree growing to 100 feet in height.

Stem; mature bark is shiny yellow to silver gray, shredding into horizontal papery strips; twigs slender, hairy, and greenish-brown.

Leaves; alternate, elliptical, with doubly toothed margins, and green above, yellowish below with hairs on both surfaces only when young.

Flower; wind pollinated, the male being yellow, small and narrow in a drooping catkin at branch tips with the female green and in broader upright catkins placed back from the tip which matures into a brown cone.

Habitat; wooded swamp often with Hemlocks, also in floodplains, ravines and moist uplands.

WIS; FAC

Yellow Birch Interactions

Community Interaction; commonly found in wetlands, often demarcating the transition zone between upland and wetland; being reasonably shade tolerant, it can form a fairly well developed understory during its early years, contributing to verticle stratification and thus habitat diversity in swamps; it eventually grows to be among the tallest trees in the wetland, reaching over 100 feet; copious seed production provides food for wildlife; roots are large and spreading which stabilizes the soils against erosion on slopes of ravines; occasionally may be found growing in pure stands, as a pioneer after forest destruction through fires or clear cutting; the female cones are an important food source for birds, releasing their seeds throughout the winter and into the spring.

Mammals; the bark and wood is food for Porcupine and Beaver; Chipmunks can be seen eating the seeds whereas Whitetail Deer eat twigs and foliage; Keen's Bat has been spotted nesting inside holes in Yellow Birch.

Plants; frequently mixed in with Hemlock in swamps and along slopes of ravines.

Birds; One can expect to see Wood Duck, Wild Turkey, Ring-necked Pheasant, Herons, and Goldfinch among the many which eat the seeds; the Red-shouldered Hawk and Yellow-bellied Sapsucker find cover and nesting sites in trees along with the Prothonotary Warbler which nests in holes or stumps; where there is growth of the lichen *Usnea*, one might find this warbler nesting here and using this lichen as nesting material; although caterpillars are a favored food, both the Black-billed and Yellow-billed Cuckoos feed on its seeds and buds.

Amphibians; Gray Treefrogs rest and forage in Yellow Birch; Redback, Two-lined and occasionally N. Dusky Salamanders may forage, at night, around the base of these trees.

Insects; serves as a major larval food source for a large number of moths including the Twin-Spotted Sphinx, Blinded Sphinx, Small-eyed Sphinx, Imperial, Io, Polyphemus, Spicebush Silkmoth, Cecropia, Large Tolype, Lappet, Maple Looper, and the Unadorned Carpet; this is also the larval food plant for several butterflies including the Compton Tortoiseshell, White Admiral, Mourning Cloak and the Dreamy Duskywing; Bud gall of Birch caused by gall-mites *Eriophyes betulae* (Family Eriophyidae) are common on branches resulting in checked terminal growth and masses of undeveloped buds.

(continued)

Yellow Birch Interactions

Human/Economic Use; because of the presence of methyl salicylate, twigs are chewed to relieve toothaches and gum inflammations; a decoction is made from boiled bark which reduces pain from burns and sore muscles; this is a strong and heavy close grained wood used as a fuel, for box building, furniture, and flooring ; the wood is subject to decay if used in such a way as to put it in contact with the soil; sap is collected in late spring to make a sweet syrup.

Need To Know about interactions involving reptiles and spiders.

SHRUBS

Alder Buckthorn *Rhamnus frangula* L.

RHAMNACEAE (Buckthorn Family)

General Description -
Introduced from Europe and now a naturalized shrub growing to 18 feet in height.

Stem; moderately branching, older bark is gray with white dots while younger branches are slightly hairy and have naked end buds.

Leaves; alternate, elliptic to oblong, stalked and with very slightly toothed margins and very distinct pinnate veins.

Flower; small, stalked 5-petaled greenish flowers, some borne singly while others are in clusters, appearing May-June.

Habitat; shrub swamp, and also invades tree swamps and upland slopes.

WIS; FAC

Alder Buckthorn Interactions

Community Interactions; a very aggressive species introduced from Europe and Western Asia; there are many invasive hybrids making identification difficult; its fast growing root and stem systems out compete other endemic shrubs displacing them and thus reducing species diversity; of limited food value; since it loses its leaves late in the season, it is of some value to wildlife as a source of protective cover.

Mammals; it is possible one might observe Whitetail Deer and Black Bear browsing on the buds and fruits.

Plants; a shade tolerant introduced species which displaces Azaleas, Arrowwood, Highbush Blueberry, and others.

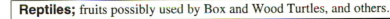

Birds; you may infrequently observe a Catbird or Wood Thrush taking the fruits; Starlings will commonly eat these fruits.

Reptiles; fruits possibly used by Box and Wood Turtles, and others.

Amphibians; useful as cover and perching site for Gray Treefrogs; Redback Salamanders may climb to lower branches to feed at night.

Human/Economic Use; CAUTION! fresh bark contains a strong cathartic property (a glycoside) which becomes milder and more useful for medical purposes when it is dried and aged; this preparation is used less for humans today, having been replaced by Cascara Sagrada.

Need To Know about interactions involving spiders, and insects.

A. Cranberry *Vaccinium macrocarpon* Aiton

ERICACEAE (Heath Family)

General Description -
Native prostrate evergreen shrub with fruiting stems possibly reaching 5 inches in height.

Stem; long, delicate, and trailing with many branches and upright fruiting stems.

Leaves; evergreen, flat to rolled edges, small, up to 3/4 inches long, alternate, oblong with rounded tips and whitish-green lower surfaces.

Flower; an insect pollinated flower, drooping, stalked, with four curved-back light pink petals revealing a yellow center, and appearing July-Aug.

Habitat; typically in bogs, occasionally damp edges of marshes and swamps.

WIS; OBL

American Cranberry Interactions

Community Interactions; although insect pollinated primarily by bees, Cranberries also self pollinate; can cover a Sphagnum or peat mat but contributes little to creating functional wildlife habitat except for fruit which is eaten by some wildlife; plant is primarily part of an agriculturally managed wetland with significant commercial impacts.

Mammals; although Black Bear are occasionally observed in and around such bogs and possibly consuming the berries, it is generally felt that they contain mammal antifeedants (chemicals making them not so tasty).

Birds; the Ruffed Grouse will eat berries.

Reptiles; The Bog, Snapping, Spotted, Redbelly, Blandings, Eastern Painted, and the Eastern Box Turtles are possible bog residents and are occasionally observed consuming various berries, among them may be Cranberries.

Amphibians; Green Frogs, Bullfrogs, Mink Frogs, and American and Fowler's Toads may take refuge beneath thick mats of Sphagnum and Cranberry.

Insects; the Bog Copper Butterfly lays eggs that overwinter on cranberry; serves as larval food plant for Rubbed Dart Moth especially near coastal salt marshes; also a larval food plant for the Cranberry Spanworm and Spotted Fireworm moths; the larvae of an uncommon Owlet moth *Hemipachnobia subporphyrea monochromatea* feeds first on a Sundew *Drosera spatulifolia*, and, avoiding the trap hairs of this insectivorous plant, it then reportedly switches to Cranberry for the remainder of its development; bees and Bumblebees visit these flowers for pollen and assist in their pollination.

Human/Economic Value; Did you drink your canberry juice or eat cranberry sauce today and get your Vitamin C? this is a fruit of high commercial value; American Natives used this as a food item and the juices to treat wounds and bowel disorders; juice can reduce nausea.

Need To Know about interaction with other plants and spiders.

Bog Laurel *Kalmia polifolia* Wangenh.

ERICACEAE (Heath Family)

General Description -
Native low evergreen shrub growing to 2 feet in height.

Stems; slender, 2-edged branches.

Leaves; evergreen, opposite, thin, lanceolate or linear, sessile, shiny green on top and white beneath and with rolled leaf margins.

Flower; pink to crimson, approximately 3/4 inches in diameter, borne in clusters at tips of branches and appearing June-July.

Habitat; bogs.

WIS; OBL

84

Bog Laurel Interactions

Community Interactions; bees will pollinate these flowers; presence indicates acidic soils with a pH ranging from 4-5; this is one of the least common of the evergreen bog shrubs; its relatively small size and low fruit and seed production make it of limited value to wildlife in terms of protective cover or food; see Sheep Laurel regarding its fire tolerance.

Mammals; interactions with mammals very similar to that expected for Labrador Tea.

Amphibians; Wood Frogs and Green frogs may forage in this plant.

Insects; this, as with Labrador Tea, is a larval food plant for the Chain-Dotted Geometer Moth and serves as a source of food for various bees.

Human/Economic Value; CAUTION-VERY POISONOUS, with same toxic principles as Sheep Laurel and Bog Rosemary.

Need To Know about interactions with plants, birds, reptiles, and spiders.

Bog Rosemary *Andromeda glaucophylla* Link

ERICACEAE (Heath Family)

General Description -
Native evergreen reclining to erect shrub growing to 2 feet in height.

Stem; smooth, slender, not highly branched which when reclined will often root along its length.

Leaves; alternate, short stalk, narrow, evergreen and up to 2 inches long, with rolled edges and white lower surfaces.

Flower; clusters of small, stalked, roundish, pink to white insect pollinated flowers dangling from a stalk at branch tips, appearing June - July.

Habitat; primarily bogs.

WIS; OBL

Bog Rosemary Interactions

Community Interactions; Bee pollinated; when present, it is found in association with other bog ericads including Leatherleaf, Sheep Laurel, and Labrador Tea; although it roots rather freely from creeping rhizomes, it is not a particulary densely growing species; these plants make little more than a modest contribution to habitat function, affording only limited cover for nesting and breeding and small amounts of food.

Mammals; seeds eaten by Southern Red-backed Vole; also see Labrador Tea for other mammal interactions.

Birds; observations for this plant are similar to those interactions expected for Leatherleaf, Sheep Laurel, Sweet Gale, Bog Laurel, and Bog Rosemary; seeds eaten by the Ptarmigan.

Amphibians; you can expect to observe the same here as those for Bog Laurel.

Insects; possible larval food plant for Andromeda Underwing Moth; Bees obtain some pollen from flower.

Human/Economic Value; CAUTION, POISONOUS; plant contains andromedotoxin- see Sheep Laurel and others for comment on toxicity; some claim boiling the leaves in making a tea removes the poisonous glycoside, but I suggest extreme caution in its use.

Need To Know about interactions with reptiles, spiders, and other plants.

Buttonbush *Cephalanthus occidentalis* L.

RUBIACEAE (Madder Family)

General Description -
A deciduous shrub growing to 6 feet in height.

Stem; highly branched and upright, reddish-brown and rounded or occasionally ridged and often bearing round flower heads at tip.

Leaves; oblong to oval with pointed tip, 3-4 inches long and alternate or whorled, stalked and with shiny green upper and pale green lower surfaces with pronounced veins.

Flower; ball-like tight cluster of small white insect pollinated flowers appearing in Aug; seeds wind and water dispersed.

Habitat; fresh marshes, occasionally wet meadows, swamps, and along edges of ponds, lakes, and streams.

WIS; OBL

Buttonbush Interactions

Community Interactions; light independent plant meaning that it can grow in full shade or in direct sun; plants have been known to withstand total submergence for up to 45 days and still survive, one of the only shrubs known to be able to withstand such inundation; even though it tends to grow better when roots are not submerged as in the higher marsh, it can frequently be seen standing in the shallow water of the low marsh, ponds and rivers; roots are quite tolerant of warm water discharge effluent, implying their selection for planting in thermally impacted areas; this shrub is often found at the margins of wetlands where it creates an edge or ecotonal community providing excellent cover for breeding and nesting as well as a source of protection for migratory waterfowl; although it may show signs of recovery following fuel oil spills into wetlands, ultimately there may be a decline in growth in such cases.

Mammals; the fruits, twigs, leaves, and wood are eaten by Muskrat, Beaver, and Whitetail Deer.

Plants; although this plant may be the dominant cover in shrub swamps and occasionally in high marshes, it usually is out competed in mid and lower marshes by such plants as Stick-tight and Spatter-dock respectively.

Birds; serves as occasional nesting site for Pied-billed Grebe near shallow water; Red-winged Blackbirds, Least Bitterns, Mallards, King Rails, and Sora Rails will nest and/or hide in and amongst these shrubs while the Wood Duck may be seen roosting in them day or night regardless of stand size; Mallards, Virginia Rails, and Wood Ducks eat the seeds.

Reptiles; the Eastern Ribbon Snake and the N. Northern Water Snake may be seen basking in the branches as may the Musk Turtle (Stink Pot) on horizontal branches hung out over the water.

Amphibians; a common egg attachment site for Wood, Leopard, and Pickerel Frogs and also the Spotted and Jefferson's Salamanders if branches are submerged in vernal or temporary pools.

Insects; careful examination might result in the observance of the cacoons of the Promethea, Polyphemus, and Luna Moths on the branches; this is the larval food plant for the Hydrangea Sphinx, Beautiful Wood-Nymph, and Connubial Underwing Moths; the adult Hessel's Hairstreak butterfly has been observed visiting these flowers as have various bees; dog ticks are likely to jump off the branches of this onto you if you get too close.

(continued)

Buttonbush Interactions

Spiders; one might expect to see a Fishing Spider waiting on a low branch just over the water.

Human/Economic Use; CAUTION; contains poisonous glucoside Cephalin; the Fox Indians prepared a bark infusion for use as a laxative, astringent (an agent which contracts tissue thus reducing secretions) and emetic (to induce vomiting); bark is chewed to reduce toothache pain.

Need To Know about interactions involving fish.

Wetland Replication

Henry David Thoreau said "Nature is not only more complex than we know; it may be more complex than we can know." Wetlands have taken thousands of years to evolve a multitude of interactions and functions of which only a few are really known as witnessed by the findings in this field guide. With this in mind, it is not to be expected that once destroyed, we can fully recreate this wetland and all its functions. While there are some examples of very conscientious efforts in this area, it has been estimated that less than half of all those wetlands destroyed have been even partially successfully replicated. If the destruction can not be avoided, then some important questions must be asked about this natural wetland so we can know in part what is needed in the recreated wetland. We need to ask such questions as (1) what are its functions, (2) of these functions, which are essential to replace, (3) can the plant and animal life forms obtained be identical to those present in the existing wetland, (4) can these wetlands be maintained at a reasonable cost, (5) and are we going to destroy valuable upland habitat to create a wetland? If the decision to try to replicate is made, then there should be a long-term plan in place to effectively monitor the success of this project.

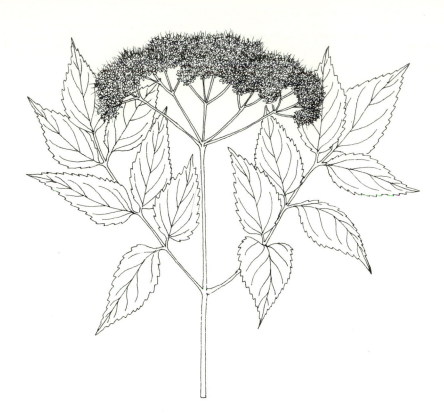

Common Elderberry *Sambucus canadensis* L.

CAPRIFOLIACEAE (Honeysuckle Family)

General Description -
Native shrub growing to 12 feet in height.

Stem; densely growing, erect, with brownish colored bark which has distinct raised dots and a white, spongy central pith.

Leaves; opposite, pinnately compound with 5-7 ovate opposite leaflets having sharp-toothed margins and smooth upper surfaces with some hairs on the bottom side.

Flower; small, 5-petaled white insect and wind pollinated flowers in dense wide 5-branched flat cluster appearing June-July.

Habitat; shrub swamp, tree swamp, marsh borders.

WIS; FACW-

Common Elderberry Interactions

Community Interactions; does quite well in moist soils and is sun and shade tolerant; provides valuable food and cover at edges of communities for a variety of wildlife which can seek cover from adjacent open fields.

Mammals; twigs and leaves are browsed by Whitetail Deer which may also bed down amongst these shrubs; fruits are eaten by the White-footed Mouse, Chipmunk, Red Squirrel, Woodchuck, and Red fox.

Birds; over 40 birds are known to enjoy the fruits of this shrub with some of the more frequently observed ones noted here; for example, the fruits are eaten by the Red-bellied Woodpecker, White-eyed Vireo, Phoebe, Veery, Wood Thrush, Tufted Titmouse, Robin, Starling, Swamp Sparrow, Cardinal, Blue Jay, and Alder Flycatcher; it provides cover and nesting for some of the previously mentioned birds as well as the Ruffed Grouse and Pheasant.

Reptiles; Wood and Box Turtles can be expected to eat the berries.

Amphibians; Gray Treefrog egg clusters and Wood Frog egg masses may be found attached to stems reaching out over and dipping under water; the surface egg masses of Bullfrogs may become passively entangled and attached to stems in water.

Insects; Honey bees, Flies, various wasps, and moths may function as pollinators; this is the larval food plant for the Elder Shoot Borer Moth the larvae of which bore into new growth; adult Elderberry Longhorn Beetles *Desmocerus palliatus* eat the pollen and nectar and lay eggs at the base of the stem with the resulting larvae making their way to the roots which they consume for food; another beetle, the Sap-feeding *Brachypterus* (*urticae*) adults, may be found on the flowers eating nectar, pollen, and sap; the Green Ground Beetle *Chlaenius sericeous* feeds on plant lice (probably from the family Psocidae) found on stems, leaves, and flowers; a Treehopper *Stitocephala diceros* feeds on the stems; one may note the Blackhorned Tree Cricket *Oecanthus nigricornis* which lays its eggs in the bark; larvae of the sawfly *Macrophya trisyllaba* can be seen crawling over the leaves where one may also observe the Ichneumon wasp *Rhyssa lineolata* laying eggs in these larvae.

Human/Economic Use; the berries are used to prepare wine, jams, and pie fillings; the flower yields a decoction which works as a diuretic or can be used to treat eye irritations and insect bites; the

(continued)

Common Elderberry Interactions

 Human/Economic Use (continued); Cherokee used various preparations of the leaves and flowers to treat colds, fevers, and burns; the Delaware made an extract from the flowers which was used to treat colicy babies.

Need To Know about interactions involving other plants and spiders.

Vegetative stratification.

Highbush Blueberry *Vaccinium corymbosum* L.

ERICACEAE (Heath Family)

General Description -
Native shrub growing to 12 feet in height.

Stem; main stem highly branched with younger twigs showing a zig-zag growth pattern; growing in clumps, stem bark is green to greenish-red and tends to shred.

Leaves; elliptical, alternate, green on both sides, with entire (smooth) margins and small hairs along veins on underside of leaf.

Flower; dense cluster of small white urn-shaped insect pollinated flowers which appear June-July.

Habitat; shrub swamp, tree swamp, bogs, other low wet areas and even occasionally uplands.

WIS; FACW-

Highbush Blueberry Interactions

Community Interactions; shade tolerant, grows singly or in dense clusters which form understory in woods providing excellent wildlife cover; also may be found growing at an edge where it creates a valuable ecotone, providing great cover for nesting, breeding, and overwintering; its presence generally indicates soil pH range of 4 - 4.5; berries are an excellent food source; plant easily propagates from suckers.

Mammals; many mammals including Black Bear, Muskrat, Otter, Skunk, Chipmunk, Rabbits, Whitetail Deer, Red Fox, Raccoon, Opposum, and White-footed Mice enjoy eating the fruits; Black Bears will visit bogs if this shrub is present; Beaver will cut branches for use as food or in den construction.

Plants; in some Vermont shrub swamps, this is found growing as a codominate with Winterberry Holly and Mountain Holly *Nemopanthus mucronata.*

Birds; many birds will be seen eating these fruits including Black-capped Chickadee, Baltimore Oriole, Blue Jay, Cardinal, Robin, Tufted Titmouse, Wood Thrush, Veery, Phoebe, Pheasant, Dove, Ruffed Grouse, Gulls, Wild Turkey, Red-bellied Woodpecker, and a host of others you can look out for; some of the above mentioned birds can be expected to nest or find cover here where indeed one can occasionally find the Red-bellied Woodpecker hiding.

Reptiles; the Eastern Box Turtle along with the Wood Turtle, Blandings Turtle, and Spotted Turtle may be expected to eat the fruits; Ribbon Snakes and N. Water Snakes bask on the branches.

Amphibians; you can expect to observe Redback Salamanders foraging amongst its branches at night; Spring Peepers and Gray Treefrogs climb into the branches.

Insects; Juvenal's Dusky Wing Butterfly emergence in the spring is timed with the opening of these flowers which it visits to drink nectar; serves as a larval food plant for such butterflies as the Pink-edged Sulphur, Brown Elfin, Henry's Elfin, possibly the Striped Hairstreak, and the Spring Azure; one occasionally observes the flowers being visited by adult Hessel's Hairstreak butterflies; it also serves as a food plant for the Azalea Sphinx, Apple Sphinx, Purple Arches, Andromeda Underwing, Graceful Underwing and the Sordid Underwing moths; Bumblebees and honey bees take nectar and pollen in return for pollinating the flowers; over 90% of insects visiting these shrubs is the Honey bee which tends to even work around bird netting.

(continued)

Highbush Blueberry Interactions

Spiders; see Appendix D.

Human/Economic Use; to the blueberry picker, this one goes without introduction as a fruit loved by most and is used in pies, muffins, cakes, etc.; the fruits are also the source of an excellent blue-gray dye; these fruits are a very good source of iron in the diet; they are one of the major small fruit crops in agriculture, accounting for tens of millions of dollars of income.

Need To Know about interactions involving spiders.

Wetland Value to Fish and Shellfish

Nearly all fish and shellfish are to some degree connected with vegetated wetlands. Many marine fish and shellfish spawn offshore and then move upstream to wetlands which serve as nurseries. Freshwater species usually prefer the shallow areas for spawning such as those found in marshes and swamps bordering streams, ponds and lakes. These wetlands also afford protection from predators which are usually not as abundant in the shallow water. As adult fish move to deeper water, they become part of the food chain. Such freshwater fish as carp, trout, perch, and pickerel and those salt water species including oysters, clams, shrimp, bluefish, and others, are found in the waters of vegetated wetlands at some point in their life cycle.

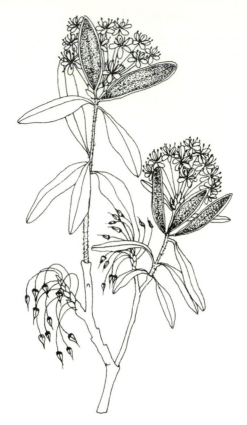

Labrador Tea *Ledum groenlandicum* Oeder

ERICACEAE (Heath Family)

General Description -
Native evergreen shrub growing to 3 feet in height.

Stem; many branched, with a very fuzzy (hairy) surface.

Leaves; evergreen, thick, oblong , to 2 inches long, stalked to sessile, dark green on top with curled edges and brown woolly bottoms, alternate and crowding at branch tips and fragrant when crushed.

Flower; small (3/8 inches wide), white, stalked with 5 sepals and petals, flowers crowded at branch tips and appearing June-July.

Habitat; bogs.

WIS; OBL

Labrador Tea Interactions

Community Interactions; insects including bees are involved in pollination; seeds need light for germination therefore the plant is typically found on open mats; not found in large numbers except in more northerly bogs; its root system tends to weave through the sphagnum serving to stabilize it; not particularly important in terms of wildlife value, although it may serve as a food source for a few animals.

Mammals; leaves and buds occasionally browsed by Whitetail Deer and Moose.

Birds; observations very similar to those expected for Sheep Laurel and other bog shrubs (ericads).

Amphibians; newly transformed Peepers may climb this plant in search of food, or for cover; Bull, Mink Frogs, and Gray treefrogs may hide beneath this shrub.

Insects; larval food plant for Chain-Dotted Geometer moth while bees obtain nectar and pollen from flowers; see Leatherleaf for its importance as part of the habitat of the Bog Fritillary butterfly.

Human/Economic Use; a leaf tea can be used externally to treat burns, itching, and head lice and internally to soothe stomach ailments; a brown dye is obtained from leaves.

Need To Know about interactions involving reptiles and spiders.

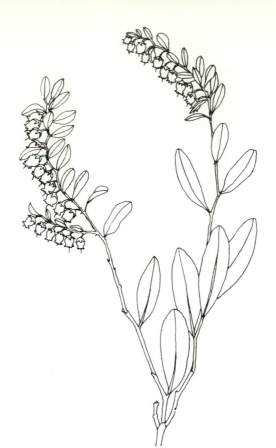

Leatherleaf *Chamaedaphne calyculata* L.

ERICACEAE (Heath Family)

General Description -
Introduced from Europe and Asia, an evergreen shrub growing to 3 feet in height.

Stem; highly branched, 1-2 inches in diameter.

Leaves; evergreen (leaves actually last for 2 years), up to 2 inches long, alternately arranged on stem and becoming smaller in size towards the tip of branch, usually stalked and leathery with brown scales on bottom.

Flower; small urn-shaped, insect pollinated white flowers hanging from the tips of stalks, appearing in May.

Habitat; bogs, fresh marshes, pond edges.

WIS; OBL

Leatherleaf Interactions

Community Interactions; prefers full sun and peaty soils; can observe bees taking nectar and pollen as they carry out pollination; in addition to sexual reproduction, plant can be propagated by division; plant adapted to the low nitrogen levels of a bog by hanging on to leaves a second growing season during which time they translocate hard earned nitrogen from these older leaves to newly developing leaves; its very extensive root system aids in stabilizing the floating Sphagnum matt; a highly branching shrub which creates thick stands covering vast areas; this habit of growth affords excellent wildlife cover; many leaves persist through the winter making the plant important as wildlife cover; the fruit is available throughout the winter as a food supply for wildlife.

Mammals; leaves and buds browsed upon by Whitetail Deer, Moose, and Cottontail rabbits.

Plants; often grows with Labrador Tea.

Birds; Ruffed Grouse are known to use the fruits as food throughout the winter.

Amphibians; the interactions expected here are similar to those observed for Labrador Tea.

Insects; the larval food plant for several moths including the Chain-dotted Geometer, a Looper *Syngrapha mirogamma*, and a leaf minor moth *Coptodisca kalmiella* which takes advantage of the two year leaves by laying eggs the first year with larvae mining leaves the second; known to house the nests of the Baldfaced Wasp *Vespula maculata*; this plant along with Labrador Tea, Tamarack, Sphagnum Moss, and other acid bog plants form the favored habitat of the Bog Fritillary Butterfly *Proclossiana eunomia* from Maine and north.

Human/Economic Use; Caution! may contain andromedotoxin a deadly cardiac glycoside; American natives concocted an infusion of the leaves for use as a drink (tea) to reduce feaver and inflammation.

Need To Know about interactions with birds, reptiles, and spiders.

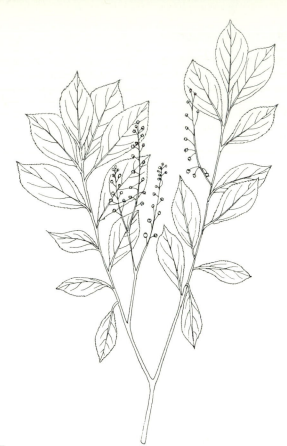

Maleberry *Lyonia ligustrina* (L.) DC

ERICACEAE (Heath Family)

General Description -
Native shrub growing to 18 feet in height.

Stem; moderately branching, with older gray bark having white dots and younger twigs appearing slightly hairy.

Leaves; alternate, elliptic to oblong, stalked, and with very slightly toothed margins and loosely pinnate leaf veins.

Flower; small, stalked, with 5 green petals borne either singly or in clusters (umbels), appearing May- June.

Habitat; shrub swamps, will invade tree swamps, is found in upland thickets and on slopes.

WIS; FAC

Maleberry Interactions

 Community Interactions; in some areas this is a fairly common member of the woody understory in wooded swamps.

 Amphibians; *Lyonia* provides perching sites and foraging areas for Peepers, Green Frogs, Pickerel Frogs, Leopard Frogs, and Cricket Frogs.

Need To Know about interactions involving mammals, other plants, birds, amphibians, reptiles, spiders, insects, and human/economic uses.

Marsh Elder *Iva frutescens* L.

COMPOSITAE (Aster Family)

General Description -
Native perennial deciduous shrub generally growing very low but occasionally reaching 1 foot in height.

Stem; branching, smooth or with sharp straight stiff hairs.

Leaves; lower leaves opposite although upper smaller leaves found within the inflorescence are alternate, with all tending to be short-stalked, fleshy and oblong with toothed margins.

Flower; small greenish-white on a leafy spike, appearing Aug-Sept.

Habitat; upper edges of salt marshes.

WIS; FACW+

Marsh Elder Interactions

Community Interactions; this and Sweetgale can grow in the higher marsh and often indicate the transition zone between upland (dry) areas and marsh; they grow in clumps, which affords some wildlife cover.

Need To Know about interactions involving mammals, birds, amphibians, reptiles, insects, spiders, other plants, and economic values.

Meadow-sweet *Spirea alba* var. *latifolia* (Aiton) Dippel

ROSACEAE (Rose Family)

General Description -
Native short perennial shrub growing in dense colonies and reaching 2-3 feet in height.

Stems; strongly single and unbranched (except occasionally towards the top where branching may occur), and having a smooth surface with red or purplish-brown coloration.

Leaves; reaching 3 inches, alternate, short stalked, oblong and tapering to the base with toothed margins and pointed to rounded tips.

Flower; a pyramidal cluster of white to pinkish 5-parted small bee, wasp, beetle and Cranefly pollinated flowers borne at stem tip.

Habitat; marshes, wet meadows.

WIS; FAC+

Meadow-sweet Interactions

Community Interactions; a very common shade to full sun tolerant plant which often grows in dense, vigorous stands providing cover for animals moving through wet meadows; the dried stems persist through winter offering some wildlife protection.

Mammals; may see the Whitetail Deer eating this plant in both summer and winter.

Plants; often seen growing with Swamp Milkweed.

Birds; dense stands are occasionally used as a nesting site by Field Sparrows and Swamp Sparrows and is often considered a favored perching site of Henslow's Sparrow.

Reptiles; Garter, Redbelly, Northern Brown, Black Racer, and occasionally Eastern Milk Snakes forage in meadows around this plant.

Amphibians; in wet meadows, Pickerel and Leopard Frogs forage around Meadowsweet in search of crickets, grasshoppers, and other insects.

Insects; this appears to be another larval food plant for the Spring Azure Butterfly whose larvae are attended by ants (*Formica* spp.) which by touching them, cause these larvae to release sweet fluids the ants consume; this is the adult nectar source for the Acadian Hairstreak and Two-spotted Skipper butterflies, the New England Buck Moth, and the Sharp-lined Yellow Moth; you may observe leaves bound together in the flower head which is the work of Tortricid Moth larvae that use this as a gallery; this plant is home to gall forming flies including the Spirea Cabbage Gall *Contarina (spiraeina)* that overwinters here and the Spirea Pod Gall Midge *Rhabdophaga (salicifolia)* that visits in summer; aphids such as the native North American *Aphis spiraecola* are often found grouped on the young shoots drinking in the sugar laden sap; several beetles including the adult False Darkling and Rove are common in the flowers.

Spiders; see Appendix D.

Human/Economic Use; a tea prepared from the leaves was used by early settlers and American Natives including the Mohegan and Osage, to treat bowel disorders such as diarrhea and nausea; a poultice from the flowers was used to treat wounds and halt bleeding.

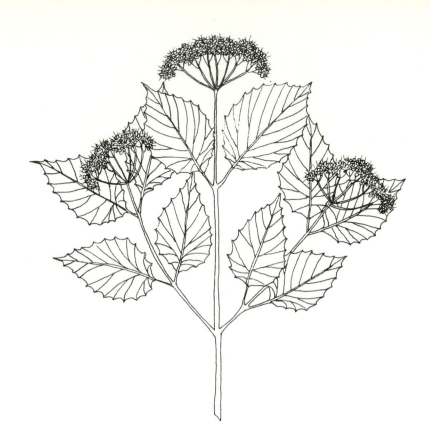

N. Arrowwood *Viburnum dentatum* var.*lucidum* Aiton

CAPRIFOLIACEAE (Honeysuckle Family)

General Description -
Native shrub growing to 12 feet in height.

Stem; highly branched, forming thickets, with extremely straight and erect twigs and smooth grayish bark and small hairs along upper edge of leaf scar.

Leaves; opposite, ovate, stalked, with sharp-toothed margins and very prominent veins having small tufts of hair in their axes and which terminate directly at the leaf margin teeth.

Flower; insect pollinated, small with five white petals in a somewhat dense terminal flat cluster, appearing June-July.

Habitat; shrub swamp also wooded swamps, thickets, and edges of streams, ponds, and marshes.

WIS; FACW-

Northern Arrowwood Interactions

 Community Interactions; one of the more air pollution tolerant woody species; quite flexible in its environmental requirements, thriving in dry to moist soils and in shade or full sun and is therefore very useful in urban plantings; often grows in dense stands providing protective cover for breeding, nesting, and overwintering sites for wildlife; fruits are eaten by a variety of animals.

 Mammals; fruits may be eaten by Chipmunk, White-footed Mouse, Skunk, Black Bear, and Red and Gray Squirrels; the twigs, fruits and buds are browsed by Whitetail Deer and eaten by Raccoon; in many instances, the seeds remain viable in the scat (dung) of these animals which thereby play an important role in plant dispersal.

 Plants; while you may observe this with many swamp plants, there is a very high degree of association to be observed between this shrub and Sensitive Fern.

 Birds; you can expect to find several birds nesting in Arrowwood including the Willow Flycatcher, White-eyed Vireo, and Catbird; although there are probably many more you will find if diligent, expect that Ruffed Grouse, Cardinal, Robin, Ring-necked Pheasant, Wild Turkey, Starling, Swainson's Thrush, and the Hermit Thrush will eat the fruits.

 Reptiles; Box and Wood Turtles are likely to consume the fruits; Garter, Ribbon, N. Water, and other snakes will climb (at least a short way) into Arrowwood to hunt for food and to bask.

 Amphibians; fallen or broken branches are useable as egg attachment sites for Wood Frogs, Spotted, Jefferson's, and Blue-spotted Salamanders; Treefrogs (Peepers, Gray Treefrogs) climb the branches to hunt food and use as calling perches.

Insects; various beetles, flies, ants, bees, wasps, and possibly butterflies and moths are known to participate in pollinating this shrub; this is the larval food plant for the Spring Azure Butterfly and the Azalea Sphinx Moth and Rose Hooktip Moth; a Click Beetle *Ampedus (collaris)* spends most of its time in the bark but can occasionally by seen as it forages in flowers; you may spot the Net-winged Beetle *Calopteron reticulatum* on flowers and foliage; the Dogwood Twig Borer Beetle *Obera tripunctata* may find conditions suitable to breed here; adult Pale Soft-winged Flower Beetles *Attalus scinetus* may feed on the pollen and the Tumbling Flower Beetle *Mordella marginata* adults feed on the flowers.

(continued)

111

Northern Arrowwood Interactions

Spiders; see Appendix D.

Human/Economic Use; Native Americans made a tea from the inner bark for a treatment of stomach disorders such as flatulance and cramps; the straight branches were used by Native Americans as arrow shafts, hence the plant name.

Need To Know about interactions involving spiders.

Likely nesting site in matted vegetation of marsh floor.

Poison Ivy *Toxicodendron radicans* (L.) Kuntze

ANACARDIACEAE (Cashew Family)

General Description -
Native trailing, climbing to the top of the tallest trees, or an erect woody shrub reaching 5 to 6 feet in height.

Stem; bushy, or runners with aerial roots that can function in clinging.

Leaves; alternate, in groups of 3, dark to light green, with entire (smooth) margins and smooth leaf surfaces except for some hairs on mid-vein.

Habitat; often found climbing trees, in swamps but also found throughout.

WIS; FAC

114

Poison Ivy Interactions

Community Interaction; a cosmopolitan species found in nearly all habitats; when it grows as a dense woody shrub, it provides cover for breeding and nesting in addition to being a food supply in winter; it is a great erosion control plant along shorelines and stabilizer of sand dunes.

Mammals; Black Bears and Muskrats eat the stems and leaves and Eastern Cottontails nest and seek protection in this; for other similar interactions, please refer to Poison Sumac.

Plants; one interesting observations shows that these plants do not compete well with Speckled Alder for space and light; refer to Jewelweed regarding its value in controlling the dermatological problems associated with this plant.

Birds; the berries are eaten by a large number of birds including the Brown Thrasher, Black-capped Chickadee, Crow, Starling, Purple Finch, White-eyed Vireo, Hermit Thrush, Phoebe, Catbird, Ruffed Grouse, andYellow-shafted Flicker; other interactions are similar to those for Poison Sumac may be expected.

Reptiles; it is possible that Box Turtles may feed on the fruit; Black Racers commonly hunt songbirds that are attracted to thick growth of poison ivy.

Insects; this is a larval food plant for several moths including the Beautiful Eutelia, the Light Marathyssa, and the Eyed Paectes; the Grape Flea Beetle *Altica chalybea* adults and larvae feed on the leaves; there is even a Poison Ivy Gall Mite *Eriophyes rhois* (Family Eriophyidae) that creates thin elongated string-like galls that are constricted at the point of attachment on the leaf.

Human/Economic Use; this is very similar in its poisonous nature to Poison Sumac; of medical interest is research showing that the active ingredients in this plant inhibit prostaglandins, a hormone-like chemical which plays a role in fertilization in humans; believe it or not, American Natives including the Chippewa, Delaware and Potawatomi rubbed leaf and root poultices into wounds to heal them or to reduce swelling; the Iroquois used a leaf extract to thin the blood while the Algonquin were known to treat Poison Ivy with Poison Ivy.

Need To Know about interactions involving amphibians and spiders.

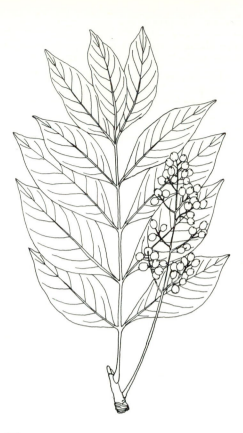

Poison Sumac *Toxicodendron vernix* (L.) Kuntze

ANACARIACEAE (Cashew Family)

General Description -
Native shrub or small tree growing to 20 feet in height.

Stem; loosely branching with a gray, smooth bark characterized by dark spots on older and yellow spots on younger stems.

Leaves; alternate, pinnately compound, with 12-13 opposite ovate leaflets having smooth edges, dark green upper and light green lower surfaces.

Flower; small drooping clusters of greenish, stalked flowers appearing May-June.

Habitat; shrub swamp, tree swamp.

WIS; OBL

116

Poison Sumac Interactions

Community Interactions; fruits provide food for wildlife well into the winter; depending upon its growth and density, it can provide some limited wildlife protection; the spreading root systems help stabilize wetland soils.

Mammals; very much like Poison Ivy.

Plants; Jewelweed and Sweetfern juices found in crushed leaves and stems break up the Urushiol and help control dermititis.

Birds; Pheasant and many thrushes eat the fruits and then deposit viable seeds in their scat (guano) thereby playing a role in seed dispersal.

Reptiles; N. Water Snake, Ribbon, Redbelly, and Smooth Green Snakes forage and hide in sumac areas; fruits can be expected to be eaten by Box and Wood Turtles.

Amphibians; Green Frogs, Wood Frogs, and Spring Peepers forage around Sumac swamps and lay their eggs in the water.

Insects; the Beautiful *Eutelia* Moth uses this as a larval host plant.

Spiders; see Appendix D.

Human/Economic Use; CAUTION! poisonous; contains a toxic oleoresin Urushiol to which it is estimated that 70% of the U.S. population would elicit dermititis on just casual contact (this same substance is in Poison Ivy , Poison Oak, and all plants in this same genus and Family Anacardiaceae); refer to Poison Ivy because this was put to similar use by American Natives; to cure this and poison ivy, American Natives used a varieity of plants including Jewelweed, dogwoods, Verbena, and Beech.

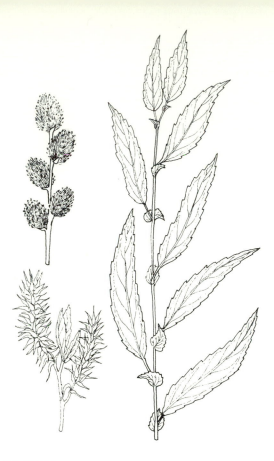

Pussy Willow *Salix discolor* Muhl.

SALICACEAE (Willow Family)

General Description -
Native shrub growing to 12 feet in height with a rounded crown.

Stem; very short and much branched trunk with bark smooth and gray, younger branches have green to reddish-tinged bark, flat side buds appressed (laying against stem) and have a single scale fitting over them much like a hood.

Leaves; alternate, stalked, lance-shaped with pointed tips and round-toothed margins, bright green above and whitish below and often having one or two small leaf-like structures at the point where stalks meet the stem.

Flower; wind and insect pollinated, with male and female on separate plants in spikes (pussies) which open April-May.

Habitat; shrub swamps, wet swales, stream banks.

WIS; FACW

Pussy Willow Interactions

Community Interactions; an important edge plant which usually has many branches providing superior cover for nesting, breeding, and overwintering wildlife; catkins, leaves, and twigs provide a source of food for wildlife; its spreading strong root system functions as an excellent soil anchor along the banks of even the swiftest moving streams; rapid growing, with stems which can quickly produce adventitious roots above a rising water table.

Mammals; you may see Beaver, Muskrat, and Red Squirrels eating bark, wood, and buds as food; Meadow Mice take catkins and leaves for food, while the Whitetail Deer, Moose, and Snowshoe Hare eat twigs.

Plants; tends to grow in association with other shrubs and less often in pure stands unless planted in this manner.

Birds; at one time or another, you may observe this as nesting site for one or more of the following: the Tricolored Heron, Cattle Egret, Alder Flycatcher, Willow Flycatcher, and the Veery; the American Woodcock will often use such thickets for breeding, the Yellow Warbler is known to use the seed fibers in nest construction, and the Ruffed Grouse eats the seeds as do perhaps many other birds which you might observe.

Reptiles; Wood Turtles are known to occasionally eat the leaves.

Amphibians; Peepers often use this plant as perching sites, as do newly metamorphosed Gray Treefrogs.

Insects; the following long list of insects which in one way or another use this plant testifies to its great value in the community; this is the larval plant for such butterflies as the Acadian Hairstreak, Bog Fritillary, Striped Hairstreak, Compton Tortoiseshell, Mourning Cloak, Viceroy which you may find wrapped up in a leaf in the larval form, occasionally the Dreamy Duskywing, and Titania's Fritillary; this is also the food plant for such moths as the Small-eyed Sphinx, Big Poplar Sphinx, Io, Luna, Cecropia, Lappet, Large Looper, Darling Underwing, and One-spotted Variant; this is food for the Cottonwood Leaf Beetle *Chrysomela scripta* and the Willow Longhorn Beetle *Xylotrechus insignis*; the Imported Willow Beetle *Plagiodera versicolor* goes through its entire life cycle on this plant; Honey bees, Bumblebees, Hover flies, and various aphids and even ants visit this plant which produces both nectar and pollen; in the fall you might observe a leafy looking gall on the branches often caused by the Willow-beaked Gall Midge *Mayetiola rigidae* or perhaps by

(continued)

Pussy Willow Interactions

Insects (continued); the Willow Cone Gall Gnat *Rhabdophaga strobiloides* or Petaled Willow Gall Gnat *R. (brassicoides)*; although it often hides in the bark, the harmful Click Beetle *Ampedus (nigri-collis)* may be found feeding in the flowers; the Flea Weevil *Rhynchaenus* spp. larvae mine the leaves while the adults eat the leaves and most other parts of the plant; various sawflies are responsible for galls on the stems; commonly feeding on the flowers are the adult Pollen Feeding Beetle *Asclera (ruficollis)*; adults of a False Antlike Beetles *Macratia* spp. feed on the leaves and flowers.

Spiders; see Appendix D.

Human/Economic Use; although not a chief source, the glycoside salicin is present in the bark; salicin is antirheumatic in its action; it was chewed by American Natives to treat toothaches, stomachaches, and headaches; salicin eventually lead to the discovery of acetylsali-cylic acid and "Bayer" aspirin; these plants also have value in horti-cultural floral arrangements; forcing the 'pussies' or silver fuzzy fruits, is of value commercially to florists.

Need To Know about interactions involving spiders.

Wetland Plant Adaptation to Anoxia (low oxygen)

Oxygen levels in water and water-logged soils are 10-30 times lower in concentration than in upland soils. As a result, wetland plant root systems which need oxygen for nutrient uptake and metabolism must cope with very low oxygen levels. Interestingly, many wetland plants do not depend upon the soggy soil or watery milieu as their source of oxygen. Instead, these plants have large air spaces called aerenchyma which run throughout the roots, stems, and leaves. These spaces allow oxygen absorbed by the aerial portions of the plant to be sent down to the roots where it is used in metabolism. Research has shown that such air spaces in upland plants average about 5 percent of the overall volume, whereas such spaces in wetland species may exceed 60 percent of the plant volume. Other plants avoid anoxia by developing surface roots which grow above the low oxygen zone. These roots have lenticels which are small openings equipped to absorb oxygen from the air. Other wetland plants lack aerenchyma, and yet their roots are capable of metabolizing at very low internal oxygen levels. Such low oxygen levels often pose a different problem for the plant roots-fermentation and the resultant production of toxic alcohol. Remarkably, these plants have evolved mechanisms to diffuse the alcohol to the outside, thus avoiding the accumulation of toxic levels.

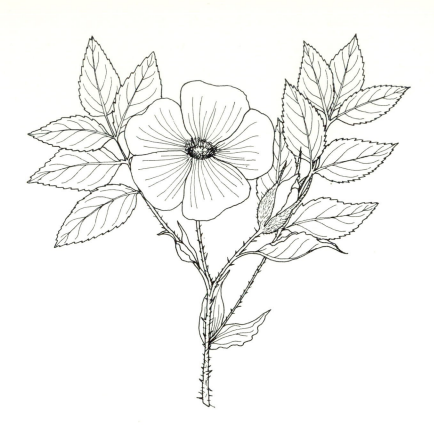

Rugosa Rose *Rosa rugosa* Thunb

ROSACEAE (Rose Family)

General Description -
Introduced and naturalized deciduous shrub growing to 6 feet in height.

Stem; highly branched, in dense clumps, with upper branches woolly and covered with prickles.

Leaves; shiny, dark green, pinnately compound with 5-9 leaflets which have toothed margins.

Flower; 5 white, red, pink or rose purple colored petals up to 5 inches wide which are insect pollinated.

Habitat; salt marshes, also on sand dunes and along roadsides near coast.

WIS; FACU

Rugosa Rose Interactions

Community Interactions; invasive, rugged shrub resistant to wind, salt spray, intense sun, wave action and dry soils; have deep branching root systems and grow in dense thickets, features which serve to make it a valuable stabilizer of soils around marshes; although not a direct wetland function, it also is a tremendous builder and stabilizer of sand dunes.

Mammals; its dense growth offers protection, breeding sites, and overwintering cover for wildlife including Raccoon, Stripped Skunk, and E. Cottontails, all of whom eat the large rose hip fruits; Whitetail Deer will browse leaves and occasionally twigs.

Birds; it is certain that one will observe many birds nesting or hiding in these shrubs including the Mockingbird and the Bobwhite which eat the fruits and buds.

Reptiles; Eastern Box Turtles probably eat some fruit; Black Racers commonly hunt rodents and birds in these thickets.

Insects; since this is a larval food plant for the Striped Hairstreak Butterfly, you can expect to observe this from time to time.

Human/Economic Use; the large reddish-orange rose hips (fruits) are quite high in Vit. C and are used to make Vitamin C tablets, pills etc., as well as drinks, jams, and sauces; the hips can also be eaten as is or steeped in tea; the presence of the citrus bioflavonoid 'hesperidin' has been indicated in the treatment of capillary fragility.

Need To Know about interactions with other plants, amphibians, and spiders.

Shadbush *Amelanchier canadensis* (L.) Medikus

ROSACEAE (Rose Family)

General Description -
Native shrub or small tree growing to 25 feet in height.

Stem; several thin, erect gray bark stems forming a clump.

Leaves; oblong, alternate, stalked, with rounded tips, toothed margins near-ly to the leaf base and having white hairs on lower surface.

Flower; small, white self and/or insect pollinated flowers borne in an ascending cluster with hairy flower stalks and petals, appearing April-June.

Habitat; found in wooded swamps, low wet areas including floodplains, banks of water courses and occasionally uplands.

WIS; FAC

Shadbush Interactions

 Community Interactions; a very shade tolerant plant that grows in thickets in swamps where it establishes excellent understory which provide food, breeding, and nesting sites for wildlife.

 Mammals; the twigs and fruits are known to be eaten by Beaver, Skunk, Chipmunk, Red and Gray Squirrel, White-footed Mice, Whitetail Deer, and possibly Red Fox.

 Birds; many birds including Ruffed Grouse, Blue Jay, Baltimore Oriole, Song Sparrow, Wood Thrush, Veery, Tufted Titmouse, Cardinal, Rose-breasted Grosbeak, Black-capped Chickadee, Brown Thrasher, and Catbird eat the fruits; Robins, and the Eastern Kingbird use it for cover and nesting.

 Reptiles; although none known, the Box and Wood Turtles may feed on fruit that has fallen.

 Amphibians; Wood Frogs and Spring Peepers are found near Shadbush in early spring- perhaps hunting insects attracted to the early spring flowers.

 Insects; this is a larval food plant for the Dark-Spotted Palthis Moth and the Praeclara Underwing Moth and for at least two butterflies including the White Admiral and the Striped Hairstreak; the flowers may also be visited by Hessel's Hairstreak adult butterflies; a Wooly Aphid *Prociphilus* spp. may be found on leaves and stems; gall-mites *Eriophyes amelanchieri* (Family Eriophyidae) cause June-berry Mite-gall which appear as light green tubes on the lower leaf surface and reddish globular structures on the upper.

Human/Economic Use; fruits are high in Vitamin C and are used to prepare jams and jellies; valued as an ornamental for planting, especially for those interested in feeding birds and mammals.

Need To Know about interactions involving other plants and spiders.

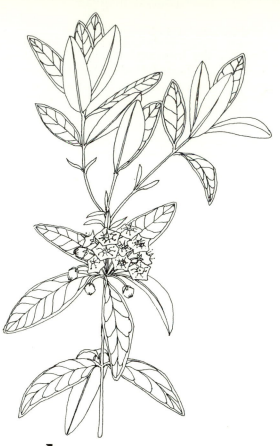

Sheep Laurel *Kalmia angustifolia* L.

ERICACEAE (Heath Family)

General Description -
Native evergreen shrub growing to 2 feet in height.

Stems; branching, upright.

Leaves; glabrous, evergreen, up to 2 inches long, oblong to elliptic and even lanceolate in shape and generally growing in whorls of three on short stalks.

Flower; up to 1/2 inch wide, cup shaped and clustered around stem towards tip and appearing July-August.

Habitat; bogs, swamps and into uplands, generally preferring acid soils.

WIS; FAC

126

Sheep Laurel Interactions

Community Interactions; insect pollinated; presence indicates acid soil conditions (pH of 4-5); this is a fire resistant plant because of the presence of vegetative propagating structures deep enough into the soil as to not be subject to surface fire damage; as a result, they often succeed quickly into a burn area forming a dense growth; plant equally at home in a bog as it is in an acid upland; provide some cover for small ground dwelling wildlife.

Mammals; similar to Leatherleaf, Sweet Gale, Bog Rosemary, Labrador Tea and Bog Laurel in value to mammals; buds and leaves occasionally consumed by Whitetail Deer and Black Bear.

Birds; Ruffed Grouse eat buds and the Black-capped Chickadee can be seen feeding on various scale insects of the Superfamily Coccoidea that live on the leaves, stems, and flowers of this plant.

Reptiles; the N. Water Snake and Eastern Ribbon Snake use the dense foliage and stands for ambush sites, for basking, and for cover.

Amphibians; Green and Bullfrogs eggs are sometimes attached to stems at the surface; also one can occasionally find Wood Frog, Spotted and Jefferson Salamander eggs attached to these stems.

Insects; Bumble and Honey bees pollinate as they go after the pollen and nectar; larval food plant for several moths including White Slant-Line, Red-Fronted Emerald, Spotted Fireworm, and the Mottled Gray Carpet; some reports indicate that this may also serve as a larval host plant for the Pink-shaded and Silver-spotted moths, which are usually found associated with various ferns; it is also the larval food plant for the Brown Elfin Butterfly.

Spiders; Look for those noted as associated with Sphagnum Moss and Pitcher Plant.

Human/Economic Use; CAUTION, DO NOT EAT- contains the cardiac glycoside andromedotoxin which can cause loss of motor coordination, hallucinations, and even heart stoppage; it is also poisonous to livestock; honey made from this pollen is poisonous; some American Natives made a paste of the leaves to relieve muscle aches; the Abenaki prepared a powder from its leaves and mixed it with Sassafras to use as a nasal decongestant snuff.

Need To Know about interactions involving other plants.

Silky Dogwood *Cornus amomum* Miller

CORNACEAE (Dogwood Family)

General Description -
Native shrub growing to 12 feet in height.

Stem; much branching, lower portions gray while more recent growth is reddish -purple and silky; the pith (central tissue core) is brown.

Leaves; opposite, petiolate,rounded at base, with pointed tips and having veins branching off midvein which follow up the smooth (entire) leaf margin without reaching edge.

Flower; insect pollinated, small , white, with four petals borne in a broad spray or cluster towards branch tips, appearing June-Aug.

Habitat; shrub swamp, tree swamp, banks of streams.

WIS;FACW

Silky Dogwood Interactions

Community Interactions; one of the most highly regarded woody plants for value to wildlife; it branches profusely from the base creating dense thickets that provides extremely valuable cover for nesting and breeding wildlife; plants easily propagated from stem cuttings; shrub often borders swamps, streams, etc. forming an edge with food and cover available to wildlife year round and providing shelter to animals migrating along such stream channels; commonly reflowers in same season following pruning.

Mammals; buds, twigs, and fruits browsed by Whitetail Deer and Black Bear while Skunk, Raccoon, Gray Squirrels, Chipmunks, and White-footed Mice eat fruits.

Birds; whether in preparation for migration or not, there are many birds you can expect to feed on the high fat content fruits of this shrub including Red-Bellied Woodpeckers, Wood Thrushes, Ruffed Grouse, Wild Turkey, Brown Thrashers, Cardinals, Purple Finches, Bluejays, Catbirds, Starlings, Mockingbirds, Pheasants, Blue Jays, Grackles, and Cedar Waxwings; many of these birds may find cover and nesting sites in this shrub as well; others, including the Alder Flycatcher and Willow Flycatcher may nest here.

Reptiles; young Snapping Turtles forage underwater along streambanks, where overhanging foliage provides cover for aquatic insects and other prey; Water and Ribbon Snakes bask along horizontal branches.

Amphibians; along streambanks, Bullfrogs, Green Frogs, and Leopard Frogs may take refuge in dense stands; Gray Treefrogs may climb into shrubs for food (insects).

Insects; this is one of the larval food plants for the Spring Azure Butterfly and a nectar source to the adult Hickory Hairstreak Butterfly and occasionally the Dark-Spotted Palthis Moth; several other moths use this as the larval food plant and thus may be seen or expect to be seen visiting including the False Crocus Geometer, Dogwood Probole, and Dogwood Borer; the spindle shaped cocoons of the Cecropia Moth are occasionally found overwintering on these plants as well as those of the White-marked Tussock Moth; the Pale Soft-winged Flower Beetle *Attalus scinetus* adults may be observed in the flowers where one may also find the Dogwood Twig Borer Beetle *Oberea tripunctata* breeding; Click Beetle *Ampedus rubricus* and Tumbling Flower Beetle *Mordella marginata* adults may be found feeding on the flowers; in addition to many of the aforementioned, Honey bees, Wasps, Bumblebees, and Hover Flies may be involved as vectors of pollination.

(continued)

Silky Dogwood Interactions

 Spiders; the Ray Spider *Theridiosoma radiosa* has been observed to suspend egg sacs from branches of this shrub along stream banks; this spider may build its snare web here that it pulls into a cone shape because of a thin thread it attaches to its middle that it lets go to capture prey passing by.

 Human/Economic Use; the bark of this plant can be powdered and used as toothpowder; a decoction of the bark was used in folk medicine and by the Chippewa and Menominee to treat diarrhea and indigestion; the inner bark was dried and smoked by the Menominee who found it slightly hallucinogenic.

Need To Know about interactions involving other plants.

Scattered dark clumps of Soft Rush typical of a wet meadow.

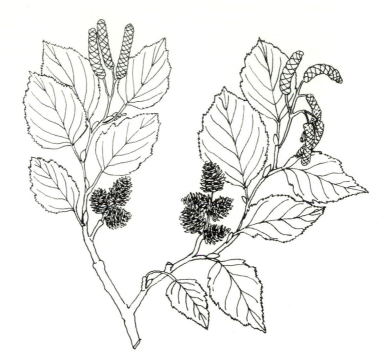

Speckled Alder *Alnus incana* var. *americana* **Regel**

BETULACEAE (Birch Family)

General Description -
Native shrub growing to 18 feet in height.

Stem; several to many, branching and upright with grayish-brown bark covered with raised spherical to elongated bumps (lenticles), and reddish-brown stalked buds.

Leaves; alternate, usually single toothed, stalked, ovate, with reddish-brown stalked buds in axils.

Flower; wind or self pollinated with the female upright in clusters, stalked and resembling a small pine cone whereas male is elongate, finger-like, drooping and on short stalks, with both appearing April-June.

Habitat; shrub swamps, tree swamp edges, and margins of streams and ponds.

WIS; FACW+

Speckled Alder Interactions

Community Interactions; although often considered a 'weed', it is a valuable early successional species which appears to play an important role in increasing nitrogen in soil through both leaves which contain high nitrogen levels and nitrogen fixation in root nodules; prefers neutral to slightly acid conditions, not growing as well in alkaline soils and waters; has both dense surface and deep roots which serve to stabilize soils on banks; these plants reproduce readily from buried roots or stems; surface roots can be produced in response to increased water table which in turn adapts alder to water logged soils; its deeper roots permit them to persist in drier, lower water tables resulting from human impacts on the hydrology; their tolerance of flooding and the resulting low oxygen levels may relate in part to their ability to synthesize glycerol rather than toxic alcohol in its root cells during fermentation metabolism; alder is sensitive to increased levels of sulfur dioxide in the air; evidence indicates that it absorbs arsenic from polluted waters thus reducing contamination of the food chain; prescribed burning recommended for management of alder thickets if basal diameter is less than 3 inches; game management provides spaced alder thickets as food and cover sources for both the Snowshoe Hare and Whitetail Deer; alder lined banks are prime habitat for Beaver.

Mammals; Beaver, Whitetail Deer, Snowshoe Hare, and Black Bear will eat bark, wood, and leaves; Beaver use the twigs in the construction of dams; Muskrat are known to establish tunnels through the roots of this plant.

Plants; one of the few plants which can out compete Poison Ivy for space and light; may be observed as a small tree or tall shrub in Red Maple dominated swamps.

Birds; with patience and time, you may observe any one or more of many birds that nest in or near this shrub including Goldfinch, Red-winged Blackbird, Alder Flycatcher, Catbird, Hermit Thrush, Yellowbellied Flycatcher and sometimes on the ground beneath these shrubs, the Tennessee, Hooded, and Wilson's Warbler; alder thickets are the favored breeding habitat of the American Woodcock, the rare Hoary Redpoll, Pine Siskin, Swamp Sparrow, and serve as the favored drumming site of the Ruffed Grouse; Mallards and Bufffleheads not only eat the seeds but utilize the shrub for cover; the seeds are eaten by a number of other birds including the Ruffed Grouse, Woodcock, Goldfinch, and Ring-necked Pheasant.

(continued)

133

Speckled Alder Interactions

Reptiles; it is quite possible that one could observe the Eastern Ribbon Snake basking on a branch; also, the Stinkpot Turtle may be seen basking on horizontal branches overhanging water; Wood Turtles forage in thickets near streams.

Amphibians; Green Frogs, Leopard Frogs, and occasionally Bullfrogs rest in the shade of Alder thickets; male Spring Peepers and Gray Treefrogs use Alders as calling perches.

Insects; an incredible array of insects interact with alder in a variety of ways as the following show: this is the larval food plant for the One-Spotted Variant Moth, Doubleday's Baileya Moth, the Sordid Bomolocha Moth, the Renounced Hydriomena Moth, the Nameless Pinion Moth, Large Looper Moth, the Luna Moth, Variegated Cutworm Moth, Purple Arches Moth, the Lappet Moth, American Dagger Moth, and the Rusty Tussock Moth; the Silver-Spotted Ghost Moth bores into the roots; the Eastern Dobson Fly *Corydalus cornutus* can be seen resting and hunting on this shrub and the Oak Lace Bug *Corythuca arcuata* may feed on plant juices; the Alder Leaf (Flea) Beetles *Altica bimarginata* adults feed on the leaves, lays eggs here and the larvae upon hatching continue feeding on the plant; the sap is eaten by the Woolly Alder Aphid *Prociphilus tesselatus* while the Orange Harvester Butterfly *Feniseca tarquinius* feeds on its honeydew (liquid excreted from the rear end of the aphid) and also lay eggs on these aphids which in turn upon hatching feed on their host- a rare instance of carnivory among butterflies; this same aphid *Prociphilus tesselatus* is a source of honeydew for ants which in turn will protect them against the Harvester Butterfly and other insects; this plant plays host to many beetles such as the Lurid Flathead Beetle *Dicera lurida* that eats and breeds here, the Golden-haired Flower Longhorned Beetle *Leptura (chrysocoma)* adults that eat the pollen and larvae that consume the wood, a Soldier Beetle *Cantharis* spp. and Flathead Borer Beetles *Chrysobothris* spp. feed on its leaves, a Longhorned Beetle *Saperda (obliqua)* breeds at the base of the plant and adult False Antlike Flower Beetles *Macratria* spp. feed on the leaves and flowers; a fly *Dasyneura* spp. causes alder bud-gall whereby the terminal buds become rounded, large, hairy, and brown.

Spiders; I have seen the Brownish-gray Fishing Spider *Dolomedes tenebrosus* sitting on the leaves.

Fish; I have seen trout congregate along stream edges under low hanging branches that provide shelter.

(continued)

Speckled Alder Interactions

Human/Economic Use; a bark infusion prepared by the Chippewa was used to induce vomiting, the Cree prepared a poultice of the inner bark as an astringent to reduce infectious secretions and to stop bleeding while the Lumbee used this plant to control Poison Ivy and to reduce swellings and rashes; this plant is a source of wool and leather dyes including brown from the roots, yellow-green from the leaves and brownish-yellow from the bark.

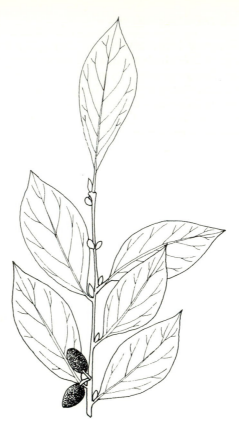

Spicebush *Lindera benzoin* (L.) Blume

LAURACEAE (Laurel Family)

General Description -
Native shrub growing to 10 feet in height.

Stem; older portions with smooth gray-brown bark while younger growth is green, leaf buds are borne singly and are pointed whereas flower buds are spherical, yellow and borne in pairs near a leaf scar.

Leaves; alternate, ovate, with smooth (entire) margins, pointed tips, aromatic when crushed, dark green, and turning bright yellow in fall.

Flower; small yellow male and female flowers borne in clusters on separate plants; are insect pollinated and appear April-May.

Habitat; shrub swamp, tree swamp, pond and stream edges.

WIS; FACW-

Spicebush Interactions

Community Interactions; presence generally indicates a soil pH in range of 5-6; shade tolerant and one of the earliest plants to flower in New England; grows as moderately dense woody understory in swamps providing cover for breeding and nesting and with berries serving as food; also contribute moderate wildlife cover in winter; have flushed Whitetail Deer from these thickets.

Mammals; Whitetail Deer observed nibbling on leaves and can be expected to eat fruits.

Birds; berries are eaten by Robins, Wood Thrush, Veery, and Ring-necked Pheasant which are known to spread the seeds through their scat; a late fall fruit for the Red-eyed Vireo; this and other low shrubs of the swamp are nesting sites for the Hooded Warbler.

Reptiles; Box Turtles may forage here; N. Ringneck snakes may be common in spicebush swamps.

Amphibians; N. Dusky Salamanders may be abundant in seepages that flow through Spicebush stands.

Insects; this is the primary larval food plant for the Spicebush Swallowtail Butterfly, that folds a leaf around itself during maturation to adulthood; the Spicebush Silkmoth uses this as a larval food plant; A Longhorned Beetle *Obera (ruficollis)* breeds on this plant.

Human/Economic Use; the dried and powdered red berries are used as a substitute for allspice in cooking; bark and twig extracts are used in folk medicine and homeopathy to treat colds, fevers, coughs, dysentery, and intestinal worms; the Cherokee were known to treat measles with a mixture of whiskey and a tea made from this, and the bark of cherry and dogwood; other parts of this plant were used by the Cherokee for such illnesses as colds and coughs.

Need To Know about interactions involving other plants and spiders.

Swamp Azalea *Rhododendron viscosum* (L.) Torr.

ERICACEAE (Heath Family)

General Description -
Native shrub growing to 8 feet in height.

Stem; multiple whorled branching with gray to brownish-gray bark.

Leaves; vary in shape but tend to be elliptic to oblong, alternate, smooth, greenish with bristly margins.

Flower; fragrant insect pollinated with white tubular petals frequently having pinkish stripes and sticky bases borne in clusters towards ends of branches and appearing June-July.

Habitat; shrub swamps, damp areas including tree swamps and rarely bogs.

WIS; OBL

Swamp Azalea Interactions

Community Interactions; presence of this species generally indicates acid soils in a pH range of 4-4.5; these plants often grow in rather dense stands and although they serve limited value as food for wildlife, they provide cover for breeding, nesting, and overwintering; these very shade tolerant understory shrubs create verticle stratification that results in increased habitat diversity.

Mammals; leaves browsed by Whitetail Deer and White-footed Mouse.

Plants; very often find Cinnamon Fern growing under these shrubs.

Birds; Wood Thrushes seem to prefer nesting in these shrubs if there is an accompanying thick growth of Cinnamon Fern; flowers very rarely seen being visited for nectar by the Ruby-throated Hummingbird; buds may be eaten by Ruffed Grouse.

Reptiles; Smooth Green, Redbelly, and Garter Snakes hunt for insects and other prey here and may climb into branches for cover, basking, or resting sites.

Amphibians; Gray Treefrogs and Peepers utilize thick foliage for food and cover.

Insects; flowers may be a nectar source for the Pipevine Swallowtail and Tiger Swallowtail Butterfly; the Azala Sphinx Moth also visits for nectar and may be the chief vector of pollination; this is a larval food plant for the Major Datana Moth; perhaps you could find the Spined Stink Bug *Podisus maculatus* waiting for one of its favorite meals - the caterpillar of the Swallowtail Butterfly.

Spiders; see Appendix D.

Human/Economic Use; CAUTION! contains poisonous cardiac glycoside andromedotoxin which is capable of stopping the heart; this toxic agent is also found in honey produced by bees utilizing this flower; the Cherokee prepared a water extract of the branches in the making of a solution to rub on sore muscles and as a treatment for rheumatism and would also tie leaves to the head to cure head pain.

Need To Know about interactions involving spiders.

Swamp Loosestrife *Decodon verticillatus* (L.)Elliott

LYTHRACEAE (Loosestrife Family)

General Description -

Native shrub becoming herbaceous towards tips and growing to 4-5 feet in height.

Stem; long, 4-6 sided and arching with a smooth to slightly hairy surface; can root at tips of arching stems resulting in establishment of dense stands.

Leaves; opposite, whorled, 3-4 inches long, sessile to short stalked, lanceolate and tapering to a point at the tip.

Flower; insect pollinated, small, 5 petaled, pinkish-purplish flowers having 5-7 sepals and borne in clusters in axils of mid to upper leaves; appearing July-Aug.

Habitat; fresh marshes, wet meadows, pond and lake margins, and swamp edges.

WIS; OBL

Swamp Loosestrife Interactions

Community Interactions; growing in dense stands it can act as a water filter trapping organics and also as a natural substrate for the attachment of algal and diatom communities; while its dense growth can serve to stabilize banks, it is a very aggressive, problematic, and wide ranging herb often dominating marshes, shrub swamps, stream and pond borders resulting in a reduction of plant species diversity, a restriction of water flow and the subsequent lowering of detrital exchange between open water and emergent wetlands; it is one of the first to invade areas subjected to an altered hydrology with prolonged flooding; the plant speeds up succession from wetland to upland (dry) if it grows out of control and is often found in swamps which have recently succeeded from a marsh or wet meadow; it is also known to invade the acid open water of bogs and to be present in many sunny open spots within the larger well established swamps; may provide protective cover, nesting material, and food for some wildlife.

Mammals; Muskrats and rabbits feed on all parts of this plant.

Plants; see comments regarding its invasive quality under 'Community Interactions'; there are several plants including Duckweed and Rice-cut Grass which seem to hold their own against the intrusion of this plant and are therefore often found growing with it; it may be associated with many shrubs found in shrub swamps including Sweet Pepperbush, Blueberry, Azalea, and Spicebush.

Birds; this along with other marsh plants acts as nesting material for the American Coot and Common Moorhen, while Black Duck, Mallard, Blue-winged Teal, and Wood Duck may be seen consuming the seeds.

Reptiles; Snapping and Painted Turtles forage near dense *Decodon* mats as occasionally do Musk (Stinkpot) Turtles; young N. Water Snakes, Ribbon Snakes and adult Redbelly Snakes hunt for prey in the dense mats.

Amphibians; various frogs can be found hiding among the stalks of this emergent along wetland edge; the long stalks provide submerged egg deposition sites for Wood Frogs, Spotted and Jefferson's Salamanders; also Pickerel Frogs and Red-spotted Newts can be found to place their eggs on these branches.

Insects; the Greenhead Fly and the Black Horse Fly lay eggs on leaves and stems overhanging fresh water into which they can fall for further development; the Burdock Borer Moth *Papaipema cataphracta*

(continued)

Swamp Loosestrife Interactions

Insects (continued); lives in the stems and, known only from Massachusetts, it serves as the larval food plant for the borer moth *P. sulphurata*; plant also serves as the larval food plant for the Hog Sphinx Moth *Darapsa myron* and the Hydrangia Sphinx Moth *D. versicolor*; bees visit flower and bring about pollination; I have seen the Fork-tailed Bush Katydid sitting on this from where they call at night.

Spiders; for similarly expected interactions, see the Pond Lily.

Fish; when growing as an emergent, one can often observe small fish hiding among the submerged parts of the stems.

Human/Economic Use; its impacts on wetlands as noted above in 'Community Interactions' section results in monetary costs for its eradication and the restoration of the natural community.

Cinnamon Fern with vegetative frond on right and reproductive frond on left.

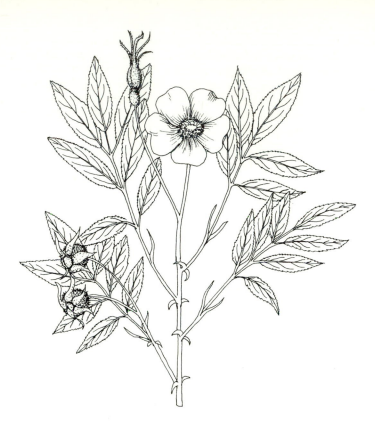

Swamp Rose *Rosa palustris* **Marshall**

ROSACEAE (Rose Family)

General Description -
Native thorned shrub growing to 6 feet in height.

Stem; commonly much branched, greenish, stout and somewhat reclining and typically with paired backward curved thorns at each leaf base.

Leaves; alternate, pinnately compound with ovate, toothed leaflets having some hairs on the lower surface with its petioles sheathed by stipules at the base.

Flower; large, insect pollinated, with five pink petals which are borne singly or in clusters (corymbs) with many thread-like structures in the center representing male and female reproductive parts, appearing July-August.

Habitat; shrub swamps, marshes, along stream borders and occasionally scattered in tree swamps.

WIS; OBL

Swamp Rose Interactions

Community Interactions; an invasive species which sends out many canes resulting in extremely dense growth that provides excellent cover along an edge where they typically grow; provides breeding, nesting, hiding, and overwinter cover for wildlife; the branching canes can be so thick as to act as a form of insulation along banks protecting them from erosion; also refer to *R. rugosa* for additional roles to be expected.

Mammals; you will probably add many species to this list which includes the fruits serving as food for Black Bear, Whitetail Deer, Skunk, Red Squirrel, White-footed Mouse, and Humans; I have noted Eastern Cottontail Rabbits hiding in such thickets.

Plants; its growth is usually so dense as to effectively eliminate most species of ground cover beneath it.

Birds; although my list includes fruits being consumed by Catbird, Cardinal, and Mockingbird, you will undoubtedly add to this; such dense growth serves as cover and nesting sites for Mockingbirds and the Alder Flycatcher; the fruits persist into winter as a food source for birds and mammals.

Insects; there is no end to the number of visits made by insects during flowering when you can expect to see such insects as Honey bees, Bumblebees, Flies, Wasps, Ants, Hover flies, Moths, Butterflies, and probably beetles; specifically, the Common Hyppa Moth, Morning-Glory Prominent Moth, and Obtuse Euchlaena Moth use this as a larval food plant as does the Striped Hairstreak Butterfly; the observer may find the mossy gall caused by the Mossy-Rose Gall Wasp larva *Diplolepis rosae*.

Human/Economic Use; in most respects, this is quite similar to that of *R. rugosa*; the Cherokee made a tea from the bark and used as a treatment for intestinal worms.

Need To Know about interactions involving amphibians, reptiles, and spiders.

Sweet Gale *Myrica gale* L.

MYRICACEAE (Wax-Myrtle Family)

General Description -
Very densely growing native shrub to 6 feet in height.

Stems; many branched and upright with brown bark and fragrant stems when crushed.

Leaves; alternate, up to 2 inches long, wedge-shaped and rounded at tip, with toothed margins towards ends and with white hairs and yellow resin dots on lower surface.

Flower; rather small, borne towards ends of last year's branches, appearing April-May.

Habitat; bogs, and both salt and fresh marshes.

WIS; OBL

146

Sweet Gale Interactions

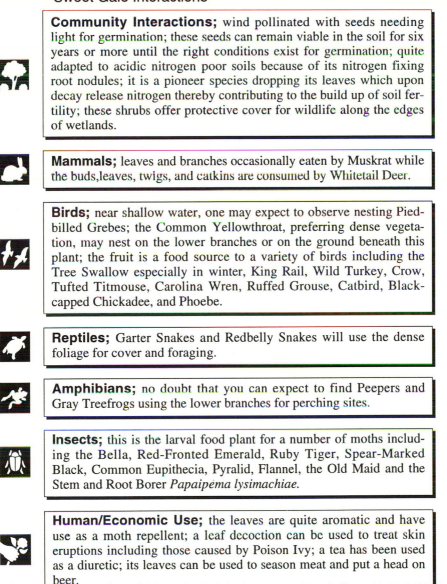

Community Interactions; wind pollinated with seeds needing light for germination; these seeds can remain viable in the soil for six years or more until the right conditions exist for germination; quite adapted to acidic nitrogen poor soils because of its nitrogen fixing root nodules; it is a pioneer species dropping its leaves which upon decay release nitrogen thereby contributing to the build up of soil fertility; these shrubs offer protective cover for wildlife along the edges of wetlands.

Mammals; leaves and branches occasionally eaten by Muskrat while the buds, leaves, twigs, and catkins are consumed by Whitetail Deer.

Birds; near shallow water, one may expect to observe nesting Pied-billed Grebes; the Common Yellowthroat, preferring dense vegetation, may nest on the lower branches or on the ground beneath this plant; the fruit is a food source to a variety of birds including the Tree Swallow especially in winter, King Rail, Wild Turkey, Crow, Tufted Titmouse, Carolina Wren, Ruffed Grouse, Catbird, Black-capped Chickadee, and Phoebe.

Reptiles; Garter Snakes and Redbelly Snakes will use the dense foliage for cover and foraging.

Amphibians; no doubt that you can expect to find Peepers and Gray Treefrogs using the lower branches for perching sites.

Insects; this is the larval food plant for a number of moths including the Bella, Red-Fronted Emerald, Ruby Tiger, Spear-Marked Black, Common Eupithecia, Pyralid, Flannel, the Old Maid and the Stem and Root Borer *Papaipema lysimachiae.*

Human/Economic Use; the leaves are quite aromatic and have use as a moth repellent; a leaf decoction can be used to treat skin eruptions including those caused by Poison Ivy; a tea has been used as a diuretic; its leaves can be used to season meat and put a head on beer.

Need To Know about interactions with other plants, and spiders.

147

Sweet Pepperbush *Clethra alnifolia* L.

CLETHERACEAE (White Alder Family)

General Description -
Native shrub growing to 8 feet in height.

Stem; highly branched, forming dense erect thickets, with the older bark shredding; characterized by long pointed end buds.

Leaves; alternate, with toothed margins towards tip and smooth at base, being prominently straight-veined, green on both sides, and tending to cluster towards branch tips.

Flower; dense, erect clusters of white to pink small, insect pollinated, stalked, aromatic flowers appearing July- August.

Habitat; shrub swamps, tree swamps.

WIS; FAC+

148

Sweet Pepperbush Interactions

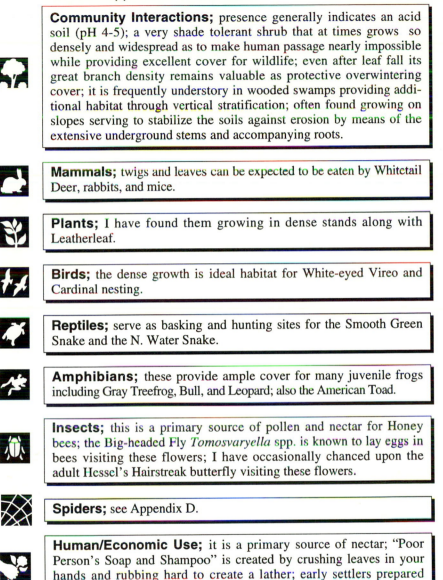

Community Interactions; presence generally indicates an acid soil (pH 4-5); a very shade tolerant shrub that at times grows so densely and widespread as to make human passage nearly impossible while providing excellent cover for wildlife; even after leaf fall its great branch density remains valuable as protective overwintering cover; it is frequently understory in wooded swamps providing additional habitat through vertical stratification; often found growing on slopes serving to stabilize the soils against erosion by means of the extensive underground stems and accompanying roots.

Mammals; twigs and leaves can be expected to be eaten by Whitetail Deer, rabbits, and mice.

Plants; I have found them growing in dense stands along with Leatherleaf.

Birds; the dense growth is ideal habitat for White-eyed Vireo and Cardinal nesting.

Reptiles; serve as basking and hunting sites for the Smooth Green Snake and the N. Water Snake.

Amphibians; these provide ample cover for many juvenile frogs including Gray Treefrog, Bull, and Leopard; also the American Toad.

Insects; this is a primary source of pollen and nectar for Honey bees; the Big-headed Fly *Tomosvaryella* spp. is known to lay eggs in bees visiting these flowers; I have occasionally chanced upon the adult Hessel's Hairstreak butterfly visiting these flowers.

Spiders; see Appendix D.

Human/Economic Use; it is a primary source of nectar; "Poor Person's Soap and Shampoo" is created by crushing leaves in your hands and rubbing hard to create a lather; early settlers prepared extracts of the blossoms to treat coughs and muscle cramps.

Need To Know about interactions involving spiders.

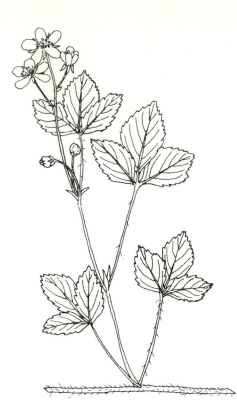

T. Swamp Blackberry *Rubus hispidus* L.

ROSACEAE (Rose Family)

General Description -
Small native ground cover, 3-4 in length.

Stem; slender, trailing, and prickly.

Leaves; 3-parted, obovate, toothed mostly evergreen leaflets on stalks with prickles.

Flower; insect pollinated with 5 white petals borne in loose clusters on a prickly stalk and appearing June-August.

Habitat; shrub swamps and tree swamps, to open areas in woodlands and occasionally dry swales.

WIS; FACW

Trailing Swamp Blackberry Interactions

 Community Interaction; its primary role is to provide some food for wildlife; if growth is dense enough, it can supply cover for small animals; quite tolerant of shade and while preferring moist soils, it is often found in slightly drier spots in wooded swamps.

 Mammals; although you may eventually add many others to this list, it is considered an important food source for Whitetail Deer in spring; the observer may also note that the fruits are consumed by Skunk and Eastern Cottontail Rabbit.

 Birds; among those expected to feed on these fruits are Ruffed Grouse, Ring-neck Pheasant, Henslow's Sparrow, and various Thrushes.

 Reptiles; among the turtles, the Box and Wood Turtles are known to eat the fruits and seeds.

 Insects; various Bees become pollinators upon visiting the flower for food; this is a larval food plant for the Toothed Brown Carpet Moth; somewhat commonly, the gall wasp *Diastrophus bassettii* causes Bassett's Blackberry Gall, a spherical swelling at the base of the stem.

 Human/Economic Use; the fruits are rather seedy and not tasty so normally not consumed much by humans, however, the Mohegans used the berries to treat for dysentery.

Need To Know about interactions involving other plants, amphibians, and spiders.

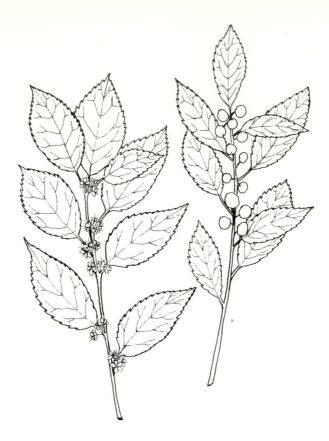

Winterberry *Ilex verticillata* (L.)

AQUIFOLIACEAE (Holly Family)

General Description -
Native shrub growing to 12 feet in height.

Stem; moderately branched, erect, with gray bark having small lateral blunt-tipped buds.

Leaves; ovate, alternate with forward pointing sharp toothed margins with somewhat downy lower and dull upper surfaces, and frequently with stipules (leaf-like structures) at base of leaf petiole (stalk).

Flower; very small, fly pollinated, white petaled and short-stalked with male and female flowers on separate plants and with males in clusters and females borne singly; appearing June-July.

Habitat; shrub swamp, tree swamp, and edges of ponds and streams.

WIS; FACW+

Winterberry Interactions

Community Interactions; a very shade tolerant shrub characteristic of poorly drained acid soils; its branching habit establishes some cover with its persistent red berries serving as a winter food supply for many birds.

Mammals; Black Bear can be expected to eat the fruits as well as can the Raccoon, White-footed Mouse and possibly the Red Fox, Whitetail Deer, and Skunk; quite likely that Beaver would use stems for den construction and bark as food.

Plants; this along with Maleberry are common elements of the woody understory of wooded swamps.

Birds; in early winter the red fruits are favored food to Mockingbird, Red-winged Blackbird, Ruffed Grouse, Catbird, Cardinal, and Brown Thrasher; also provides nesting sites for many birds including the Red-winged Blackbird.

Reptiles; Spotted Turtles have been seen basking at the base of these shrubs.

Amphibians; Wood Frogs, Spotted and Jefferson's Salamanders, and Red-spotted Newts may attach eggs to submerged stems.

Insects; the Striped Hairstreak Butterfly uses this as its larval food plant.

Spiders; see Appendix D.

Human/Economic Use; this is a useful landscaping shrub in areas where high soil moisture is a problem; the red berries are poisonous to humans; an antiseptic and astringent was made by the Iroquois from the bark juices; a tea with little or no caffeine can be made from the leaves.

Wetland value as Pollution Filters

There is some evidence that vegetated wetlands can remove organic and inorganic pollutants from waters flowing through such wetlands. In fact, a number of experimental investigations have shown that various wetlands including marshes, bogs, and swamps can function effectively in wastewater treatment, the result of which is in a significant lowering of nitrogen, phosphorous and heavy metal levels. Other research has shown that wetlands can reduce harmful coliform bacteria and viruses before they enter the ground water. Part of this reduction results from dilution, but there are many other reasons why wetlands are successful reducers of organic and inorganic pollutants in wastewater. Floating and emergent plant life effectively slow water velocity and allow for suspended sediments to fall into the wetland muck soils. Some of the wetland plants then actually absorb the inorganics and incorporate them into their tissues, thereby effectively removing them from the water. Wetland waters and soils have a variety of microorganisms which feed on organic pollution and break down nitrogen compounds to elemental nitrogen gas. As our understanding of the functions of wetlands increases, we find evidence that some are more effective than others in pollution abatement. Part of this difference is reflected in variables including the types of plants, soils, and microbes associated with different wetlands. Eventually, it is conceivable that we may be able to create artificial vegetated wetlands engineered to reduce water pollution in a manner far exceeding traditional wastewater treatment methods.

HERBS

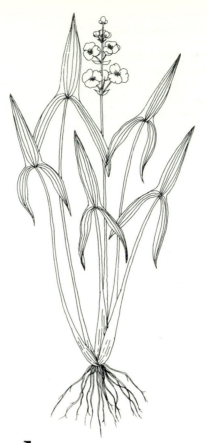

Arrowhead *Sagittaria latifolia* Willd.

ALISMATACEAE (Water-plantain Family)

General Description -
Native perennial emergent herb growing to 4 feet in height.

Stem; with no upright visible stem, however there are underground tubers (stems).

Leaves; submerged leaves are long (2-4 feet) and ribbon-like with emergent leaves that are arrowhead shaped and borne at ends of long petioles that clasp the flower stalk.

Flower; insect pollinated (flies, etc) in whorls of three flowers with three white petals and a yellow center and having male flowers at the top with female ones lower on the flower stalk.

Habitat; fresh marshes, ponds, lakes, and river edges.

WIS; OBL

Arrowhead Interactions

Community Interactions; propagates by tubers and if necessary are easily transplanted by these; has been shown to be very resistant to oil spills, actually spreading at the expense of less tolerant species; can withstand brackish water thus frequently found in estuaries; since this plant looses great quantities of water through their leaves, their elimination is often sought at reservoirs under conditions where water supplies need to be conserved; they do establish ecotones at wetland edges providing nesting and breeding sites and modest food sources for wildlife.

Mammals; the stems, tubers, and roots are eaten by Porcupine, Beaver, and Muskrat.

Birds; may serve as nesting material for Black Tern; the seeds and tubers can be expected to be eaten by Wood Duck, Canvasback, Mallard, Black Duck, Blue-winged Teal, King Rail, and the Gadwall.

Reptiles; both the Plymouth Redbelly (Federally Endangered) and Painted Turtles (both Eastern and Midland) will eat this plant.

Amphibians; one may spot the Northern Leopard, Green, and Pickerel Frogs among these plants at an edge during breeding season.

Insects; similar to Cattails and Burreeds, this too is host to the Cattail Borer Moth *Bellura obliqua;* you may also see the Golden Looper Moth using this as food and for egg laying; this is a larval food plant for Crane flies *Tipula spp.*; a Snout Beetle *Listronotus caudatus* may also be seen breeding on the Arrowhead and smartweeds.

Spiders; expected use by spiders is similar to that observed for the Pond Lily.

Human/Economic Use; Native Americans eat the rhizomes, which can get as large as a white potato, as a food source high in starch; the rhizomes are used to prepare a tea for treating indigestion; a leaf tea was reportedly effective in reducing fever; plant effective in waste water cleansing by absorbing large amounts of ammonia; it has been planted in wildlife management procedures to improve feeding and cover.

Need To Know about interactions involving other plants and fish.

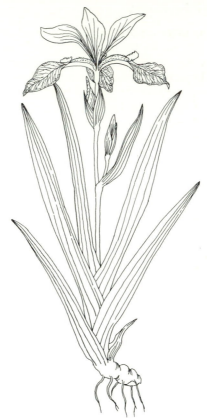

Blue Flag *Iris versicolor* L.

IRIDACEAE (Iris Family)

General Description -
Native perennial herb growing to a height of 2 feet or more.

Stem; robust, erect, and possibly flat on one side.

Leaves; up to 1 inch wide with sword shaped basal leaves which are fan-like in their arrangement, growing to 3 feet with those growing on the stems being alternate and sheathing.

Flower; blue, insect pollinated, with 3 sepals and upright petals in center, appearing May-June.

Habitat; wet meadows, marshes, and sunnier spots of shrub swamps.

WIS; OBL

Blue Flag Interactions

Community Interactions; although not usually growing in large abundance, it is among the most common of the irises; its chief role is that of anchoring the soil along the lower marsh and constantly flooded wetland margins with its rather stout, creeping rhizome; not being overly grazed, it does persist as protective cover for wildlife; not tolerant of fuel oil spills.

Mammals; the Muskrat will be seen eating all parts of the plant.

Birds; this is visited by the Ruby-throated Hummingbird for its nectar; the seeds may be taken by Gadwalls, Blue-winged Teal, and Wood Ducks.

Reptiles; Ribbon, Garter, and N. Water Snakes search for amphibians, earthworms, insects, and other invertebrates in thick stands of Iris.

Amphibians; in areas where Blue Flag is abundant, adult, juvenile, and recently metamorphosed frogs and salamanders find great cover and probably food in the form of insects and other invertebrates.

Insects; one may see the Burdock Borer Moth visiting its larval food plant; the observer may, upon close inspection, see the Gladiolus Thrip *Thrips simplex* on the plant where it eats and injures the flowers and stems; while not easily seen, upon hatching, the Iris Borer Moth *Macronoctua onusta* works its way internally to the root and devours it; Two-spotted and Arctic Skippers adult butterflies nectar here; this is also the larval food plant for the White Slant-line Moth; one may see the adult Snout Beetle *Mononychus vulpeculus* eating leaves or flowers; various bees are attracted to the purple flower for nectar and in the process of obtaining it, play a role in pollination.

Human/Economic Use; according to many, this was one of the most widely used herbal medicines by Native Americans; the Cree, Missouri and others used the dried rhizomes as a laxative, to induce vomiting, and as a diuretic; the Penobscot, Rappahannock, and others used the roots extensively to cure colds, prepare poultices to soothe burns and itches despite the presence of a poisonous chemical 'iridin', a phenol glycoside; there is some evidence that this plant has properties which increase fat breakdown and that during ancient times the root was eaten to reduce obesity.

Need To Know about interactions involving other plants, and spiders.

Blue Vervain   *Verbena hastata* L.

VERBENACEAE (Vervain Family)

General Description -
Native herb growing to 4 feet in height.

Stem; grooved, four-sided, rough, fairly straight and growing in small groups.

Leaves; opposite, stalked, lanceolate, toothed, tapering to a point and with a rough surface.

Flowers; 5 small blue petals in a pencil-like spike borne singly or in clusters with individual flowers blooming periodically from the base to top of spike.

Habitat; fresh marsh, wet meadow, and edges of ponds and slow moving streams.

WIS; FACW+

Blue Vervain Interactions

 Community Interaction; although not seen in abundance, its presence adds a vigorous strong plant with a dense flower head which provides perches and hiding places for birds and other wildlife; it also contributes to soil stability by having a well developed fibrous root system; sensitive to fuel oil spills, often dying off after such incidents.

 Mammals; the Eastern Cottontail Rabbit in known to eat this plant and Muskrat and the Eastern Harvest Mouse can be expected to feed on the shoots.

 Birds; you can see Cardinals and Swamp Sparrows feeding on the seeds.

 Reptiles; none known; Box and Wood Turtles might feed on the flower stalks.

 Amphibians; adult and juvenile frogs and salamanders are expected to feed on insects attracted to the flowers and leaves.

 Insects; this is the larval food plant for the Verbena Moth and occasionally for the Buckeye Butterfly.

Human/Economic Use; the Chippewa and Delaware used the dried leaves from which an expectorant was prepared to clear sinuses, induce sweating, to treat stomach pain, fever, and coughs.

Need To Know about interactions involving other plants and spiders.

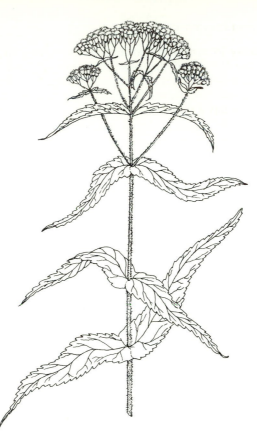

Boneset *Eupatorium perfoliatum* L.

COMPOSITAE (Aster Family)

General Description -
Native perennial herb growing to 5 feet in height.

Stem; robust, erect, hairy.

Leaves; lanceolate, pointed, toothed, and opposite, with the base surrounding (perfoliate) the stem, heavily veined.

Flowers; small white flowers in 3-4 terminal clusters.

Habitat; wet meadows, marshes, and pond edges.

WIS; FACW+

Boneset Interactions

Community Interactions; similar in many ways to the roles of Spotted Joe-Pye-weed; fruits are a source of food in winter to some birds and mammals; it is very sensitive to drying out if soil water is lowered through drainage and other disturbances to the hydrology; it has a fibrous root system which is important in binding the very wet soils and resisting erosion in the higher marsh where this predominates.

Mammals; often seen growing with Spotted Joe-Pye-weed, it interacts in much the same way with mammals.

Plants; often a companion with Spotted Joe-Pye-weed.

Birds; seeds occasionally eaten by Wild Turkey and Swamp Sparrow; Mallards and Ruffed Grouse eat leaves and fruits.

Amphibians; Pickerel and Leopard frogs commonly forage in areas where Boneset occurs; young Gray Treefrogs may rest on the leaves.

Insects; Boneset is a larval food plant for several moths which you might catch visiting, including the Clymene Moth, Burdock Borer Moth, Ruby Tiger Moth, and the Curved-lined Angle Moth; you may see Lace Bugs of the genus *Galeatus spp.* feeding on this plant; a small gallfly *Neolasioptera perfoliata* causes Boneset Stem-galls which are elliptical swellings, often two to three times the stem diameter.

Human/Economic Use; found widespread use by 19th century U.S. physicians in the preparation of hot teas to relieve colds, arthritis, gout, epilepsy, and as a substitute to quinine in the treatment of malaria; Cherokee also used a tea from this to treat colds, reduce fever, and to soothe sore throats; this plant was as much a part of the standard home medicine cabinet as aspirin is today; contains a glycoside 'eupatorin' which has emetic qualities.

Need To Know about interactions involving reptiles, and spiders.

Bulrush *Scirpus atrovirens* Willd.

CYPERACEAE (Sedge Family)

General Description -
Native herb growing to 8 feet in height.

Stem; erect and robust, growing from a thick well developed rhizome.

Leaves; lacking or reduced to sheaths.

Flower; tiny flowers in spiklets which are grouped in large clusters at tips of stems and which have a single leaf-like bract at the base, appearing July-August.

Habitat; fresh to brackish marsh, and wet meadows.

WIS; OBL

Bulrush Interactions

Community Interactions; creating excellent habitat shelter, food, and nesting sites, this is commonly found with Wool-grass playing similar roles within the community; although many of the interactions with the various animals groups are comparable as well to those of Wool-grass, I have observed some specifically related to the Bulrush; interestingly, this plant is equally as tolerant of flooding as it is of short (several months) periods of drought, implying its adaptibility to short term changes in hydrology; the highly matted root system plays an important role in soil stabilization.

Mammals; Bulrushes form an important part of the overall habitat of the Muskrat which also consumes the stems and roots and uses the stems for nesting material; Meadow Jumping Mice are known to eat the seeds.

Birds; one can expect to see the seeds eaten by many ducks including Blacks, Mallards, Teals (Blue-/Green-winged), the Canadian Goose, Whistling Swans, Rails (including the Clapper, Virginia, and Sora), the Common Snipe, Gadwalls, and the Ring-necked Pheasant; it is a favored habitat for Black Ducks; the observer may find birds nesting among these plants such as Boat-tailed Grackles, the Red-winged Blackbird, and the Long Billed Marsh Wren; in addition, the Common Loon, Sora Rail, American Bittern and American Coot utilize this plant for nesting material; Snow Geese will eat the tubers which also serve as a winter food source for Buffleheads.

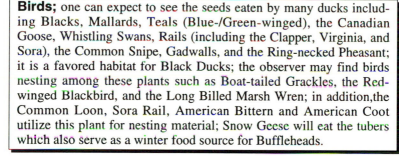

Reptiles; interactions expected to be similar to that of Wool-grass.

Amphibians; expected to be similar to that of Wool-grass.

Spiders; spiders find this quite similar to Wool-grass in terms of structural advantage for web building, hunting, etc.

Insects; in addition to those noted for Wool-grass, one might notice that it is a larval food plant for the Ignorant Apamea Moth, the Oblong Sedge Borer Moth, the Subflava Sedge Borer, and also the Cattail Borer Moth; the rare Mitchell's Satyr butterfly larvae feed on this plant.

Fish; plant contributes food and cover for a variety of fish as well as nesting sites for Bluegills and Bass.

Human/Economic Use; uses very much like that of Wool-grass.

Need To Know about interactions involving other plants.

165

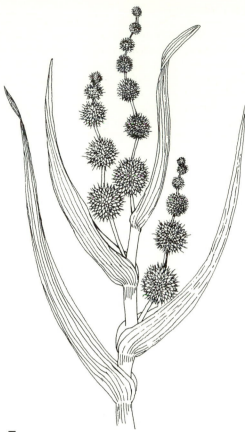

Bur-reed *Sparganium americanum* Nutt.

SPARGANIACEAE (Bur-reed Family)

General Description -
Native perennial emergent robust herb growing to 6 feet in height.

Stem; erect, zig-zagging at end, and arising from an underground rhizome.

Leaves; submerged leaves long (to 4 feet), linear and floating whereas emergent stem leaves are alternate, narrow, elongate and keeled (ridged) on their back side.

Flower; the lower bulbs or burs are clusters of greenish wind pollinated (rarely insect) female flowers while the upper smaller heads are white petaled male inflorescences.

Habitat; fresh marshes, along pond, lake and river edges in shallow water to 1 foot deep.

WIS; OBL

166

Bur-reed Interactions

 Community Interactions; these propagate by creeping fibrous root-stocks which serve to anchor soil along pond edges and act as a buffer against wave action on beaches; also create ecotones along marsh edges where they provide excellent cover for nesting and breeding for a variety of wildlife; this is one of the last plants of the season to supply nutlets as food for waterfowl; may die off following fuel oil spills which reach wetlands; this species may be an indicator of good water quality.

 Mammals; stems and foliage used as shelter and food by Muskrat and highly favored by Whitetailed Deer.

 Birds; can expect the Common Loon to use this plant for nest building; the seeds are eaten by Wood Ducks, the Sora, Clapper, and King Rails, and the American Coot.

 Reptiles; one can expect to see the Painted Turtle feeding on leaves of this plant.

 Amphibians; habitats with this as well as other emergents, are places where one might observe Northern Leopard, Pickerel, Green, and Bull Frogs during breeding.

Insects; see the Cattail for the Cattail Borer Moth which is known to inhabit this plant as well; also can expect to observe Putnam's Looper Moth using it for food; this is a larval food plant for the Oblong Sedge Borer Moth; Skimmers *Celithemis eponina* and Black Wing Damselflies *Calopteryx maculata* have been observed laying eggs on stems just at the surface or under the water; the Giant Water Bug *Lethocerus americanus* (and other species) and Velvety Shore Bugs *Ochterus americanus* may lay their eggs on this, Cattails, and other emergents; various Leaf Beetle *(Donacia spp.)* larval and adult stages may be seen on the leaves with larvae also feeding on the stems and roots; the Bluet Damselfly *Enallagma civile* is commonly seen resting on this plant.

 Spiders; one can expect similar interactions to those found with the Pond Lily.

 Fish; role is very similar to that of Cattail; also have observed nest hollowed amongst the roots by Sunfish.

 Human/Economic Use; the tubers served as a high starch food source to American Natives, much like a potato; dense growth of this can impede flow in drainage swales.

Need To Know about interactions involving other plants.

167

Cardinal Flower *Lobelia cardinalis* L.

CAMPANULACEAE (Bluebell Family)

General Description -
Native biennial herb growing to 5 feet in height.

Stem; erect, unbranched, smooth, and occasionally growing in small groups.

Leaves; alternate, toothed, lance-shaped and coming to a point at each end, borne on a short stalk, and having smooth or downy surfaces.

Flower; Scarlet 2-lipped tubular flower with the upper lip 2-lobed and lower lip 3- lobed, and having the stamens fused into a long tube projecting through the upper lip sinus.

Habitat; shrub and wooded swamps and along shaded stream banks.

WIS; FACW+

Cardinal Flower Interactions

Community Interaction; does not grow in profusion; its major importance is as a source of food for Hummingbirds (see birds below).

Mammals; may be grazed by Whitetail Deer, Black Bear and trampled by cattle.

Birds; even though this flower is usually nectarless, it is still visited by the Ruby-throated Hummingbird which forage for insects and spiders in the flowers and in doing so may bring about pollination.

Reptiles; it is not known if the bright red flowers attract Wood and Box turtles; Ribbon Snakes search out amphibians, insects, and earthworms where this plant grows.

Amphibians; Cardinal Flower grows in the company of Leopard, Pickerel, Green Frogs as well as Spring Peepers and Gray Treefrogs; Dusky Salamanders forage nearby and Spotted and Jefferson's Salamanders pass by on their spring breeding migrations; Redback Salamanders may hunt for insects on or near the Cardinal Flower, at night.

Insects; this has been found to be a larval food plant for the Lobelia Dagger Moth.

Human/Economic Use; CAUTION! contains an alkaloid Lobeline that can cause paralysis and death; even with this concern, the Delaware and Cherokee used root decoctions for such maladys as syphilis, worms, colds, and root extracts as a love potion; its beauty has made it the subject of collection by humans, threatening its existence.

Need To Know about interactions involving other plants and spiders.

Cinnamon Fern *Osmunda cinnamomea* L.

OSMUNDACEAE (Flowering Fern Family)

General Description -
Native perennial fern growing to 3 feet in height.

Stem; stout, smooth, erect, green and covered with cinnamon colored wool.

Leaves; fronds are up to 3 feet high, erect to slightly arched, lanceolate with 20 plus opposite lance-shaped leaflets; fertile fronds (leaves) do not persist through summer whereas vegetative (sterile) fronds remain until first frost.

Reproduction; club-like fertile leaf (frond) with groups of spore cases on leaflets that hug the main axis.

Habitat; shrub and tree swamps and occasionally in wet sunny meadows and bogs.

WIS; FACW

Cinnamon Fern Interactions

Community Interactions; preferring shade and acid soils, they grow taller and frequently much more extensively than Sensitive Fern; they tend to act as a living mulch, slowing down evaporation of wetland soils by shading them; their extensive and vigorously growing, sturdy, matted rhizomes bind the soil against erosion; their height increases habitat diversity by creating vertical stratification of the herbal layer; these ferns do not respond well to long term flooding resulting from altered hydrology; one of the first ferns to appear in the spring, they along with the Sensitive Fern are among the first of the herbs to die off in the cool fall.

Mammals; in this respect they are similar to Sensitive Fern.

Plants; very similar to Sensitive Fern.

Birds; the fiddleheads are favored as food by the Ruffed Grouse; although the Yellowthroat typically nests in the crotch of a tree or shrub, it will occasionally do so in these and use the leaves for nesting material; Brown Thrashers may build nests in clumps of this fern; stem fir is used by Ruby-throated Hummingbirds to line nests.

Reptiles; not surprising, many snakes including the N.Water, Ribbon, Garter, Redbelly, Northern Brown, Milk Snakes, Northern Copperheads, and occasionally Black Racers forage here for their food; Wood and Box Turtles search for fruits and berries, fungi, insects, earthworms, and other invertebrates here; hatchling Spotted, Snapping, and Bog Turtles may linger in wet Cinnamon fern areas.

Amphibians; stands of Cinnamon Fern offer excellent cover for adult, juvenile, and recently metamorphosed amphibians; Spring Peepers, Gray Treefrogs, Green frogs, Mink, Leopard, Pickerel, and Wood Frogs, as well as many woodland (Redback, Dusky, Two-lined, Four-toed) and Mole (Spotted, Jefferson's, Blue-spotted, and Marbled) Salamanders hide, hunt, and rest in Cinnamon Fern stands; the stout stems (stipes) and wide leaves make good calling perches for male Spring Peepers and Gray Treefrogs.

Insects; this serves as a larval food plant for the Osmunda Borer Moth, which bores both stem and root stocks; the Plant Bug *Monalocoris americanus* is found on this and the Sensitive Fern; it is possible that the Pink-shaded Fern Moth and the Silver-spotted Fern Moth use this as a larval food source.

(continued)

Cinnanmon Fern Interactions

 Human/Economic Use; in the spring when the young leaves or "fiddleheads" poke up, collect and eat them raw or boiled as did the Menominee Indian tribe, tasting somewhat like fresh peas; the leaves can be boiled in milk as an aid to diarrhea; a mucilaginous extract from the rhizomes can be used to soothe coughs and in ointments for sore muscles and bruises.

Need To Know about interactions involving other plants and spiders.

Ecotones.

Cleavers Bedstraw *Galium palustre* L.

RUBIACEAE (Madder Family)

General Description -
Native perennial, prostrate herb growing over the ground, other plants and itself.

Stem; square, weak, prostrate, only occasionally with barbed prickles.

Leaves; in whorls of 6 at joints, thin, blunt, and having rough margins.

Flower; cluster of many tiny white, stalked, 3-4 petaled flowers at ends of branches, appearing June-August.

Habitat; wet meadows, swamp edges.

WIS; OBL

Cleavers Bedstraw Interactions

Community Interactions; this prostrate herb grows quite densely from horizontal rhizomes, providing excellent wildlife cover; other roles are very similar to that of the Water-Smartweed.

Mammals; the fruits and seeds are occasionally eaten by Muskrat.

Plants; frequently associate this species with Boneset, Joe-Pye-weed, New England, New York, and Small White Aster.

Reptiles; Smooth Green, Redbelly, N. Brown, C. Garter, and Ribbon Snakes hunt prey here, and also thermoregulate on the top of bedstraw mats.

Amphibians; dense stands of bedstraw provide good foraging and hiding places for Leopard and Pickerel Frogs and for American and Fowler's Toads.

Insects; several moths including the Drab Brown Wave, the Common Tan Wave, and the White-Banded Toothed Carpet can be expected to visit since it serves as its larval food plant.

Human/Economic Use; the roots have found value as a source of yellow dye; it is in the same family as coffee (Rubiaceae) and the seeds have been ground as a coffee substitute; there is mention of it as being useful as a rennet (rennin) to curdle milk in cheese making; also was used to stuff colonial mattresses, thus the name.

Need To Know about interactions involving other plants, birds, and spiders.

175

Common Bladderwort *Utricularia vulgaris* L.

LENTIBULARIACEAE (Bladderwort Family)

General Description -
Native herb growing 2-3 inches above water, or in or on a muddy or Sphagnum substrate.

Stem; elongate, slender, very much branched and can be characterized by air bladders along their length; either free-floating or imbedded in mud.

Leaves; highly filamentous, often accompanied by attached bladders and, like the stems, these too are often free-floating or imbedded in mud.

Flower; flower stalks project several inches above water (or mud) bearing 10-20 small snapdragon-like yellow flowers, appearing July-August.

Habitat; bogs, marshes, shallow ponds and lakes, and slow moving streams.

WIS; OBL

Common Bladderwort Interactions

Community Interactions; insect pollinated; interesting insectivorous plants which have small bladders along the stem which act to suck in and thereby capture water fleas and other small life forms which serve as a source of nitrogen in the nutrient poor acidic waters they may grow in; does provide cover for fish, but in general appears to be of modest value to wildlife.

Mammals; Beaver will graze on this plant.

Plants; I have noted that this plant often grows where there is an abundance of Duckweed.

Reptiles; Plymouth Redbelly Turtles may be seen feeding on leaves, flowers, and stems; the same may be expected of Painted, Chicken, and Red-eared turtles.

Amphibians; dense mats may be useful as a refuge to tadpoles of Green Frogs, Bullfrogs, and others, while some of these may actually graze on the plant.

Insects; bees seen on flowers and are probably involved in pollination.

Fish; Sunfish and Pumpkinseeds may be seen swimming amongst the bladders probably consuming insects; does afford some protective cover for these fish.

Human/Economic Use; reportedly useful as a diuretic.

Need To Know about interactions involving other plants, birds, and spiders.

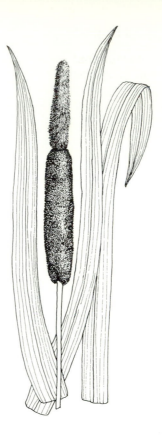

Common Cattail *Typha latifolia* L.

TYPHACEAE (Cattail Family)

General Description -
Native perennial herb growing to 10 feet in height.

Stem; stiff, growing in dense stands from underground rhizomes.

Leaves; upright, linear, 2-6 feet long and up to 1 inch wide arising from the base or are alternating along the stem; leaves have a spongy feel which represents air-filled chambers responsible for channeling air to the roots.

Flower; many small flowers, packed into tight clusters creating a lower female spike topped by a smaller male spike with no gap between the two flower types; female spike persists turning into the familiar dark brown "tail" and appearing May-July.

Habitat; fresh marshes, also wet swales, stream, pond and lake margins.

WIS; OBL

Common Cattail Interactions

Community Interactions; direct relationship between stand loss and bird brooding couple decline, thus implying impacts of wetland destruction; single flooding events can eliminate cattail stands which in turn reduce migrating duck populations and breeding waterfowl on flooded nest sites; impact of changing storm water runoff patterns to wetlands implied; creates ecotonal edge and serves food, shelter, breeding, overwintering, and migratory corridor wildlife habitat functional values; can be representative of a wetland in transition to upland field; an unusually zinc tolerant species through resistance to its uptake; this cattail occupies wetter sites than *T. angustifolia* and is less salt tolerant than the latter which invades brackish waters; plant will hybridize with other forms near coastal areas thereby adjusting to salinity changes; in winter, frozen substrate protects this plant from the effects of compaction by heavy construction equipment being driven over it with growth the next spring not varying significantly from that of the previous year-implications of how to possibly mitigate wetland impacts during construction are suggested by this.

Mammals; Muskrats build dens from leaves packed with mud for shelter, sleeping and rearing of young; they also use rootstalks, culms, and leaves as primary food source, consuming up to 10% of stand per year; Chipmunks and mice use fluff from the spike to line nests and the Whitetail Deer and occasionally Mink, will bed down in stands.

Plants; Giant Reed out competes Cattail, the favored nesting site of many birds, thus posing a threat to local population diversity; Cattail contains phenolic compounds in leaves which are released upon decay and inhibit germination of its own seeds, thus reducing competition within the stand; competes successfully with sedges and Swamp Loosestrife in or near water but less so further from the water's edge; observations support the contention that the seeds may release substances which limit the growth of blue-green algae; commonly seen growing with duck weed floating between the stalks.

Birds; Redwing Blackbird and Long-billed Marsh Wren suspends nest between stalks in dense stands 2-4 feet above the water, needing at least 3-5 adjacent stems for attachment and thus not nesting as readily in sparse stands; Swamp Sparrow attaches nest to stalks 2-4' above water; favored nesting site because it is rigid, an easy perch, and has wide spacing to allow for best defense; Semipalmated Sandpiper eat seeds; Snow, and Canada Goose eat seeds, young stalks, and starchy rootstalks; Least and American Bittern, the Sora, Virginia and King Rail, Common Moorhen, American Coot use leaves extensively for nesting sites and building material;

(continued)

Common Cattail Interactions

Birds (continued); Sanderlings may line nest with material from dried spikes; many other birds including the Boat-tailed Grackle, Common Grackle, Black-crowned Night-Heron, Canada Goose, Mallards, Mute Swan, Blue-winged Teal can be expected to nest amongst these plants; rarely one might see a Green-backed Heron nesting in cattails and in very dense stands you can expect a good nesting site for the Glossy Ibis; if in remote, safe, undisturbed area, small (less than 1/2 acre) Cattail stands support feeding, nesting, and brooding for Canvasbacks.

Reptiles; Common hiding and occasional feeding site for Common Snapping Turtle; breeding site for Spotted Turtle; Common Snapping Turtle and Painted Turtle feed on seeds and stems; Northern Water Snake is very selective in its habitat usage, preferring drier vegetative clumps in cattail marshes for sunning- it will hunt for frogs, fish, and invertebrates in the wetter areas, as will Ribbon and Garter Snakes.

Amphibians; Northern Spring Peepers, Greenfrogs, Bullfrogs and the Northern Leopard Frogs breed here (look for N. Leopard Frog eggs attached to submerged stems).

Insects; Cattail Borer Moth goes through entire life cycle on head-stalk; female lays eggs on the flower in summer, larvae feed on seeds, construct a winter home from the flower cottony hairs, build a cocoon in spring in seedhead and begin the cycle again in summer after pupation, emergence, and mating; Oblong Sedge Borer Moth is common inhabitant of Cattail as are the White-tailed Diver moth and the Pickerelweed Borer Moth; none of these is a threat to cattail nor reduces its energy production; several other moths including Henry's Marsh, the Meal Moth, and the Shy Cosmet use this as a larval food plant; Backswimmers *Notonecta undulata* may attach eggs to stems under water, and the Giant Water Bug *Lethocerus americanus* and Velvety Shore Bug *Ochterus americanus* are found on the plants where they may lay eggs.

Spiders; Elongated Long-Jawed Orb Weaver builds orb web among leaves.

Fish; serves as cover for Bluegills and Pumpkinseeds, both of which may also hollow out a nest around base of plant; Carp are known to dislodge rootstocks, thus playing a role in the vegetative propagation (reproduction) of Cattail; plant has an associated aquatic insect population which probably serves as food for fish; Northern Pike are known to spawn in waters where this and other emergent marsh grasses grow.

(continued)

Common Cattail Interactions

Human/Economic Use; one of the most famous edible and useful plants in the world, often referred to as the "supermarket of the marsh;" the young leaves are excellent salad greens and can be cooked as potherbs; before the pollen spike is ripe, it can be boiled and eaten much like corn on the cob; the pollen is high in protein and can be added to wheat flower as a nutritional supplement; the hairs of the fruit have been used to stuff pillows and life preservers; the root-stocks are high in starch and quite edible, eaten regularly by Native Americans; Cattail tea from the young spikes is used to stop diarrhea; American Natives including the Algonquin and Fox and early American pioneers used the flower down (fluff) as a wound dressing; dried leaves make excellent material for chair seats; this plant and *Phragmites* have photosynthetic rates comparable to some of our highly managed crops such as sugar beets, corn, and sugar cane; Cattails play an important role in pollution reduction by absorbing excess nitrogen and phosphorous and by slowing down the rate of water flow they allow for the settling out of suspended materials; has been implicated as an aeroallergen resulting in hypersensitivity in some humans.

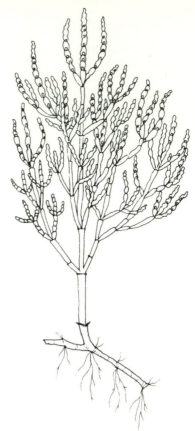

Common Glasswort *Salicornia europaea* L.

CHENOPODIACEAE (Goosefoot Family)

General Description -
Naturalized from Europe and Africa, annual herb growing to 20 inches in height.

Stem; highly branched, upright, jointed, and fleshy.

Leaves; opposite, very small and scale-like.

Flower; very small, green, and in upper stem joints; appearing August-November.

Habitat; in upper irregularly flooded salt marsh, also in saline inland soils and marshes.

WIS; OBL

Common Glasswort Interactions

Community Interactions; extremely tolerant of high salt, one of the few whose seeds are able to germinate in water with salinities higher than that of sea water and to live in the upper marsh where during warm dry periods the rapid rate of evaporation brings salt levels to very high levels; considered a pioneer plant capable of establishing itself in areas where salt levels exceed those tolerated by most other salt marsh species; its shallow root system prohibits its growth in intertidal areas where strong tides wash it away; plants are not tolerant of oil spills.

Mammals; the high salt content of this plant makes it a favored food of grazing animals such as cattle.

Plants; these are annuals which do not compete well with the perennial cordgrasses.

Birds; leaves, stems, and seeds are eaten by Canada Goose and occasionally by Buffleheads and Goldeneye.

Reptiles; Snapping Turtles and Diamondback Terrapins, especially their hatchlings, may take refuge in dense stands of *Salicornia* and related plants; it is possible that Garter Snakes, Black Racers, and even coastal populations of Eastern Hognose Snakes may forage for toads, fish, or birds here.

Amphibians; owing to the salinity of the area this plant grows in, there are few , if any, expected amphibian-plant interactions; Fowler Toads and E. Spadefood Toads may forage in or near *Salicornia* during rainy nights.

Human/Economic Use; the shoots can be pickled and eaten or used directly as a vegetable; the stems were used as a source of sal soda in soap making.

Need To Know about interactions involving insects and spiders.

C. Reed Grass *Phragmites australis* (Cav.) Trin.

GRAMINEAE (Grass Family)

General Description -
Introduced from Europe and Asia, a perennial grass growing to 13 feet in height.

Stem; robust, upright, in large numbers from underground rhizome.

Leaves; wide (2 inches or more) and up to 2 feet long, light green, with smooth surfaces, rough edges, and sheathing leaf bases.

Flower; wind pollinated, self-sterile flowers grouped into a number of spiklets resulting in a large (up to 16 inches) purplish plume surrounded by long silky hairs, appearing August-September, with most seeds being inviable.

Habitat; at upper drier edges of fresh, brackish and salt marshes and ponds, streams, and wet ditches; usually found where they are away from constant inundation.

WIS; FACW

Common Reed Grass Interactions

Community Interactions; have stout creeping rhizomes which spread quickly and are hard to dislodge and are thus good for flood control and soil stabilization on banks and slopes; often found growing in sandy, nutrient-poor soils, their invasive quality crowds out other plants reducing species diversity and often establishing pure clones that, if left undisturbed, reportedly live for 100-200 years; although generally considered to be of limited wildlife value, they do provide dense cover for breeding and nesting but limited food value because of their low seed productivity; dense dry stands are a potential fire hazard; although some temporary control of their growth is accomplished through crushing of the rootstocks, desiccation and mowing, the best control is through flooding of the young seedlings which are intolerant of such conditions; *Phragmites* is considered to have the largest geographical distribution of any species in the world, and it is a single species

Mammals; Meadow Vole runs have been observed within the stands and Muskrats are known to eat the plant.

Plants; one of the most highly competitive plants establishing itself to the exclusion of nearly all other marsh plants including tree seedlings; one of the few plants capable of growing with this is the Japanese Fleece Flower *(Polygonum cuspidata).*

Birds; stands of this are common nesting habitat for Black-Crowned Night-Herons, Snowy Egrets, Canada Geese, Mallards, and Red-winged Blackbirds; on rare occasions, one might find the Green-backed Heron nesting here too; along the coast American Oystercatchers will nest under these plants; when the stands are especially dense near water, this might be a nesting site for the Glossy Ibis; in addition,the Common Loon may use the plant as nesting material.

Reptiles; Snapping, Musk, Painted, Redbelly, and other turtles may forage near *Phragmites* stands; Ribbon, N. Water, Garter, Black Racers, and other snakes may also hunt for food and escape predators here.

Amphibians; metamorphs of N. Cricket, Upland Chorus, Spring Peepers, Gray Treefrogs, Pickerel, Leopard, Bull and Green Frogs may forage along the edges of *Phragmites* stands.

Insects; the American Ruby Spot (Broad-winged) Damselfly *Hetaerina americana* and the Common Skimmer Dragonfly *Celithemus eponina* are often seen perching on this and other marsh

(continued)

Common Reed Grass Interactions

plants; this is the larval food plant for a number of insects you might observe including such butterflies as the Broad-winged Skipper, **Insects** (continued); Prairie Ringlet, Yellowpatch Skipper, Long Dash, Zabulon Skipper, Hobomok, and Saffron Skipper; the Pepper-and-salt Skipper butterfly breeds and lives here as well; this serves as a larval food plant for the Many-lined Wainscot moth.

Spiders; see Appendix D.

Human/Economic Use; American Natives reportedly ate the starch-rich rhizomes as a vegetable or roasted and ground it into a flour for cooking; the stems are used to make mats, arrows, fishing rods, and mouth pieces for musical instruments, while string can be made by twisting the leaf fibers together; the leaves were also used as roof thatching and for cattle grazing as it grows back quite effec-tively; a poultice was prepared of cut rhizomes in vinegar to stop itching; its dense growth along banks can hinder fishing.

Need To Know about interactions involving spiders.

Wetland Value in Flood Control and Storm Damage Prevention

Land development has led to the demise of many wetlands. Often accompanying these major projects has been the paving of large areas for parking and roads as well as the construction of many roof tops. These impervious surfaces result in a direct increase in the rates of storm water run off which increases the potential for flooding and erosion. Natural wetland depressions can play a very important role in reducing the risk of flood damage by serving as temporary storage basins. Such ponding slows the rate of water movement and in turn reduces the possibilities for serious erosion. In addition, streams and rivers are often lined with wetland vegetation which acts to stabilize banks and slow water movement.

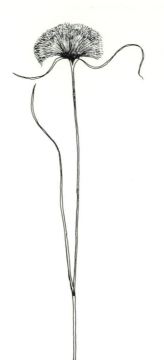

Cotton-grass *Eriophorum virginicum* L.

CYPERACEAE (Sedge Family)

General Description -
Native herb growing to 3 feet in height.

Stem; thin, from underground stem (rhizome).

Leaves; very narrow and grasslike, with several growing just beneath the flower and reaching 5 inches, other leaves longer and borne along the stem.

Flower; compact, small inflorescence characterized by white cotton-like bristles.

Habitat; bogs.

WIS; OBL

Cotton-grass Interactions

Community Interactions; an arctic plant more or less in its southern limit and interestingly is a glacial relic, having lived at the edge of the retreating glaciers during the last ice age more than 12,000 years ago, where it moved northward invading bogs; known to sprout new roots in the upper airy layers of Sphagnum which assures enough oxygen for root metabolism.

Mammals; Beaver, Southern Red-backed vole, and Whitetail Deer can be expected to feed on leaf and stem greens.

Amphibians; Mink frogs, Wood Frogs, and others may be seen searching for bog insects nearby.

Insects; occasionally serves as a larval food plant for the Jutta Arctic butterfly.

Human/Economic Use; it is suspected of causing allergic reactions by means of its wind-borne pollen; greens were eaten by Native Americans.

Need To Know about interactions involving other plants, birds, reptiles, and spiders.

Curled Dock *Rumex crispus* L.

POLYGONACEAE (Buckwheat Family)

General Description -
Herb introduced and naturalized from Europe and growing to 4 feet in height.

Stem; upright, gooved, jointed and generally unbranched.

Leaves; alternate, the lower leaves lanceolate with very wavy edges and tapering to the stalk (petiole); overall leaf size tends to decrease towards the top of stem.

Flower; small, slender cluster of green to brown wind pollinated flowers in leaf axils and stem tip, appearing May-August.

Habitat; very cosmopolitan, frequenting uplands but commonly found in wet meadows and the upper marshes where the soil is quite wet.

WIS; FACU

Curled Dock Interactions

Community Interactions; a troublesome plant having a large somewhat branching tap root; flowers produce many seeds which do provide some food for wildlife; plants can be controlled by frequent plowing; the soil seed bank (cache of seeds stored in ground after seed production) can remain viable for 80 years, so if later disturbed by soil turning, this species can become established in early stages of wet meadow succession.

Mammals; the Eastern Cottontail will eat the leaves; both the White-footed Mouse and the Meadow Mouse eat the leaves and seeds; plant contains levels of soluble oxalic acid which are toxic to many mammals.

Birds; several birds including the Sora Rail, Redwing Blackbird, and Swamp Sparrow eat the seeds.

Reptiles; female Spotted, Painted, Snapping, Wood, and Box Turtles are likely to dig their nests and deposit eggs where this plant grows; Wood and Box Turtles probably feed on the leaves.

Amphibians; the largest leaves make good perches for Spring Peepers, Gray Treefrogs, and other treefrogs; American and Fowler's Toads will forage among them at night.

Insects; expect to observe several butterflies which use this as their larval food plant including the very green colored Bronze Copper, and possibly the Great Gray and the American Copper; adults and larvae of the Rhubarb Weevil *Lixis concavus* might be observed feeding on the soft stems; one might find the Plant Bug *Adelphocoris spp.* breeding and taking juices here; this is the larval food plant for the Ruby Tiger Moth and the Dock Borer Moth *Papaipema nitela*, which is also a pest of corn, tomato, and potato.

Spiders; see Appendix D.

Human/Economic Use; although this contains toxic levels of oxalic acid known to be fatal to livestock if eaten in large quantities, a root preparation has been used as a laxative, astringent, and as a treatment for upset stomach, syphillis and jaundice; powdered roots used as a natural dentrifice.

Need To Know about interactions involving other plants.

Duckweed *Lemna sp.* L.

LEMNACEAE (Duckweed Family)

General Description -
Native small floating plant occasionally appearing singly but usually carpeting water surface.

Stem; none.

Leaves; no true leaves, but having an oval thallus which is green above and purple below with one to many hanging roots.

Flower; very tiny white flower which is uncommon to observe, appearing during summer which is insect, wind, or water pollinated.

Habitat; surface of marshes, ponds, and other areas of slow moving or stagnate water, in sun or shade.

WIS; OBL

Duckweed Interactions

Community Interactions; worldwide in distribution, these plants, although typical of the low or constantly flooded marsh system, are found throughout all types of marshes; they are outstanding in their ability to multiply and quickly cover a water surface, providing cover and food for a variety of wildlife; although it flowers rarely, pollination can be brought about in many ways including by water, wind, snails, spiders, Water Striders, Water Beetles, and self; the plant can tolerate many hours out of the water as is the case when they stick to the body of waterfowl and are carried long distances in flight; in winter, plants sink to the bottom below the ice until warmer weather returns when they refloat; although they act to filter out from water nitrogen and phosphorous brought into wetlands by stormwater runoff and are thereby an important water filtration system, they are rarely found in water with a pH higher than 8 or in those containing industrial toxicants including heavy metals - because of this, they may be useful indicators of polluted water; appear to be unaffected by fuel oil spills reaching wetlands.

Mammals; both the Muskrat and the Beaver utilize this plant for a large amount of their food intake.

Plants; among its more common associates are the Pond Lily and Spatter-dock, although it will be found associated with a number of other plants.

Birds; this plant can be a food source to a number of birds including Pheasant, Gadwells which are seen feeding on them during the non-breeding season, Canada Geese, Wood Duck, Black and Mallard Ducks, the Blue and Green-winged Teal, and the Sora Rail.

Reptiles; Snapping, Redbelly, Painted (Eastern and Midland) and probably a host of other turtles feed, at least occasionally, on *Lemna*; dense floating mats of *Lemna* provide superior cover for hatchling of juvenile turtles, including the three already named, plus Spotted, Bog and the Mink Frog.

Amphibians; Duckweed-covered pools and ponds provide superb background for the generally green-colored frogs that live in or near permanent water wetlands (Green, Bull, Leopard, Pickerel Frogs); the floating egg masses of Green and Bull frogs may slightly adhere to *Lemna* and allow these midsummer eggs to float at the surface (where there is more heat and oxygen) for longer periods of time.

(continued)

Duckweed Interactions

Insects; this is a larval food plant for the Pyralid Moth *Munroessa icciusalis*; Water Striders *Gerris remigis* and the smaller strider *Paravelia (stagnalis)* are often spotted crawling over these along with the Snout Beetle *Tanysphyrus lemnae* and the Velvet Water Bug *Merragata hebroides*; the aquatic larval stage of the horsefly finds shelter under duckweed.

Fish; dense growth provides food and cover for *Tilapia Mossambicus*, and the carp.

Human/ Economic Use; since its food value compares favorably with alfalfa, it is used as food for farm animals; added to poultry feed, there is a noticeable increase in the protein of eggs and pigmentation of the yolk; may therefore be a valuable alternative to fish and soybean based foods; some evidence that *Lemna spp.* interferes with host location by the human parasite *Schistosoma mansoni;* interestingly, this plant is a source of a human neurotransmitter acetylcholine; another fascinating aspect of this little water plant is that the mammalian sterol estrogen stimulates it to flower; Iroquois would prepare a poultice from a mixture of this plant and chickweed to reduce skin swellings; at times the growth can be extensive enough to interfere with boating and even shade out other aquatic plants.

Need To Know about interactions involving other plants and spiders.

A series of "edges" where vegetation changes from herbs to shrubs to trees.

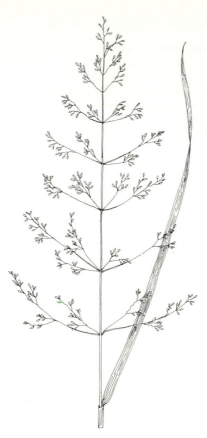

Fowl-meadow Grass *Poa palustris* L.

GRAMINEAE (Grass Family)

General Description -
Native grass growing to 3 1/2 feet in height.

Stem; smooth, purplish, prostrate to erect with a flattened base and often growing in large groups.

Leaves; thin, flat, terminating in boat-shaped tip.

Flower; a wind pollinated open cluster of small green, purple or bronze colored spiklets with cobwebby-like hairs at their base.

Habitat; wet meadows, marsh edges.

WIS; FACW

Fowl-meadow Grass Interactions

Community Interactions; its habit of growing in dense stands provides excellent cover and nesting sites for small mammals; in winter, its dry stalks continue to provide some winter cover for wildlife; seed heads and greens serve as food for a variety animals.

Mammals; the Meadow Jumping Mouse creates runs and nests throughout this grass and will consume its seeds and greens; the New England Cottontail and Muskrat will also eat the seeds and stems.

Plants; fairly competitive, frequently establishing pure stands at the expense of other meadow plants.

Birds; plant may serve as nesting material for the Northern Harrier; although at times difficult to spot, Bobolinks can be expected to be nesting in dense stands of this plant as well as another ground nester I've seen, the Song Sparrow; the seeds are eaten by Song Sparrows, Tree Sparrows, Wild Turkey, Ring-necked Pheasant, the Northern Pintail Duck, and the Blue-winged Teal.

Reptiles; although the Garter Snake is rather cosmopolitan, I have seen them resting or waiting for prey (e.g. frogs, small fish, tadpoles, and other wetland creatures) in this grass along the edges of ponds and streams.

Amphibians; frogs, especially juveniles and recent metamorphs, find excellent cover and foraging in thick stands of *Poa palustris;* this is an especially good area to look for Leopard and Pickerel frogs.

Insects; a variety of butterflies may be seen visiting their larval food plant including the following; the Prairie Ringlet, Yellowpatch Skipper, Zabulon Skipperling, Hobomok Skipper, Saffron Skipper, Least Skipperling, Long Dash, Little Wood Satyr, and the Large Wood Nymph; the Spotted Grass Moth spends much of its time in wetlands where this is a larval food plant; this is also the larval food plant for the wetland obligate Henry's Marsh Moth; occasionally Billbugs can be found feeding here along with the Toothed Flea Beetle *Chaetocnema denticulata*, which feeds on the leaves; one of the more uncomfortable experiences in wetlands is to find oneself trudging through the protective slimy foam of the Spittle Bug *Philaenus spumaris* larva deposited on this and other wet meadow plants.

Spiders; see Appendix D.

(continued)

Fowl-meadow Grass Interactions

Human/Economic Use; the primary use by humans has been as a hay and pasture grass for farm animals which also graze it in wet meadows; although it is grazed, it produces a cyanogenic glycoside which has been known to kill calves; since it is wind pollinated, it has been implicated as an allergin; an interesting yet serious note is that this plant can be infected with 'ergot', a parasitic fungus of cereals that produces a dangerous precursor to hallucinogenic LSD, which can result in death of humans; the ergot fungus can also be a threat to livestock grazing on it.

Salt Marsh Plant Adaptation to Salt

Have you ever placed your finger into a glass of water saturated with table salt for 10-15 minutes and noted how your skin appears shriveled up? This is because the salt content of the water in the glass is greater than the salt content of your finger cells. Conversely, it means that the amount of water per unit volume in the glass is less than the amount per the same unit volume in your finger. The laws of osmosis tell us quite simply that water flows from an area of higher to an area of lower water concentration. Therefore, your finger cells shrink because they lose water to the outer salty medium by osmosis. Since the principles of osmosis hold for all living organisms, a plant placed in an environment saltier than itself will also lose water. However, plants adapted to a salt water environment have developed several interesting strategies for coping with such an environment. One mechanism is for the plant cells to become saltier than the sea water that surrounds them. They do this by actively accumulating salts at slightly higher levels in their cells than in the external environment. Once this is done, it assures that the water component of sea water will move osmotically into the plant. In other words, the plant "extracts" only the water from salt water, leaving behind most of the salts. As a sort of back up, if the plants do happen to get an overdose of salts, many have salt excreting glands on their leaves and stems which allows them to balance salt at levels appropriate for survival. In fact, if you look closely, you might see small sparkles given off by sunlight striking these salt crystals on their leaves.

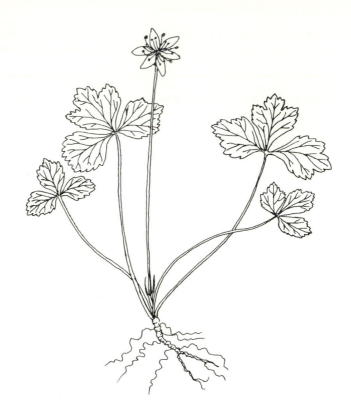

Goldthread *Coptis trifolia* var. *groenlandica* (Oeder) Fassett

RANUNCULACEAE (Crowfoot Family)

General Description -
Native evergreen prostrate herb.

Stem; underground rhizome giving rise to leaves.

Leaves; evergreen, arising in clumps of 3-5 from the rhizome, each leaf is 3-lobed, rounded, toothed, stalked, and are smooth and dark green on top and yellow-green on lower surface.

Flower; borne singly, usually with 5 white petals at end of smooth stalks which project above leaves.

Habitat; wooded swamps.

WIS; FACW

Goldthread Interactions

Community Interactions; found in cool damp woods frequenting the edges of wetlands and thus are often used as an indicator of such boundaries.

Mammals; this is a favored food of the Southern Red-backed Vole.

Plants; I often see this growing near the edge of a swamp interspersed amongst Sensitive and Cinnamon Ferns.

Birds; Ruffed Grouse eat the buds and seeds.

Amphibians; Wood Frogs, Pickerel Frogs, Mink Frogs, and Red Efts (newts) may be found nearby this plant.

Human/Economic Use; the roots are used as a source of yellow and gold colored dyes; in folk medicine, the roots were chewed to treat canker sores; reports have it that the Algonquin made decoctions from this plant which were used to treat upset stomachs and aid in digestion; the Iroquois used the root for the treatment of earaches.

Need To Know about interactions involving reptiles, spiders, and insects.

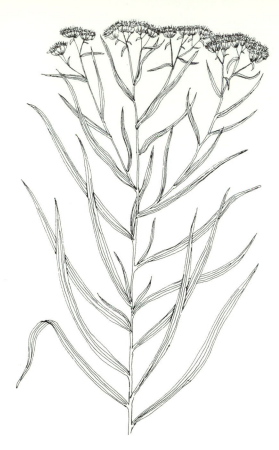

Grass-leaved Goldenrod *Euthamia graminifolia* (L.) Nutt.

COMPOSITAE (Aster Family)

General Description -
Native perennial herb growing to 4 feet in height.

Stem; erect, smooth, slightly curving.

Leaves; numerous, alternate, unstalked, narrow, lanceolate, with rough untoothed margins, and 3-5 parallel veins.

Flowers; flat- topped cluster of small, insect pollinated yellow flowers appearing July-October.

Habitat; wet meadows, damp swales, open marshes and swamp edges.

WIS; FAC

Grass-leaved Goldenrod Interactions

Community Interactions; this is the most wide ranging of the Goldenrods, capable of living in very moist soils and even occasionally in shallow water; it grows in dense stands providing cover for wildlife in open wet meadows during summer; it persists through the winter as dead upright stalks affording some cover for wildlife; plants are grazed by animals as an occasional food source.

Mammals; stems and leaves are eaten by both the New England and Eastern Cottontail Rabbits, Meadow Mice, and Whitetail Deer.

Birds; ruffed Grouse eat the seeds and leaves; one also may observe seeds being taken by Swamp Sparrows.

Amphibians; one could expect frogs to be attracted by the many insect visitors to this goldenrod; Spring Peepers and Gray Treefrogs may be able to ascend to the upper leaves.

Insects; this plant plays host to a vast array of flower visiting insects the observer might chance to see as indicated in the following list: this is the larval food plant for the Pink-Barred Lithacodia Moth, the False Crocus Geometer Moth, the Fine-lined Sallow Moth, the Ruby Tiger Moth, and the Goldenrod Gall Moth whose galls are not as globous as those created on this plant by the Gall Fly (of the Tephritidae or Fruit Fly family); another Fruit Fly, *Eurosta spp.* may also cause galls on these stems; the Plant Bug *Ilnacora (malina)* feeds on the plant juices and breeds here as well; the pollen is fed upon by adult Pennsylvania Leather-wing Beetle *Chauliognathes pennsylvanicus* and the Tumbling Flower Beetle *Mordella atrata*; Hover (Flower) Flies *Volucella bombylans*, use the nectar for food; Ambush bugs *Phymata americana* hide in the flowers for prey; the leaves are eaten by the larvae of the Goldenrod Leaf Beetle *Trirhabda spp.* and by the Lace Bug *Galeatus spp.*; a very common visitor to these flowers is the Ladybird Beetle *Hippodamia convergens* as it hunts for prey; needless to say, you will observe many honey bees and bumblebees gathering pollen and nectar from these flowers which also serve as important pollinators.

Spiders; the observer can expect to find one of the most common flower spiders, the Golden Rod Spider *Misumena vatia,* hiding in the flowers awaiting its prey which are other flower visiting insects.

(continued)

Grass-leaved Goldenrod Interactions

Human/Economic Use; the flowers are a source of a high quality yellow dye and to Native Americans, the leaves served as a source of a nutritious tea high in Vitamin A; the Chippewa prepared an extract from boiled roots to treat chest pain and lung or breathing difficulties.

Need To Know about interactions involving other plants and reptiles.

Curled Dock in flower.

Indian Poke *Veratrum viride* Aiton

LILIACEAE (Lily Family)

General Description -
Native perennial robust succulent herb growing to 7 feet in height.

Stem; robust, straight, often appearing alone or in small clumps.

Leaves; many, alternate, long and oval with deep longitudinal furrows and prominent parallel veins; with smooth surfaces, dark green in color, and with the base of the leaf stalk sheathing the stem.

Flower; small green flowers borne along stalks arising from axils of the upper leaves and appearing May-June.

Habitat; wooded swamps and stream banks.

WIS; FACW+

Indian Poke Interactions

Community Interactions; a rather tall herb which often grows in dense stands with Skunk Cabbage with which it shares many similar functions in the community (refer to Skunk Cabbage); this plant has a very well developed fibrous root system which holds soil against erosion; generally avoided by insects and other animals because of the complex lethal alkaloids; for its interactions with other animals groups including Mammals, Birds, Amphibians, Reptiles, Spiders, and Insects, please refer to the Skunk Cabbage.

Reptiles; Ribbon Snakes hunt near these plants, and may bask on the leaves.

Amphibians; the large leaves provide good cover, resting, and thermoregulation sites.

Human/Economic Use; powdered roots used as an insecticide; contains alkaloids 'jervine', 'pseudojervine', 'veratridine', and 'cevadine' that are poisonous to most animal life; tinctures have been used as fairly reliably in the treatment of hypertension, reducing blood pressure and heart rate.

Need To Know about interactions involving mammals, other plants, birds, spiders, and insects.

Jack-in-the-pulpit *Arisaema triphyllum* (L.) Schott

ARACEAE (Arum Family)

General Description -
Native perennial herb growing to 2 feet in height.

Stem; underground tuber.

Leaves; usually one, but possibly two 3-parted leaves with leaflets that are elliptic, entire (smooth margins), and pointed at both ends.

Flower; bee, gnat, and fly pollinated with male and female flowers clustered into a dense spike which is in turn enclosed within a greenish purple spathe (canopy-resembling a "pulpit"), and appearing May-June.

Habitat; shrub swamps, and at edges of tree swamps, and moist upland woodlands.

WIS; FACW-

208

Jack-in-the-pulpit Interactions

Community Interactions; this plant is extremely shade tolerant, in some cases having grown up to four years in nearly total darkness as long as they had sufficient moisture and nutrients such as is found in moist woods; characterized by fibrous roots systems which help bind soils; find that this plant can change sex from male to female or visa-versa depending upon the growing conditions - on poor nutrient, low light sights there is less energy available to expend on developing fruits and seeds so most flowers are male - on nutrient rich soils with adequate light, most of the flowers are female; at times, they may form very dense stands at edge of shrub swamps or high marsh where there is normally water saturated soil, where they add modestly to the variety of plant life providing cover, breeding sights, and limited food for wildlife; interestingly these plants may live 25 or more years, quite long for an herb.

Mammals; you can expect that the fruits will be occasionally eaten by Muskrat, Raccoon, Beaver, and Chipmunk.

Plants; can be found associated with Jewelweed, Marsh Fern, Sensitive Fern, and Skunk Cabbage.

Birds; the fruits and leaves are eaten by several birds including Wood Thrush, Wild Turkey, Pheasant, and Wood Duck.

Reptiles; none known; Wood and Box Turtles may be observed to either feed or reject the fruits - more observations are needed here.

Amphibians; the observer might chance to see both the Gray Treefrog and Spring Peepers sunning on the plants and awaiting for insect meals which may be attracted to this plant.

Insects; Honey bees, Bumblebees, various beetles and flies feed on pollen and may ultimately bring about pollination in the process; certain Thrips (Family Thripidae) very occasionally feed on the flowers.

Spiders; see Appendix D.

Human/Economic Interaction; although poisonous when raw, American Natives used to eat the boiled tubers; the dried tubers yield an expectorant which is used in folk medicine and by the Shawnee to treat coughs, asthma, bronchitis and ringworm; also known as Indian Turnip, the corms yield a flour similar to that of Arrowroot in being high in starch; the Malecite and Rappahannock made a root poultice to treat boils and swelling; cells contain calcium oxylate crystals which are very irritating to the tissues of the digestive tract.

Need To Know about interactions involving spiders.

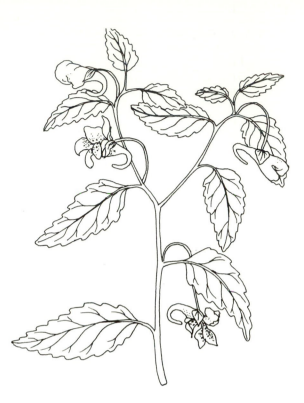

Jewelweed *Impatiens capensis* Meerb.

BALSAMINACEAE (Touch-me-not Family)

General Description -
Native annual herb growing to 6 feet in height.

Stem; slightly branching, erect, smooth, hollow, somewhat succulent, slightly transluscent, with smooth joints; often growing in dense stands.

Leaves; alternate, stalked, egg shaped, and having toothed margins.

Flowers; orange in color and bird pollinated (self pollinated flowers inconspicuous, green), with a reddish spotted spur curved inward, with flowers dangling, and borne singly or in a loose cluster; appearing in July-August.

Habitat; wet, well drained calcareous soils, and sun or shade of shrub swamps, edges of wooded swamps and stream banks.

WIS; FACW

Jewelweed Interactions

Community Interactions; one of the most important food supplies for the Ruby-throated Hummingbird east of the Mississippi River; by mid to late summer it is often one of the dominant members of its community, growing in dense stands; its very fibrous root system helps stabilize the wet soils of the higher marsh; cannot tolerate excessive flooding as seeds and seedlings do not survive anaerobic (oxygen deficient) conditions, implying negative impacts of altered hydrology on a valuable wildlife plant.

Mammals; seeds are eaten by the White-footed Mouse and the Woodland Jumping Mouse; the Meadow Jumping Mouse finds stands of this serve as valuable cover.

Plants; often found growing near Poison Ivy; their habit of dense growth often results in pure stands at the expense of other herbs; also frequently found growing with Sensitive Fern, Skunk Cabbage and their associated community members.

Birds; the Ruby-throated Hummingbird gets nectar here and serves to help in pollination; although quite secretive, you can expect that occasionally the Mourning Warbler will nest in thick stands of the plant; Veery will nest in this close to the ground; seeds are food for Ring-neck Pheasant and Ruffed Grouse.

Reptiles; Wood and Box Turtles forage near patches of Jewelweed, though it is not known if they eat the blossoms or seeds.

Amphibians; there is one report of a naturalist who watched as a Bullfrog lept up to eat a Hummingbird that was taking nectar at blossoms close to the water (That must have tasted sweet!); young Gray Treefrogs and Spring Peepers climb into the plants.

Insects; Ants and Bumblebees which are known to eat the pollen and nectar, Honey bees, and other insects play important roles in pollinating these flowers; Sphinx Moths use the nectar, and the Obtuse Euchlaena Moth and White-striped Black Moth employ this as a larval food plant; these are also host to various gall forming midges (flies) of the genus *Cecidomyia spp.* and *Lasioptera spp.*- the former creates a see-through gall near the flower base while the latter produces a swelling at the leaf base.

Spiders; see Appendix D.

(continued)

Jewelweed Interactions

Human/Economic Use; as practiced by the Cherokee, Mohegan, Nanticoke, and other American Natives, the stems and blossoms of this can be crushed and the resulting liquid which oozes out can be rubbed directly on that part of skin which was in contact with Poison Ivy or Poison Sumac, serving to dissolve the active irritant Urushiol thus avoiding serious attacks of dermititis; there are reports that a antiseptic 'methoxy-naphthoquione' is present in this plant which might be used as a natural fungicide to treat athlete's foot and itchy scalp; the Fox and Nanticoke made a poultice for dressing wounds and burns.

Biological Interactions

Plants and animals within a community interact or influence one another in positive or negative ways which can increase, decrease, or stabilize a population. Mutualism is a positive interaction between both populations. Such interactions are of benefit to both and may be nonobligatory (meaning not necessary) to the survival of each, or they may be obligatory or essential to the survival of both. If the interactions are negative or adverse to both populations, it is called competition. Commensalism is a type of interaction in which one population, the commensal, benefits while the other or host is neither harmed nor helped. If one population is negatively impacted and the other is unaffected, this type of interaction is called ammensalism or antibiosis. Parasitism/predation interactions are those which benefit one, the predator or parasite, while harming the other called the prey or host. Try to decide which of these biological interactions is represented by your field observations and note those in the guide on the "Field Data Form."

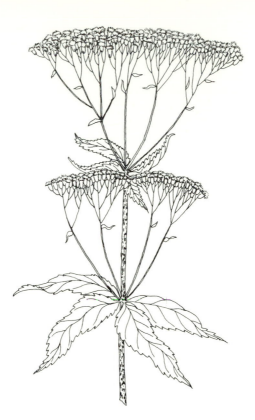

Joe-Pye-weed *Eupatorium maculatum* L.

Compositae (Aster Family)

General Description -
Native perennial herb growing to 6 feet.

Stem; robust, purple-spotted to totally purple, smooth and growing in clumps.

Leaves; in whorls of 3-7, lanceolate, toothed, short-stalked with a rough surface and a large single mid vein.

Flowers; insect pollinated, terminal purple/pink in a more or less flat cluster, appearing June-September.

Habitat; wet meadows, marshes, edges of thickets and ponds.

WIS; FACW

Joe-Pye-weed Interactions

Community Interactions; at times, it can grow in dense stands contributing to the overall value of wildlife cover in a wet meadow; its fibrous root system helps stabilize the wet soils of the high marsh where it is most abundant; the seeds persist into winter, serving as an emergency food source for wildlife; this weed is easily controlled by cultivating, mowing, or draining of the soil.

Mammals; growing along edges of small stream channels, I have seen the Meadow Jumping Mouse hiding in this; expect to see other wetland mammals including Muskrat using it as cover while others such as the Eastern Cottontail and Raccoon could eat the young shoots.

Plants; often found growing with Boneset.

Birds; seeds occasionally eaten by Wild Turkey and Swamp Sparrow.

Reptiles; hatchling Wood, Box, Snapping, and Painted Turtles may find good cover here.

Amphibians; Gray Treefrogs and Spring Peepers may climb the plant to escape predation or to hunt for food.

Insects; the Buffalo Treehopper *Stictocephala bisonia* feeds on its leaves; can observe Cottony Cushion Scale *Icerya purchasi*, introduced from Australia, on the stems which are in turn preyed upon by Lady Bugs; the Three-lined Flower Moth, Eupatorium Borer Moth, Once-married Underwing, and Red Groundling Moth may be seen feeding on this plant at night; the Cocklebur Weevil *Rhodobaenus tredecim punctatus* may breed here.

Spiders; see Appendix D.

Human/Economic Use; preparations of the leaf, flower, and shoot are used in folk medicine as a kidney stone remedy; hot tea from the leaves produces sweating to break fever and to overcome impotence; the Cherokee used a section of the hollow stem as a means of applying medication and they, along with the Iroquois, used the root to treat rheumatism.

Marsh Fern *Dryopteris thelypteris* (L.) Gray

POLPODIACEAE (True Fern Family)

General Description -
Native herb (fern) growing to 2 feet in height.

Stem; thin, flexible.

Leaves; delicate, divided into 12 or so nearly opposite pairs of leaflets which are yellow-green and lanceolate with deeply divided lobes, the fertile leaves(fronds) are taller than vegetative fronds.

Reproductive; groups of spherical spore cases on bottoms of fertile leaflets, appearing July-August.

Habitat; wet meadows to possibly shaded swamps, swales and stream borders.

WIS; FACW+

Marsh Fern Interactions

Community Interactions; a very common fern which prefers the sunny exposures of bogs, high marshes, and wet meadows where it establishes itself slowly over the years and may eventually grow in fairly dense clumps interspersed throughout the area where it provides some temporary cover for smaller wildlife; rootstocks are shallow, forking and not many in number affording only limited soil binding and stabilization; as do other ferns, they too serve as soil builders.

Mammals; very similar to the Sensitive Fern in its interactions with mammals.

Plants; this is frequently noted growing in association with Stick-tight.

Birds; of value to birds in a manner similar to that of Cinnamon Fern.

Reptiles; Water, Ribbon, Garter, and other snakes are known to search for prey among these plants.

Amphibians; dense stands provide excellent cover for hiding, hunting, thermoregulating, and body moisture control; the fronds are strong enough to support treefrogs; Woodfrogs cruise Marsh Fern stands in search of fruits and invertebrates.

Insects; use here is very similar to that of the Cinnamon Fern.

Human/Economic Use; fronds are not hardy and have little commercial value.

Need To Know about its interactions with other plants and spiders.

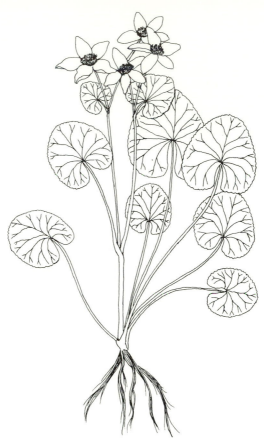

Marsh Marigold *Caltha palustris* L.

RANUNCULACEAE (Butttercup Family)

General Description -
Native perennial herb growing to 2 feet in height.

Stem; hollow, thick, and succulent, growing in small to large groups.

Leaves; heart or kidney shaped, growing to 4 inches in width with a long stalk and generally finely toothed margins.

Flower; insect pollinated, 1-2 inches wide with 5-9 bright yellow sepals (no petals); appearing April-June.

Habitat; fresh marshes, shrub or wooded swamps and occasionally wet meadows, often growing in the water.

WIS; OBL

218

Marsh Marigold Interactions

Community Interactions; its presence in a wetland indicates a pH range of 5-6; although of limited wildlife value, they do have branching filamentous roots systems which serve to stabilize wetland soils thereby protecting against erosion.

Mammals; the entire plant is eaten by Moose and Whitetail Deer.

Birds; occasionally one might observe Mallards feeding on the seeds as well as some upland game birds including Pheasant and Ruffed Grouse.

Reptiles; there is good hunting habitat for snakes (Water, Garter) and turtles (Wood, Box, Bog).

Amphibians; the large leaves provide both cover and perch sites for Green frogs, Spring Peepers, Gray Treefrogs and others.

Insects; flower reflects ultraviolet light that attracts Honey bees and Bumblebees active in pollination; the Hover Flies *Volucella bombylans* may be seen wondering over the flowers facilitating pollination; the Marsh Beetle *Cyphon collaris* is occasionally found on this plant; the Yellow Plant Bug *Horcias dislocatus* may be found on this plant in shadier areas.

Spiders; relates to spiders in the same manner as does the Pond Lily.

Human/Economic Use; Caution! contains a poisonous alkaloid Jervine and a glucoside Helleborin which have proven fatal to cattle browsing on them; both of these poisonous principles are reported to be rendered noninjurious upon proper drying and cooking as witnessed by the fact that some people use the stems and leaves as potherbs; others have used the roots as food; Chippewa prepared a tea from the roots to treat colds and a root poultice to use on open sores.

Need To Know about interactions invovling other plants.

219

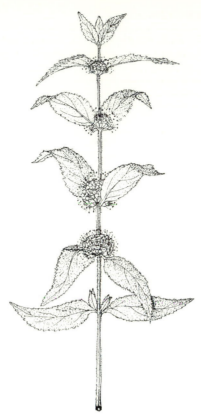

Mint *Mentha arvensis* L.

LABIATAE (Mint Family)

General Description -
Native perennial aromatic herb growing to 3 feet in height.

Stem; erect, square, with hairs.

Leaves; opposite, hairy, oval with toothed margins, stalked, and pointed at tips.

Flower; insect pollinated small tubular flowers in dense whorls in the upper leaf axils, lilac in color and with anthers (filaments) extending beyond the floral tube.

Habitat; shrub swamps, also wet meadows and fresh marsh edges.

WIS; FACW

Mint Interactions

Community Interactions; shade tolerant and occasionally occurring in large clumps growing from runners; in growing to 3 feet, they contribute to protective cover for small mammals and birds.

Mammals; Muskrat enjoy eating the entire plant including the pollen.

Birds; the Green-winged Teal and Ruffed Grouse can be expected to feed on the seeds.

Reptiles; Redbelly, Northern Brown, Northern Water, Ribbon, and Garter Snakes are likely to find food in these stands.

Amphibians; thick stands of tall mint create a moist and cool microhabitat, important to most amphibians.

Insects; although not a significant larval food plant, it is expected that various beetles and flies feed on nectar and pollen.

Human/Economic Use; contain volatile oil peppermint which is used in chewing gum, candies, and pharmaceutics; used as a carminative; the leaves and stems are high in Vitamin C and can be eaten raw or as a potherb.

Need To Know about interactions involving other plants and spiders.

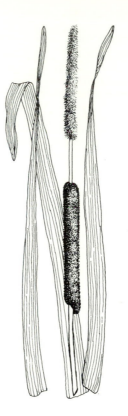

Narrow-leaved Cattail *Typha angustifolia* L.

TYPHACEAE (Cattail Family)

General Description -
Native very similar to Common Cattail with some key differences noted among the following.

Stem; more or less same Common Cattail.

Leaves; narrower than Common Cattail, growing to 1/2 inch wide.

Flower; upper male and lower female parts of spike have a gap between them.

Habitat; more coastal and although in fresh marshes, is more tolerant of brackish water than Common Cattail.

WIS; OBL

Narrow-leaved Cattail Interactions

 Community Interactions; please refer to the Common Cattail, as the roles are very much the same when found in similar habitats; it is tolerant of sewage polluted water; this plant is fairly common in the upper edges of salt marshes.

 Mammals; expect very similar observation to Common Cattail.

 Plants; expect very similar observations to Common Cattail; this is an inferior competitor to *T. latifolia* in fresh water wetlands.

 Birds; expect very similar observations to Common Cattail; also a nesting site for the Long-Billed Marsh Wren in brackish and possibly fresh marshes.

 Reptiles; expect very similar observation to Common Cattail.

 Amphibians; depending upon the habitat, expect very similar observations to Common Cattail.

 Insects; expect very similar observations to Common Cattail.

 Spiders; expect very similar observations to Common Cattail.

 Fish; expect very similar observations to Common Cattail.

 Human/Economic Use; expect very similar observations to Common Cattail.

223

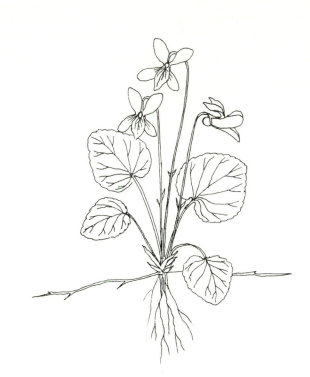

N. White Violet

Viola macloskeyi
F. Lloyd var.*pallens*(Banks) C.L.

VIOLACEAE (Violet Family)

General Description -
Native herb with leaves growing to 6 inches in height.

Stem; without upright stem, instead it has creeping runner (horizontal stem) which roots where it touches ground.

Leaves; ovate with heart-shaped base, blunt tip, round toothed margins, stalked, and smooth to slightly hairy surfaces.

Flower; solitary, stalked, white, with 5 petals, the lower three petals being dark lined and serving as 'nectar guides' for visiting insects, appear May-June.

Habitat; wet meadows, and streams, marshes, and swamp edges in sun or shade.

WIS; OBL

Northern White Violet Interactions

Community Interactions; the presence of this plant indicates a moderate soil pH range of 5 to 6; aside from providing some food, they are of limited wildlife value.

Mammals; the young shoots, flowers, and leaves are eaten by the Eastern Cottontail Rabbit, the Meadow Jumping Mouse, Muskrat, Beaver, and the Whitetail Deer.

Birds; one can expect to observe Wild Turkey eating the roots and the Ruffed Grouse and Woodcock feeding on the seeds.

Reptiles; Wood and Box Turtles probably feed on both the flowers and leaves.

Amphibians; many kinds of frogs no doubt hunt insects attracted to the blossoms.

Insects; while bees can be seen visiting the flowers for pollen, it also serves as the larval food plant for several butterflies including the Aphrodite, and most of the fritillaries including the Great Spangled Fritillary, Bog Fritillary, Regal Fritillary, Silver-bordered Fritillary, and the Meadow Fritillary.

Human/Economic Use; many *Viola* species have volatile essential oils which are used as scents in perfumes, shampoos, soaps etc.; leaves which are high in Vitamin C and magnesium, can be added to salads; the Cherokee made root poultices for wounds and boils and drank the tea for coughs.

Need To Know about interactions involving other plants and spiders.

Panic-grass *Panicum rigidulum* Nees.

GRAMINIAE (Grass Family)

General Description -
Native perennial grass growing to 6 feet in height.

Stem; upright from a more or less prostrate base, growing in dense stands.

Leaves; long (to 18 inches), alternate, with a prominent mid vein and other parallel veins and a leaf-like structure (ligule) at axis of leaf and stem.

Flower; delicate, loose cluster of small branches with many spiklets creating a dense green wind pollinated head.

Habitat; wet meadows, damp pond edges.

WIS; FACW+

Panic-grass Interactions

Community Interactions; a fairly sturdy plant which grows in clumps providing cover in summer and persisting as upright dead material through winter where it affords some protection for wildlife; its fibrous root systems serve to stabilize soil against erosion.

Mammals; Cottontail Rabbits will eat the entire plant; one could expect other herbivores such as mice, Muskrat, Whitetail Deer, and Beaver to eat this plant.

Birds; the Ring-neck Pheasant, Wild Turkey, Red-winged Blackbird, Henslow Sparrow, and Swamp Sparrow have been observed eating the seeds.

Reptiles; Ribbon, Garter, Red-bellied, and other snakes search for food here; it is possible, but not known, that Wood and Box Turtles graze on this plant.

Amphibians; Pickerel and Leopard frogs hunt for crickets, grasshoppers, leafhoppers, and butterflies here; many juvenile frogs hunt and hide in dense Panicum stands.

Insects; this is an important larval food plant to a number of butter-flies, so one might expect to observe visits from the Northern Broken Dash, the Leonardus Skipper, the Indian Skippering, Tawny-edged Skipper, the Broad-winged Skipper, the Least Skipperling, and the Long Dash.

Human/Economic Use; it has been used as a hay and silage plant.

Need To Know about interactions involving other plants and spiders.

Pickerelweed *Pontederia cordata* L.

PONTEDERIACEAE (Pickerelweed Family)

General Description -
Native perennial, emergent herb growing to 4 feet in height.

Stem; robust, arising from a rhizome, bearing one leaf and one terminal spike.

Leaves; very large arrowhead to heart-shaped with prominent parallel veins, blunt tip, and borne on a spongy leaf stalk.

Flower; solitary spike of small blue flowers with 2 lips and 3 lobes.

Habitat; fresh marshes, edges of ponds and slow moving streams.

WIS; OBL

Pickerelweed Interactions

Community Interactions; similar to the Arrowhead, this too loses great quantities of water from leaves and must be controlled where it often slows water movement and clogs reservoirs; has a fairly wide tolerance to salinity, often invading estuaries; this is an aggressive species which does provide wildlife protective cover; while it may decline in abundance following fuel oil spills, ultimately it returns at abundance levels higher than those prior to the spill.

Mammals; seeds, which are occasionally eaten by deer, serve as an important food source for the Muskrat.

Birds; one might observe Black Duck, Mallard, and Wood Duck eating the seeds.

Reptiles; if lucky, you may see the Spotted Turtle feeding under-water on these, along with the Snapping Turtle which eats these leaves and rotting stems.

Amphibians; the Northern Leopard and Pickerel Frog tadpoles often develop in large numbers among these plants where egg masses may be attached to submerged plant parts.

Insects; as the Cattail, this too serves as host to the Cattail Borer Moth, the White-tailed Diver moth and the Pickerelweed Borer moth; adult Black Dash Butterflies visit here; the adult Waterlily Beetle *Donacia piscatrix* feed on the leaves while the larvae eat submerged parts; backswimmers *Notonecta undulata* attach eggs to underwater stems and the Waterlily Leaf Beetle *Galerucella nymphaeae* may be seen eating this plant; one can expect to see the Spined Stink Bug *Podisus maculata* sitting in wait for its favored food, caterpillars; the Black-wing Damselfly *Calopteryx maculata* may be seen flying around this where the female may land and lay eggs in the sub-merged stems; also look for one of the more common Bluet Damselflies *Enallagma civile* in these same haunts.

Spiders; expect similar observations to those noted for Cattail.

Fish; this plant affords shade and shelter and is similar to the Cattail in serving other interactive roles for fish.

Human/Economic Use; the fruits formed in the spikes are starchy and edible and were ground into flour for bread making by Early Americans; the entire plant may be cooked as a potherb for food or used raw as salad greens.

Need To Know about interactions involving other plants.

Pitcher Plant *Sarracenia purpurea* L.

SARRACENIACEAE (Pitcher Plant Family)

General Description -
Native perennial herb growing l-2 feet in height.

Leaves; basal, purple to purple green, liquid-containing and pitcher-shaped with a flared bristled upper lip at the opening.

Flower; dark red to purple with five sepals and petals nodding on a stalk l-2 feet high and appearing in June.

Habitat; typically in bogs.

WIS; OBL

Pitcher Plant Interactions

Community Interactions; sun-loving plant of modest overall value in the community and which is of interest for its ability to capture insects and extract nitrogen from their soft body parts to supplement the generally low levels of their acidic nutrient poor environment; plant has a very slow growth rate, thus extirpation (local removal) through wetland disturbances will result in very limited recovery; these are rooted in the Sphagnum mat rather than the soil, so are an important part of the overall bog mat vegetative community.

Birds; have observed Golden-crowned Kinglet swoop in and take insects hovering around flower.

Reptiles; N. Water Snakes and Ribbon Snakes are the typical reptiles hunting near Pitcher Plants.

Amphibians; Spring Peepers occasionally observed sunning on these; Mink Frogs and American Toads are known to live in or near Sphagnum and these plants.

Insects; some Pitcher Plant mosquitos *Wyeomyia smithii* are immune to a volatile alkaloid 'coniine' found in the liquid of the trap which would kill most other insects, and as a result, are able to spend their larval stages in here in relative protection; the Pitcher Plant Borer Moth larvae can be found boring into leaves as can the larvae of the Tortricid moth *Olethreutes spp.*; also serves as the larval food plant for The Half-Yellow moth *Tarachidia semiflava*; red and purple flower colors along with nectar serve to attract insects.

Spiders; members of the genus *Dictyna spp.*, cribellate or snare building spiders, have been noted to build webs over apertures of flower traps to catch insects attracted to flower, a process which decreases the overall capture rate by the plants.

Human/Economic Use; a decoction prepared from the leaves has been used as a treatment for constipation, dyspepsia, liver, and kidney disorders; although many disagree, some consider the root to have curative properties over chicken pox and small pox, purposes to which the Algonquin put it; vapors of this plant are quite reactive and cause severe mucosal irritation and skin rashes; the pitcher shaped basal leaves have been used as drinking cups; the Penobscot and Cree made preparations from the plant to treat kidney disorders.

Need To Know about interactions involving Mammals and other plants.

Pond or Waterlily *Nymphaea odorata* Aiton

NYMPHAEACEAE (Pond Lily Family)

General Description -
Native perennial herb with floating leaves and flowers.

Stem; creeping, branching rhizome buried in mud.

Leaves; round floating blade 10-12 inches in diameter with a slit or sinus; green upper and purplish lower surfaces, and connected to a petiole (stalk) which can be 3-4 feet long, arising from the buried rhizome.

Flower; floating, borne singly on a very long stalk and having many white petals, flowers insect pollinated; appearing July-August.

Habitat; fresh marsh, also in ponds, lakes, stream borders.

WIS; OBL

Pond or Waterlily Interactions

Community Interactions; each floating leaf actually creates a mini edge community where one can see wildlife congregating; growing along the margins and in the openings of deep marshes, the leaves provide protective cover and breeding areas for aquatic life; this single plant establishes a series of habitats vertically stratified from the mud bottom through the water column to the floating leaves where one can find different organisms distributed at each level; however, even the floating leaf provides an amazing array of interactions as you will notice in the following examples; in addition, these plants have a stout, creeping, and branching rootstock which stabilizes the muddy bottoms of ponds, low marshes and slow moving streams; the upper leaf surface of these plants has many tiny openings or stomata which serve to bring in oxygen and carbon dioxide needed for survival.

Mammals; plant forms an important part of the habitat of Beavers and Muskrats which feed on leaves and rootstocks; the Whitetail Deer, Moose, and Porcupine may also be observed feeding on these plants.

Plants; usually you will observe this growing in abundance under conditions supporting the presence of Duckweed and Spatter-dock.

Birds; one can expect to observe the Lesser Scaup, Wood Duck, and Blue-winged Teal eating parts of this plant including seeds and rootstocks.

Reptiles; hatchlings and juvenile Painted, Redbelly, Red-eared Slider, and E. Softshell turtles bask on the larger, floating leaves.

Amphibians; Bullfrogs often bask on the leaves; also, egg masses of Leopard and Pickerel frogs may be attached to the leaves.

Insects; in general, flowers produce no nectar but copious amounts of pollen which is attractive to beetles including the adult Waterlily Beetle *Donacia piscatrix* and the Waterlily Leaf Beetle *Galerucella nymphaeae* that eat foliage and pollen while the larvae eat submerged plant parts (not so easily observed unless you pull up such parts and cut into them for evidence of their presence); you may also see Marsh Flies *(Tetanocera* spp.*)* running over the leaves of the plants; leaves of this are also a larval food plant for the Burdock Borer moth, the White-tailed Diver moth and for the Pyralid moths *Munroessa gyralis* and *Synclita obliteralis,* the latter of which makes a protective casing out of such plant parts; the observer will undoubtedly notice Whirligig Beetles resting on and swimming about the leaves; other

(continued)

Pond or Waterlily Interactions

 Insects (continued); insects including Honey bees, Bumblebees, beetles, and flies, probably quite important in pollination, can be seen visiting the flowers .

 Spiders; Look for the Six-spotted Fishing Spider *Dolomedes triton* darting over the leaves positioning itself to catch its prey.

 Fish; at one time or another you might spot Catfish, Golden Shiners, panfish, bass, and the ubiquitous Carp hiding under its leaves.

 Human/Economic Use; the leaves have been boiled and eaten as potherbs while its roots are the source of a soap substitute and a brown dye; a tea made from the leaves can be used as a throat gargle, eyewash, and, vaginal douche; roots and leaves have been used as a poultice for dressing wounds; the tubers are a rich source of starch and the seeds are a good source of starch, oils, and proteins; heavy growth of this can create obstructions to boating and fishing.

Water-lily on open water adjacent to a fresh marsh.

Purple Loosestrife   *Lythrum salicaria* L.

LYTHRACEAE (Loosestrife Family)

General Description -
Introduced from Europe and naturalized, a perennial herb growing to 5 feet with terminal purple inflorescence.

Stems; erect, tall, smooth to hairy.

Leaves; lance shaped, opposite to whorled (three) and tending to have clasping leaf bases and hairy surfaces.

Flower; insect pollinated, with 5-6 purple petals and green hairy sepals held in a dense terminal spike, appearing July-August.

Habitat; fresh marshes, wet meadows, pond and swamp edges, and usually in full sun.

WIS; FACW+

Purple Loosestrife Interactions

Community Interactions; research has shown that this plant can take up PCB (polychloro-biphenyls) pollutants, thus implicating it as an environmental filter; this is an highly invasive plant in all marshes where it gets started, propagating not only by seed but also vegetatively through growth of the strong fleshy roots; it normally out competes most other emergent plants, thereby reducing the high species diversity of both plants and animals which is usually characteristic of a marsh; this plant persists for many years and grows successfully in standing water; Loosestrife cheerfully colonizes the upper edges of salt marshes and the entirety of brackish ones; generally considered to be of low value to wildlife.

Mammals; the normal movements of Muskrats and Beavers along the water's edge often results in these plants being knocked down where the seeds may then be passively spread by water or become attached to animal coats and carried to new locations.

Plants; through rapid growth, it often establishes pure stands at the expense of other emergents.

Birds; Red-winged Blackbirds have been seen perching and nesting among these.

Amphibians; little information is available on interactions with this plant.

Insects; as a plant which produces large amounts of pollen and nectar high in sucrose, Honey bees, flies, beetles, and Bumblebees are often seen visiting the flowers and are probably involved in its pollination; one may chance to see the Water Scavenger Beetle *Hydrobius fuscipes* crawling over the leaves of this and other nearby plants; members of the Snout Beetle family Curculionidae may be involved in pollination; this is also the larval food plant for the Pearly Wood-nymph moth.

Human/Economic Use; the leaves can be consumed as a vegetable; infusions or extracts of the herb are reportedly used to control diarrhea; research has revealed that leaf extracts can stop internal bleeeding; beekeepers have planted this herb in waterways because it is a valued source of nectar and pollen for their hives.

Need To Know about interactions involving amphibians, reptiles, fish, and spiders.

Reed-Canary Grass *Phalaris arundinacea* L.

GRAMINEAE (Grass Family)

General Description -
Native perennial grass-like herb growing to 7 feet in height.

Stems; upright, stiff, and often growing in dense stands.

Leaves; alternate, long and narrow (12-14 inches long and 3/4-1 inch wide) with an open sheath and ligule at the leaf axis.

Flower; wind pollinated green to greenish-purple spike borne singly on a short stalk and appearing May-August.

Habitat; wet meadows, swales, marsh edges.

WIS; FACW+

Reed-Canary Grass Interactions

Community Interactions; a very aggressive invader capable of spreading from a widely creeping and branching rhizome which serves to hold soil and build humus; it can grow well in either sun or shade; has been shown to respond well to municipal solid waste leachate irrigation with resultant increase in height and leaf size; plant does not appear to accumulate excessive heavy metals.

Mammals; although I have occasionally observed Meadow Voles seeming to nibble on stems and leaves, there is a limited record of animals feeding on this which is probably due to the bitter tasting alkaloids it contains.

Plants; where this gets established, it seems to grow in pure stands at the expense of other members of the wetland plant community.

Birds; the Common Yellowthroat uses the plant for nesting material; the plant also serves as nesting material for the Northern Harrier; seeds are known to be consumed by Ring-neck Pheasant; one can expect certain ducks including Mallards and Black Duck to eat the seeds.

Reptiles; the Water Snake is very selective in its habitat usage, preferring flooded meadows with a cover of this grass and sedges or a Cattail dominated marsh; Ribbon Snakes, Garter Snakes, and Redbelly Water Snakes may hunt in *Phalaris* meadows.

Amphibians; many newly metamorphosed frogs, including Spring Peepers, Gray Treefrogs, Leopard Frogs, Pickerel Frogs and Spadefoot Toads hide and hunt small invertebrates in meadows dominated by this plant.

Insects; this is the larval food plant to a number of butterflies you can expect to see visiting this plant at one time or another including the following: the Prairie Ringlet, the Yellowpatch Skipper, the Long Dash, the Zabulon Skipper, the Hobomok Skipper, and the Saffron Skipper; since this plant is often associated with mosquito larvae, its eradication can potentially lead to mosquito control; a Vampire Leafhopper *Draeculacephala spp.* can be seen on this.

Spiders; the Orb Weaver *Argiope (riparia)* has been observed building its web on this plant; also look for this spider's cocoons.

Human/Economic Use; serves primarily in pastures and haying fields and thus is a potentially useful agricultural plant; flour from the seed is used to make a glue for sizing cotton.

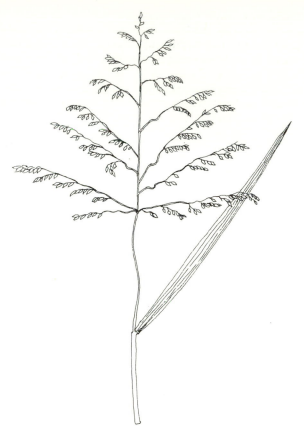

Rice-Cutgrass   *Leersia oryzoides* (L.) Swartz

Gramineae (Grass Family)

General Description -
Native perennial grass growing to 4 feet in height.

Stem; reclining to ascending, branching, and arising from a slender, elongated rhizome.

Leaves; elongated (up to 12 inches) and very rough to the touch on the surface and margins and with a ligule (leaf-like structure) at axis of leaf and stem.

Flower; wind and sometimes self pollinated, single-flowered, short stalked, with overlapping flat spiklets borne on one side of crooked branches of the inflorescence.

Habitat; primarily fresh marshes.

WIS; OBL

Rice-Cutgrass Interactions

Community Interactions; although this emergent is often characterized by high frequency, it affords only limited cover and some vertical stratification for breeding and nesting at water's edge - the prolific seed head is a valuable food source; when growing in dense stands, its short shallow roots form a network system to help reduce erosion of channels and banks; usualy declines abruptly following fuel oil spills into wetlands; research has shown that this plant is tolerant of very acidic (pH 3) marsh waters, actually showing an increase in biomass.

Mammals; the seeds and greens are regularly consumed by Moose, Deer, and Muskrat.

Plants; although it may be found growing with a wide variety of marsh plants, there are those with which it is more frequently associated including Swamp Loosestrife, Duckweed, Sensitive Fern, and when present, Wild Rice.

Birds; the seeds and inflorescences are eaten by a variety of water fowl including Mallards, Blue and Green-winged Teal, Red-winged Blackbirds, Canadian Geese, the American Coot, Wood Duck, and Black Ducks; it is one of the top duck foods in the area but only seasonally available; several other birds including the Virginia and Sora Rails might also be seen dining on this plant.

Reptiles; Wood Turtles, Ribbon Snakes, N. Water Snakes, Redbelly and N. Brown Snakes commonly hunt for food here; Wood Turtles may spend large amounts of time resting, and/or thermoregulating in large, open meadows.

Amphibians; dense *Leersia* stands are excellent foraging areas for Pickerel and Leopard frogs; excellent cover for many recently metomorphosed amphibians, such as Spring Peepers, Gray Treefrogs, and American Toads.

Insects; at one time or another one might observe a number of butterflies visiting cutgrass since it serves as their larval food plant; some of those butterflies include the Yellowpatch Skipper, Long Dash, Zabulon Skipper, Hobomok Skipper, Safron Skipper, Broad-winged Skipper, and the Prairie Ringlet; the Toothed Flea Beetle adults *Chaetocnema denticulata* feed on the leaves along with Billbugs of the genus *Shenophorus (calendra)*; adult Lesser Water Weevils *Lissorhoptrus oryzophilus* feed on the leaves of this plant as well as on other aquatic grasses.

(continued)

Rice-Cutgrass Interactions

Human/Economic Use; the ripe fruit (grain) can be dried and ground into flour or eaten as regular rice; it is considered quite a delicacy, more valuable per pound than many of the top meat cuts; American Natives still have licensed rights to harvest the plant; it is planted along waterfowl migratory flyways to supply them with food; occasionally the seed heads become infected with a fungus known as *Claviceps purpurea* that causes a disease called "Ergot", poisonous because it produces Lysergic Acid (a precursor to the infamous LSD hallucinogen).

Need To Know about interactions involving other plants, and spiders; compare this plant with Wild Rice for similarities of interactions.

Pragmites at Edge of salt marsh.

Rose Mallow *Hibiscus moscheutos* L.

MALVACEAE (Mallow Family)

General Description -
Native or possibly introduced from England, herb growing to 8 feet in height.

Stem; fairly stout and covered with fine hairs.

Leaves; alternate, with wedge shaped base, tapering to a pointed tip and often coarsely toothed to lobed at edges and reaching 8-10 inches in length.

Flower; insect pollinated, very distinctive and large (6 inches or more in width) with 5 large white to whitish-pink petals with a long style (column) in flower center which has 5 spherical structures (stigmas) on the end; appearing August-September.

Habitat; fresh to brackish marshes, and upper edges of salt marshes.

WIS; OBL

Rose Mallow Interactions

Community Interactions; often seen on slopes in wetlands, it has a deep growing fibrous root system which serves to hold the soil against erosion.

Birds; the more frequent visitors to this plant for seeds are Mallards and Black Ducks; less frequently the observer may find Wood Duck, Blue-winged Teal, and Bobwhite eating these seeds.

Amphibians; one might expect semiaquatic frogs, such as Pickerel, Leopard, Green, and Bullfrogs to hunt insects attracted to this plant.

Insects; the Common Checkered Skipper Butterfly regularly uses this as a larval food plant; the Gray Hairstreak and Painted Lady butterflies occasionally use this as a larval food plant; this plant is also a larval food plant for the Delightful Bird-Dropping Moth and a rather inconspicuous noctuid moth *Bagisara rectifascia*; the flower is visited by the Digger Bee *Ptilothrix bombiformis* for its pollen.

Human/Economic Use; a gargle is made from a leaf infusion; tea made from the entire plant is made to treat bronchial disorders including cough and asthma as well as digestive disorders such as ulcers and colitis; a soothing poultice is made from leaves.

Need To Know about interactions involving other plants, mammals, reptiles, and spiders.

Rose Pogonia *Pogonia ophioglossoides* (L.) Ker Gawler

ORCHIDACEAE (Orchid Family)

General Description -
Native slender, upright, often growing in clumps and reaching a height of 1.5 feet.

Leaves; generally only one which is 6-8 inches long and clasping at the mid point of the stem.

Flower; borne singly, insect pollinated, with five large spreading pink sepals and petals of similar appearance and above a drooping fringed lip.

Habitat; bogs and acid wet meadows.

WIS; OBL

Rose Pogonia Interactions

 Community Interactions; is limited in population numbers and nearly an obligate resident of the bog; it responds negatively to human impacts, usually dying if stepped upon or transplanted.

 Mammals; would expect to see Southern Red-backed voles and Beaver feeding on these plants.

 Amphibians; hardy species such as Green Frogs, Spring Peepers, Mink Frogs, and possibly Wood Frogs would be expected to feed on insect visitors to the flower.

 Insects; have observed mosquitos, bees, and flies hovering around the flower where they may play a role in pollination.

Human/Economic Use; a small fragrant orchid to be enjoyed aesthetically but left unpicked.

Need To Know about interactions involving other plants, birds, reptiles, spiders, and insects.

Salt Marsh Bulrush *Scirpus robustus* Pursh

CYPERACEAE (Sedge Family)

General Description -
Native perennial upright grass-like herb growing to 4 feet in height.

Stem; triangular shape, robust.

Leaves; several long, narrow pointed grass-like leaves

Flower; small cone-shaped spiklets some stalked, others sessile and accompanied by erect leafy bracts, appearing July-October.

Habitat; most common in upper salt marsh where irregularly flooded, but also occasionally seen in lower regularly flooded areas with Saltmarsh Cordgrass.

WIS; OBL

Salt Marsh Bulrush Interactions

Community Interactions; grows towards the upper marsh edge where there is a higher organic base, doing less well in sandier substrates; it has a thick creeping rhizome which helps stabilize the upper marsh soils against storm or tidal impacts.

Mammals; Muskrats eat root systems.

Plants; often found growing in the same community with *Phragmites* and Japanese Fleece Flower.

Birds; seed production is high enough to serve as water fowl food for many of those already mentioned for other salt marsh plants including the cordgrasses; Mute Swans dislodge the rootstocks which they consume as food.

Insects; this is the larval food plant for the Salt Marsh Skipper Butterfly and a place where the Greenhead Fly attaches its egg masses.

Human/Economic Use; the dried rootstock was used by American Natives who ground it into flour.

Need To Know about interactions involving amphibians, reptiles, and spiders.

Saltmarsh Cordgrass *Spartina alterniflora* Loisel

GRAMINEAE (Grass Family)

General Description -
Native perennial grass growing to 8 feet in height.

Stem; hollow, robust, and round.

Leaves; smooth to slightly rough-edged, grass-like, growing to 16 inches, curling at tips and having edges of lower leaf sheath slightly hairy.

Flower; inflorescence composed of spikes appressed (hugging) to the terminal axis, appearing July-September.

Habitat; twice daily flooded lower zone of salt marsh.

WIS; OBL

Saltmarsh Cordgrass Interactions

Community Interactions; has large air spaces in leaf sheaths which probably play a role in transporting oxygen to roots deep in the low oxygen marsh soils thereby keeping them alive; plant is reportedly endowed with flexible genetic material that allows it considerable adaptive success to many environmental stresses; for example, they can oxidize the reduced toxins which accumulate in anaerobic soils (e.g. ethylene, monocarboxylic acid as well as heavy metal compounds including zinc, lead, mercury, iron, and copper); however, they are adversely affected by oil spills, with growth and development especially retarded the year following the incident; spreads by rhizomes and seeds, establishing dense stands; while generally dominating in salt marshes, seeds from this plant can also germinate and grow in fresh water; plants have several strategies for dealing with salt including excess salt excretion from special glands or by concentrating salt in cells so as to become saltier than the surrounding salt water, causing only water to move into their cells by osmosis; interestingly, its major ecological role is achieved upon death, when it becomes food for bacteria through decay, thus starting the detritus food chain which supplies food for plankton which in turn become food for clams and Fiddler Crabs *Uca pugilator, U. minax, and U. pugnax* which may then be eaten by birds; 2/3 of fish and shellfish of East Coast spend part of their life in a salt marsh as free swimming larvae; a salt marsh snail has lungs rather than gills and can be seen migrating up stems to avoid drowning by incoming tides as it feeds on decaying stems; this is the dominant plant of most N. American coastal marshes; has very wide range of temperature tolerance from O degrees in the Bay of Fundy to 35 to 50 degrees centigrade in the tropics; a pioneer species which along with Glasswort stabilize the substrate and promote soil build up thereby preparing the way for the eventual invasion by other salt marsh plants.

Mammals; both the Whitetail Deer and the Muskrat eat entire plant, while the the Short-tailed Shrew burrows in this and other grasses.

Plants; please refer to ' Community Interactions' above.

Birds; nesting material for the Northern Harrier and the Clapper Rail, which tends to nest close to incoming tides along channels; the Seaside Sparrow can also be counted on to nest in clumps of this grass; a wide diversity of birds can be expected to nest in this grass including Common Terns which can be seen chasing away other predatory birds, Black Skimmers, Gadwalls, Willets, Sharp-tailed sparrows, and Oystercatchers; one may catch sight of a Great Blue Heron standing among this and other cordgrasses along with the Cattle Egret, Snowy Egret, and Canada Goose; Snow Geese eat the

(continued)

Saltmarsh Cordgrass Interactions

 Birds (continued); succulent shoots and rootstocks, whereas the seeds and roots may be consumed by Mallards, Black Ducks, Canada Geese, Green- and Blue-winged Teal, the Clapper and Sora rails and the Seaside Sparrow.

 Reptiles; Diamondback Terrapin hatchlings may be found in and near *Spartina* marshes, in early to late autumn; occasionally cold stunnned Atlantic Loggerhead, Atlantic Green, and Atlantic Leatherback turtles are stranded in *Spartina* marshes at low tides.

 Amphibians; none known or expected.

 Insects; this is the host plant and overwintering site for the intertidal plant hopper *Prokelisia marginata,* one of the most abundant herbivores of the Atlantic salt marshes; a Saltmarsh Grasshopper *Orchelimum* spp. feeds on the stems and leaves of the *Spartina*; male Golden Saltmarsh mosquitos *Aedes taeniorhynchus* feed on plant juices and breed among these and *S. patens* where tidal inundation does not exceed 8-10 days per month, yet failing to develope where it exceeds 25 days per month; a rather obscure Owlet moth *Spartiniphaga inops* uses this as a larval food plant.

 Spiders; often find Marsh Fiddler Crabs around the base of plants in burrows they create which also serve as conduits for nutrient flow to the plant roots; the Fishing Spider, *Dolomedes striatus,* may be found fishing from these leaves; the Line-weaving Spider *Linyphia clathrata* can be seen with its web among the leaves.

 Fish; during high tide, many fish including the Sheepshead Minnow and Atlantic Silversides move in amongst these grasses to feed and gain some protection.

Human/Economic Use; used for thatching, as a garden mulch and for cattle feed.

252

Animals as agents of Flower Pollination

Pollination is the transfer of pollen from the male flower part (anther) to the female part (stigma). Plants have enlisted many pollination vectors or agents to help carry out this process vital to reproduction. Many of these vectors are animals including insects, spiders, mammals, and birds. The relationship between the flower and animals in this process might be considered a mutualistic biological interaction, one beneficial to both populations. Plants offer a variety of "primary attractants" or rewards to animals for helping out with pollination. These primary attractants are of direct need to animal life and include such things as pollen, nectar, egg laying sites, and protection. Other ways plants attract animals for pollination is through "secondary attractants" that are olfactory or visual cues, such as fragrances, colors, and shapes. Bees are among the most important pollinators. The adults eat primarily nectar while the larvae consume honey (converted nectar) and some pollen. Bees are usually attracted by the sight of blue/violet or yellow colors, and therefore not the best colors to wear into the field if you are allergic to bee stings. Bee pollinated flowers typically reflect ultraviolet light which bees also see. Flies are often attracted by the odor of rotting meat. Moths are generally nocturnal and often visit dull or white colored evening to night blooming flowers which are usually very sweetly scented. Butterflies are strongly attracted to red/orange colored flowers. Birds do not normally have well developed senses of smell but do perceive colors in the red region. As a result, bird pollinated flowers are generally red and pretty much unscented, a combination usually unattractive to many insects. This close ecological interrelationship between flower and pollinator is the result of coevolution, whereby selective forces in nature work on both populations creating a partial dependence of one upon the other.

Saltmeadow Cordgrass *Spartina patens* (Aiton) Muhl.

GRAMINEAE (Grass Family)

General Description -
Native perennial grass growing to 3 feet in height.

Stem; thin, stiff, hollow, growing in clumps.

Leaves; grass-like,very narrow, growing to 18 inches in height and tapering to a very slender tip with involute (rolled in) leaf margins.

Flower; terminal inflorescence composed of spikes alternately arranged and diverging from the main axis with many spiklets overlapping each other on one side of stalk and appearing June-October.

Habitat; in the upper salt marsh behind *S. alterniflora* where irregularly flooded.

WIS; FACW+

Saltmeadow Cordgrass Interactions

 Community Interactions; this fulfills many of the same roles as those ellaborated upon for *S. alterniflora.*

 Mammals; the Muskrat and Whitetail Deer graze on this; the observer might spot the Masked Shrew and various mice running quickly through this grass; the Marsh Rice Rat creates runs in grasses, is somewhat amphibious, a good swimmer, and makes nests of this, other grasses, rushes, and sedges.

 Plants; for this, refer to *S. alternifolia.*

 Birds; this is nesting site for the Snow Goose and Gadwell and occasionally for the Short-eared Owl; constitutes nesting material for Willets which nest on the ground in drier spots and for other birds including Great Black-Backed and Herring Gulls, Common Yellowthroats, and Savannah and Seaside Sparrows; the Seaside and Sharp-tailed Sparrows along with the Clapper Rail, Shoveler and American Bittern nest here and throughout the marsh, usually on higher dry spots; this is important habitat material for the Marsh Wren; also a favored habitat and food source for Mallards and Black Ducks.

 Reptiles; I have observed the Northern Water Snake emerge from this grass along the edge of the marsh, a snake which seems to inhabit all types of clean water wetlands; also, the wide ranging Eastern Garter Snake may be spotted here; Diamondback Terrapin hatchlings may be seen hiking through the grass to the low tide mark.

 Amphibians; Spadefoot Toads, American Toads, and Fowler's Toads may forage the edges of *S. patens* marshes.

 Insects; this is the larval food plant for the Double-Lined Doryodes Moth; a plant hopper *Prokelesia* spp. can be found sucking juices from stems and leaves; Horse Flies *Tabanus atratus* lay eggs in stems and leaves as do Deer Flies *Chrysops callidus* and where males of both species take nectar, pollen or suck juices.

 Spiders; see Appendix D.

 Human/Economic Use; this and *S. alternifolia* are known to reduce nitrogen and phosphorus levels from effluents before such water enters the sea; as nitrogen levels increase plants grow and in turn increase habitat and food supply which is reflected in herbivore faunal increases; since it can be walked on without detriment to survival, cattle can graze here without permanent injury to the plants; it was harvested for cattle feed by New England farmers.

Need To Know about interactions involving spiders.

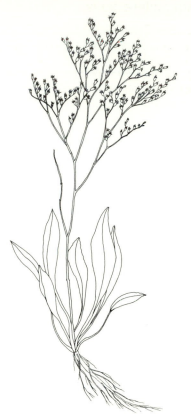

Sea Lavender *Limonium carolinianum* (Walter) Britton

PLUMBAGINACEAE (Leadwort Family)

General Description -
Native herb growing to 2 feet in height.

Stem; not readily visible.

Leaves; basal, entire margins, lance-shaped with a reddish- brown stalk.

Flower; 5 small lavender petals, stalked, and lining one side of the floral stem of the many branched inflorescence.

Habitat; upper edge of salt marsh.

WIS; OBL

Sea Lavender Interactions

 Reptiles; Diamondback Terrapin adults and especially hatchlings, may forage at high tide near *Limonium.*

Need To Know; much is left for you to discover about this plant.

Seaside Goldenrod *Solidago sempervirens* L.

COMPOSITAE (Aster Family)

General Description -
Native perennial herb growing to 7 feet in height.

Stem; erect, smooth.

Leaves; oblong to lance-shaped, thick and fleshy with smooth margins and lacking a stalk or petiole.

Flower; showy, yellow, insect pollinated with a terminal inflorescence of smaller curved one-sided clusters, appearing August-September.

Habitat; upper irregularly flooded portions of salt marsh.

WIS; FACW

Seaside Goldenrod Interactions

Community Interactions; this is a highly salt tolerant plant of the upper edges of the salt marsh community, withstanding salt spray and adding to the species diversity of plant life in this zone; its fleshy fibrous root system serves to stabilize the marsh border.

Mammals; foliage is browsed by the Eastern Cottontail, Meadow Jumping Mouse, and the Whitetail Deer; the presence of certain diterpenes proves to be toxic to sheep and many other mammals.

Birds; I have observed Goldfinches eating the seeds.

Insects; Bumblebees and honey bees can be seen taking the pollen and nectar; possibly find Leaf-eating Beetles *Trirhabda* spp. adults eating the leaves; Common Carpenter Bees and Black Blister Beetles can also be seen visiting this plant; as was noted for the Grass-leaved Goldenrod, Pennsylvania Leather-wing Beetle *Chauliognathes pennsylvanicus* may be observed here too; keep a look out for some of the other insect visitors listed for Grass-leaved Goldenrod, you can expect to find some here for sure.

Spiders; can expect observations similar to those for the Grass-leaved Goldenrod; also see Appendix D.

Human/Economic Use; this species, as for other goldenrods, may cause allergic reactions if sensitive individuals come into direct contact with the flowers; this is not wind pollinated and thus airborne pollen is usually not the culprit; the leaves can be boiled to prepare a tea high in Vitamin C.

Need To Know about interactions involving other plants, amphibians, and reptiles.

259

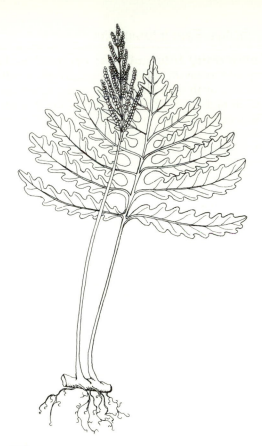

Sensitive Fern *Onoclea sensibilis* L.

POLYPODIACEAE (True Fern Family)

General Description -
Native herb (fern) growing to 3 feet in height.

Stem; robust, erect.

Leaves; sterile leaves grow to 3 feet and are light green and divided into 12 or so opposite pairs of leaflets which have wavy edges.

Reproduction; fertile fronds (leaves) grow to 1 foot that terminate in a dark brown spike consisting of hard sphericle spore cases that appear in July-August and persist through the winter.

Habitat; wet meadows, shrub and wooded swamps.

WIS; FACW

Sensitive Fern Interactions

Community Interactions; observations have shown that in response to environmental change, the apical cells respond by giving rise to growth tolerant of these changes; although this plant grows best in high marshes and swamps where it is not usually flooded, it will tolerate the mid marsh where water often remains at the surface between plants clumps; I have also observed that these plants will often be among the first to recolonize an area the year following a major flooding event which killed off the herb strata; although they prefer neutral soils, the fern can also tolerate acidity; it is tolerant of full sun or complete shade; they are frequently found growing in large numbers at the edge of a wetland where they provide significant cover in summer for small animals; in winter, the fertile fronds persist and serve as limited food for wildlife; the root systems are robust, many in number, fibrous, matted and creeping, which serve to bind the soils and thus reduce erosion; although it may decline following fuel oil spills to wetlands, it generally recovers to abundance levels higher than before the incident.

Mammals; plant provides cover for the White-footed Mouse and the N. Redback Vole, both of which can be seen scurrying among the leaf stalks; the fronds are eaten by Chipmunk and Whitetail Deer.

Plants; in many mid marsh communities this is commonly observed in association with Rice-cut Grass, Duck Weed, Skunk Cabbage and Swamp Loosestrife; in high or unflooded marshes and swamps, I typically observe this associated with such species as Jack-in-the-pulpit, Skunk Cabbage, Goldthread, Cinnamon Fern and Jewelweed in the herb strata.

Birds; "fiddleheads" are favored as a food by the Ruffed Grouse and Wild Turkey, while the American Woodcock nests among these near open feeding areas.

Reptiles; Wood Turtles, Box Turtles, Bog, and Spotted Turtles may feed, forage, or rest in Sensitive Fern areas. Redbelly, Ribbon, Garter, and N. Water Snakes hunt for adult and juvenile amphibians, insects, worms, and other invertebrates.

Amphibians; when flooded, the fertile fronds may be used as egg cluster attachment sites for several species of vernal pool breeders, including the Spotted, Jefferson's, Blue-spotted Salamanders, Wood Frogs and Spring Peepers.

(continued)

Sensitive Fern Interactions

Insects; its relationships to insects is quite similar to that of Cinnamon Fern; serves as the larval food plant for the Sensitive Fern (Root) Borer Moth; also is a larval food plant for the Pink-shaded and Silver-spotted Moths; the Japanese Beetle eats the leaves.

Spiders; see Appendix D.

Human/Economic Use; although the active ingredient is not agreed upon, it may contain 'thiaminase', an enzyme which destroys thiamine (Vitamin B which is important in nerve function and general metabolism) resulting in deficiency symptoms and thus poisoning in horses which consume them while grazing; reportedly, the Iroquois controlled venereal diseases with preparations from the rhizomes.

Need To Know about interactions involving spiders.

Plant Parts as Food for Wildlife

Nearly all parts of a plant provide food for one type of animal or another. Roots, tubers, and bulbs are underground storage organs often high in carbohydrates, such as starch. Inner bark and wood are used by some animals as a food source containing sugars, starches, and minerals. Fruits have fats, proteins, carbohydrates, and vitamins and are highly prized food sources by many forms of wildlife. Depending upon the plant species, fruits are often available spring, summer, fall, and even into the winter. Nuts are fruits with a dry wall and are a source of dietary fat. Seeds are propagating structures produced within the fruit. They are one of the most valued food supplies to wildlife that contain fats, carbohydrates, proteins, fiber, minerals, and vitamins. Vegetation generally refers to the green parts of plants, such as stems and leaves. These are eaten by a vast number of organism as a primary food item containing carbohydrates, fats, proteins, water, minerals, and vitamins.

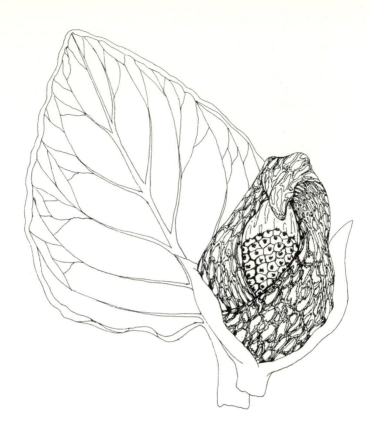

Skunk Cabbage *Symplocarpus foetidus* (L.) Nutt.

ARACEAE (Arum Family)

General Description -
Native perennial herb growing to 3 feet in height.

Stem; stout rhizome (underground stem).

Leaves; large (2-3 feet), oval, thick, dark green, prominently veined, entire (smooth) margins, stout petiole, and having a skunk-like odor upon crushing.

Flower; many small insect, carrion fly, snail, and self pollinated flowers which produce copious pollen and are clustered into a spike which is enclosed in a purple and yellow spotted sheath-like hood which remains close to the ground and appears in March.

Habitat; shrub and tree swamps.

WIS; OBL

Skunk Cabbage Interactions

Community Interaction; they are very shade tolerant and can grow in dense stands , often becoming the dominant herb in swamps; large leaves provide important cover and breeding habitat for wildlife; have deep root systems which help prevent erosion, maintaining the stability of the soil in swamps subject to the moving water accompanying flooding; a welcome sign of spring, metabolism of the inflorescence increases the plant temperature above that of the ambient air thereby allowing it to grow up through snow in late winter/early spring and to be the first plant to flower and thus be the earliest pollen source for bees.

Mammals; Porcupine are known to feed on the leaves and Muskrat on both leaves and flowers.

Plants; when in dense stands, it successfully eliminates competition from most other plants except Greenbrier, Tussock Sedge, Sensitive Fern, and Jewelweed with which it is commonly associated.

Birds; one might expect to see Wood Duck, Ring-neck Pheasant, and Ruffed Grouse feeding on the seeds; this is a favored nest cradle for the Common Yellowthroat.

Reptiles; N. Water Snakes, Ribbon Snakes, and Garter Snakes can be found foraging around the Skunk Cabbage leaves.

Amphibians; Spring Peepers have been found hiding in the spathe (flowers); Redback Salamanders and Dusky Salamanders often forage and deposit their terrestrial eggs in Skunk Cabbage swamps.

Insects; serves as a larval food plant for the Cattail Borer Moth and Ruby Tiger Moth; a rare stalk-eyed fly *Sphyracephala brevicornis* is found on the leaves and flowers where it may lay its eggs which give rise to root eating larvae; the Pomace Fly (Drosophilidae) is a very common breeder in the flower of Skunk Cabbage; some think that the heat of metabolism generated by the flower head is important in attracting pollinators such as carrion flies and bees; Ladybird Beetle *Hippodamia convergens* adults feed on lice at base of leaves; adult Smut Beetles *Phalacrus politus* are found on the leaves and flowers feeding on fungal spores; occasionally one can observe the leaves being eaten by the Waterlily Beetle *Donacia pistcatrix*.

(continued)

Skunk Cabbage Interactions

Spiders; see Appendix D.

Human/Economic Use; American Natives reportedly cooked the roots and used as a starchy food; Indians also used the fine roots as a local anesthesia for toothaches; root preparations have been useful in treating coughs, lung spasms associated with asthma, muscle spasms, and nervous disorders; American Natives boiled the roots and drank the preparation as a contraceptive; the Menominee used the smaller roots as styptik to stop external bleeding; the antispasmodic chemical found in the roots is 5-hydroxytryptamine which is a precursor to hallucinogenic poisons such as the psilocybins, the same chemicals which are also found in certain fungi; the antispasmodic qualities of the leaves and roots were employed by Mohegans and Delawares to treat epileptic seizures; leaves accumulate needle-like crystals of calcium oxalate which cause a burning sensation to the mouth and lips if chewed.

Need To Know about interactions invovling spiders.

Herbaceous ground cover characteristic of a tree swamp (Note Skunk Cabbage).

Soft Rush *Juncus effusus* L.

JUNCACEAE (Rush Family)

General Description -
Possibly introduced from Europe and naturalized, herb growing to 5 feet in height.

Stems; upright, grass-like and growing in dense clusters from rhizomes.

Leaves; not present, represented only by basal sheaths.

Flower; several branching clusters of green to brown self or wind pollinated small flowers emerging from one side of flower stalk near stem tip and appearing July-August.

Habitat; fresh marsh, wet meadow, pond edges.

WIS; FACW+

Community Interactions; although it prefers full sun and wet soils of the higher marsh and wet meadows, it can survive in brackish water of estuaries and salt marshes and is tolerant of a pH range from 4-6; although it can reproduce by seed, it is an aggressive invader by means of rhizomes, often taking over where it is too wet to grow most crop plants; in order to get rid of this plant, they must be grubbed out, the area filled with soil, and a new crop planted for several years; their tolerance to flooding and the resulting anoxia (low oxygen) may stem from their ability to avoid the synthesis of the toxic fermentation product alcohol, and instead accumulate nontoxic malate in their cells as do diving reptiles, mammals, and birds; they often grow in clumps forming good cover for wildlife in open wet meadows; the fibrous root systems and sturdy rhizomes serve to stabilize soils along pond and stream margins.

Mammals; Muskrats and Moose can be observed feeding on the roots and stems; Whitetail deer are known to browse on this.

Plants; when found in the upper marsh or even drier wet meadows, you may observe that they are the more abundant members of their wetland community associates.

Birds; this plant may be used as nesting material by the Common Loon; other birds such as the King Rail, Virginia Rail, Field Sparrow, Henslow's Sparrow, and the American Wigeon may actually be seen nesting in the clumps if you are careful and quiet; many of the aforementioned birds and possibly in addition the Pintail Duck, eat the seeds of this rush.

Insects; with the right timing, one may observe Leaf Beetle *Donacia* spp. feeding on this; the stems, which are a source of sap, regularly may be seen covered by green aphids *Aphis* spp.; this serves as a larval food plant for the Subflava Sedge Borer moth; the American Ruby Spot Damselfly *Hetaerina americana* commonly sits on this plant.

Spiders; Garden spider often utilize soft rush stems as frames for their webs; in unmaintained wet meadows, I have observed webs spun soley on the soft rush even though other vegetation of similar height was available.

Fish; this plant can form the spawning grounds for sunfish and bass.

Soft Rush Interactions

 Human/Economic Use; being primarily wind pollinated, it has been implicated as an aeroallergin, causing hypersensitive (allergic) reactions in humans; its stems are used in mat making while its pith is used in the orient as a candle wick; it is generally unpalatable to livestock who will avoid eating it since most any trip to a wet meadow where cattle are grazing will show the rush as one of the few plants left untouched- as you look out across the meadow, the dark green clumps of Soft Rush can easily be seen standing out against the grazed grasses.

Need To Know about interactions involving amphibians, reptiles, and spiders.

Oxygen, the Greenhouse Effect, and Wetlands

Photosynthesis is the process whereby green plants absorb carbon dioxide from the air and in the presence of water, light, and chlorophyll produce carbohydrates and the only source of oxygen in the world for us to breath. Nearly two-thirds of all the photosynthesis and therefore oxygen production on the planet occur in aquatic ecosystems which include the oceans, lakes, ponds, and the approximately 6 percent of the world's surface referred to as wetlands. The "greenhouse effect" is a predicted warming of the planet. This warming is thought to occur in large part through the increase in carbon dioxide in our atmosphere through human activity (such as by burning coal, oil, and other fossil fuels which release carbon dioxide). This increased carbon dioxide serves to trap infrared or heat light, and when carbon dioxide is not able to escape from our atmosphere, it leads to global warming. With increased pollution of water and the subsequent killing of its plant life coupled with wetland destruction through land development, there are fewer plants to sponge up the excess carbon dioxide for photosynthesis, leading to increased atmospheric levels of this gas and eventual warming of the planet.

Sphagnum Moss *Sphagnum palustre* and *S. rubrum*

SPHAGNACEAE (Sphagnum Moss Family)

General Description -
Highly branching and creeping, with only the upper portions alive where the reproductive structures are located; lower portions are dead and form "peatmoss".

Leaves; small leaf-like appendages which droop at tips and whorl around and cover the stem.

Reproductive; small, nearly microscopic spore cases borne at branch tips.

Habitat; bogs, marsh edges, wet meadows, shrub and tree swamps, and along pond and lake margins.

WIS; OBL

Sphagnum Moss Interactions

Community Interactions; it often blankets the floor of vegetated wetlands; have cells which can absorb enough water to increase plant weight over 100 times that of dried forms; during drier periods, its high water content helps it act as a natural mulch, maintaining soil water levels so that other plants can exist; an implication as to the negative impact of changed hydrology resulting in lower water supplies, these plants greatly reduce their photosynthetic rates to a level just required for basic survival and during this period, food storage stops, growth halts, and they appear dried out-such slow-downs have long term impacts because mat building is quite slow, proceeding at a rate estimated to be 1 inch in 100 years; much like the topical rain forest vegetation, this plant is responsible for locking up large amounts of carbon which prevents it from entering the atmosphere where this carbon might otherwise contribute to the 'greenhouse' effect and global warming-so their preservation is essential.

Mammals; the Northern Water Shrew burrows and nests in this plant along marshes and lakes; several mice including the Eastern Harvest Mouse and the Red-Backed Vole can be found scampering about or nesting in Sphagnum; you might also discover the Meadow and Woodland Jumping Mouse hiding here; it is possible for you to observe the Southern Bog Lemming tunneling in or traveling over the mat and even nesting here; one may even find a Star-nosed Mole, one of the few animals adapted to an acidic bog environment, burrowing about in the Sphagnum.

Plants; this moss serves as a stabilizer of the substrate for other plants of bogs, marshes, and swamps.

Birds: serves as occasional nesting site and material for Black Ducks; one can find the eggs of Common Snipe buried in the moss; patience can be rewarded by sighting nesting Tennessee Warblers, Palm Warblers (in Maine), Lincoln's Sparrows, and even Yellow-bellied Flycatchers; where this moss appears at the edge of a swamp, it plays an important role as a potential nesting site for other birds of woody habitats.

Reptiles; Bog Turtle known to breed and lay eggs in moss where one may also see the Spotted Turtle basking, one that is also known to hibernate in muds associated with such bogs; the wide ranging Redbelly Snake is known to hunt and sun among the mounds of Sphagnum; in bogs, one might chance upon the Smooth Green Snake and the Northern Ribbon Snake on the moss mat; the Eastern Massasuaga (Swamp Rattler) is very possibly the only poisonous snake to be found in bogs amongst the Sphagnum.

(continued)

273

Sphagnum Moss Interactions

Amphibians; many of these animals enjoy Sphagnum moss as a part of their environment including the Wood Frog which you might observe on the mat; the Rare Pine Barrens Tree Frog attaches eggs to this moss especially where Atlantic White Cedar is dominant in or around a bog; in more coastal areas, this is habitat material for the Carpenter Frog; occasionally one finds a Blue-spotted Salamander in open mat of Sphagnum in bogs and swamps; although often missed because it spends much time buried in the Sphagnum, the Four-toed Salamander can be found breeding and living here where it may lay its eggs at a depth of 3-4 inches; considered good habitat material for Northern Spring Peepers and Pickerel Frogs and even the Northern Spring Salamander which can be found in Sphagnum during non-breeding season.

Insects; the adult Bog Fritillary butterfly may be expected to be seen resting on the Sphagnum that is also home to the nymphs of the Common Skimmer *Celithemis eponina*; perhaps the smallest of all seed bugs, *Antilloccoris spp.*, eats the moss' spores; several Water Scavenger Beetles, *Hydrobius fuscipes* and *Paracymus* spp. may be found in or on the Sphagnum mat.

Spiders; may be possible to observe the reddish-orange spider *Dysdera crocata* hiding in darker patches of the moss as well as the Line Weaving Spider *Stemonyphantes blauveltae* which builds snares here; I have also chanced upon a thin-legged Wolf Spider *Pardosa makenziana* and the Crab Spider *Oxyptila conspurcata*.

Human/Economic Use; this very absorbent plant can be used as a diaper or as a wound dressing with its acidic quality creating an unfavorable habitat for bacteria and thus contributing to its highly regarded antibiotic/antiseptic properties; its water retentive nature makes it an excellent soil amendment enhancing garden moisture; has been used to as pillow and mattress stuffing.

Need To Know about interactions involving spiders.

Soft Rush in a wet meadow.

Spotted Cowbane *Cicuta maculata* L.

UMBELLIFERAE (Parsely Family)

General Description -
Native, biennial tall, shiny herb growing to 6 feet.

Stem; much branched and robust with a smooth and shiny surface streaked with purple.

Leaves; twice or three times divided, alternate, reddish-tinged, toothed margins and with base of leaf stalk sheathing the stem.

Flower; small white flowers in an umbel borne at top of stem and appearing June-July.

Habitat; fresh marsh, wet meadow, and in shallow water along pond and lake edges.

WIS; OBL

Spotted Cowbane Interactions

Community Interactions; the highly branched nature of the large stems adds to the overall cover value of a wetland; its very fleshy roots help stabilize the wet and muddy soils of the higher marsh.

Birds; Mallards will occasionally eat the seeds.

Insects; this is the larval food plant for the Black Swallowtail Butterfly so you will probably see the adults flitting around them preparing to lay eggs; the Epermeniid Moth larvae feed on this flower; this is also the larval food plant for an uncommon stem and root borer moth *Papaipema marginidens.*

Human/Economic Use; Caution! this is one of the most poisonous plants in the U.S.A., containing an unsaturated alcohol Cicutoxin concentrated in the roots which acts directly on the central nervous system - a mouthful of which will cause convulsions and death in an adult; American Natives took this when they "tired of life;" although not generally recommended now, the Cherokee would chew the raw poisonous roots for several days to induce permanent sterility.

Need To Know about interactiions involving mammals, plants, amphibians, reptiles, and spiders.

Stick-tight *Bidens connata* Muhl.

COMPOSITAE (Aster Family)

General Description -
Native annual herb growing to 4 feet in height.

Stem; single, upright, smooth, thin, and often growing in groups.

Leaves; opposite, lanceolate, stalked or not, with a smooth surface, and toothed margins.

Flowers; small tubular flowers in small, dense, erect, and solitary heads accompanied by short yellow rays at the base.

Habitat; wet meadows, ponds, and lake edges.

WIS; FACW

Stick-tight Interactions

Community Interactions; the shallow branching roots and seeds which can germinate in water, contribute to its dramatic increase in response to long term flooding; this increase is often at the expense of other plants that then effectively reduces species diversity of the community; the fruits are armed with barbed prickles that stick to animal coats, aiding in their dispersal; not very tolerant of fuel oil spills reaching wetlands.

Mammals; the Eastern Cottontail Rabbit eats the shoots as do Muskrats which also consume seeds; many mammals, including humans, carry the seeds about and thus play a role in their distribution.

Plants; note the comments under " Community Interactions."

Birds; seeds are eaten by the Swamp Sparrow, Purple Finch, Ring-necked Pheasant, Ruffed Grouse, Bobwhite, Wood Duck, Mallard, Black Duck, and Blue- and Green-winged Teal.

Reptiles; the Musk (Stinkpot) Turtle is known to eat the seeds.

Insects; this is the larval food plant for Tortricid Moths of the genus *Eucosma* spp.; although not tolerant of cold winters, you may see the Painted Lady (Cosmopolite) Butterfly visiting; the larvae of the Painted Lady have a wide host range among the composites (family to which this plant belongs).

Human/Economic Use; the leaves of this are used as pot herbs in cooking.

Need To Know about interactions involving amphibians and spiders.

Sundew *Drosera rotundifolia* L.

DROSERACEAE (Sundew Family)

General Description -
Native perennial, no stem.

Leaves; rosette of basal, stalked, plate-like leaves which are reddish-green and covered with glandular hairs exuding droplets of a sticky fluid.

Flower; flower stalk up to 10 inches long, terminating in a cluster of small white insect and self-pollinated flowers usually borne on one side of the stalk and appearing June-July.

Habitat; bogs, mud flats, and damp borders around ponds and lakes.

WIS; OBL

Sundew Interactions

Community Interactions; can reproduce vegetatively by rooting of a crawling runner; 25-30% of the nitrogen in their leaves comes from that extracted from the soft body parts of captured insects by means of a pepsin-like digestive juice; this insectivorous habit serves as an advantage in a bog or cedar swamp where acidic conditions result in low nutrient availability; increased rate of growth and development is commonly linked to higher insect capture rates; plant is sun loving, intolerant of desiccation, and has roots which serve to stabilize Sphagnum mats.

Plants; these plants do not grow well in high nutrient environments where they are out competed by other herbs that eventually shade them out.

Birds; have seen the Northern Waterthrush searching for insects around wetter edges of bogs standing near this plant probably taking insects attracted to its flower.

Amphibians; although not recorded, some adult frogs and salamanders may be attracted to struggling insects caught by the Sundew.

Insects; insects may be attracted to leaves by bright mucilage drops on tentacles; flies, mosquitos, Hover Flies, wasps, moths, and others are caught in traps; occasionally you can observe ants robbing captured insects from these traps- an important food source for the ant; one beetle, however, the Assassin Bug *Apiomerus* spp., is immune to the deadly juices of the plant and hunts throughout its surface for caught insects.

Human/Economic Use; valued in past more than in present for its juices which contain a protein digesting enzyme used for removing warts and corns; some have used the dried leaves as a treatment for coughs because of the presence of proteolytic enzymes that can break down phlegm; leaves also a source of natural purple dyes and source of high levels of vitamin C; were used as fly paper indoors by early pioneers.

Need To Know about interactions involving mammals, reptiles, and spiders.

Swamp Candles *Lysimachia terrestris* (L.) BSP.

PRIMULACEAE (Primrose Family)

General Description -
Native perennial herb growing to 4 feet in height.

Stem; erect, thin, smooth, unbranched to slightly branched,and often growing in clumps.

Leaves; opposite, narrow, elongated with smooth margins and being pointed at each end.

Flower; small, insect or wind pollinated, stalked, with 5 dark-lined yellow petals and 5 sepals and borne in a terminal cluster (spike).

Habitat; fresh marsh, also wet meadows and swamp edges.

WIS; OBL

Swamp Candles Interactions

Community Interactions; very invasive and quick spreading vegetatively through stolons, often crowding out other plants; generally of limited wildlife value although it does offer some protective cover; resistant to fuel oil spills.

Mammals; occasionally one may spot a deer grazing on this plant.

Amphibians; Frogs and salamanders may be attracted to insects that visit this plant.

Insects; chances are decent that you may see a Borer Moth *Papaipema lysimachiae* since this is food for the larva which bores the stems and roots of the plant.

Need To Know about interactions in general for this plant including other plants, birds, reptiles, spiders, as well as its economic value.

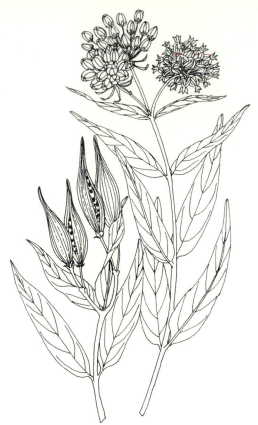

Swamp Milkweed *Asclepias incarnata* L.

ASCLEPIADACEAE (Milkweed Family)

General Description -
Native perennial herb growing to 4 feet in height.

Stem; robust, upper portions downy, with stems containing a milky sap.

Leaves; opposite to whorled, 4-5 inches long and lance-shaped with pointed tips.

Flower; small, insect pollinated, with 5 pink to purple downward-turned petals and 5 sepals occuring in a large terminal cluster; appearing July-August.

Habitat; edges of shrub swamp, also in wet meadows .

WIS; OBL

Swamp Milkweed Interactions

Community Interactions; have shallow, spreading rhizomes and deep taproots which are valuable in stabilizing soils and preventing erosion along wetland margins; although they provide some food for wildlife, their habit of growing singly or in very small clumps scattered about does not supply much protective cover.

Mammals; Muskrat may occasionally eat the entire plant including roots.

Plants; although its seeds are wind dispersed and reasonably plentiful, it is not a strong competitor with other plants and thus only establishes itself where such conditions do not exist.

Birds; several water birds including Black Ducks and Mallards will eat the seeds; the Red-winged Blackbird uses the fruit pod fibers to affix its nest to vegetation and the Ruby-throated Hummingbird lines its nest with these silky fibers.

Reptiles; E.Milk, Redbelly, Ribbon, and Garter snakes hunt frogs, insects, earthworms, and other prey near Swamp Milkweed.

Amphibians; no doubt treefrogs (Peepers, Gray Treefrogs and others) climb into this plant to hunt insects; Leopard and Pickerel frogs commonly forage around the base of this plant.

Insects; a variety of insects are involved in pollinating this flower and are assisted by special "pinch traps" on the pollen- bearing floral structures that clip them to the feet of the visiting insect assuring that the pollen will be carried away to another flower; this plant contains a poisonous cardiac glycoside 'calotropin' that gets into the invertebrates feeding on it and are immune to its effects-this chemical serves to protect these invertebrates against bird predation and grazing by mammals since both are extremely sensitive to calotropin; this is a larval food plant for the Monarch Butterfly and Queen Butterfly, and most likely a nectar supply for the adult Hickory Hairstreak Butterfly , Striped Hairstreak Butterfly, Hessel's Hairstreak, the Mulberry Wing, Pipevine Swallowtail, Acadian Hairstreak, and the Regal Fritillary; it may also be a nectar supply for the adult Milkweed Tussock Moth; the Large Milkweed Bug *Oncopeltus fasciatus* and Small Milkweed Bug *Lygaeus kalmii* find this plant its exclusive host, eating the seeds and laying eggs in the soft tissues; the Red Milkweed Beetle *Tetraopes basalis* lays eggs on the lower stem, the larvae bore inside completing its life cycle by emerging in spring; the Ladybird Beetle *Hippodamia convergens*

(continued)

Swamp Milkweed Interactions

Insects (continued); feeds on plant lice and other prey here; the Pennsylvania Soldier Beetle *Chauliognathus pennsylvanicus* may be seen feeding on the flowers; the Swamp Milkweed Leaf Beetle *Labidomera clivicolis* attacks the leaves and flowers of this and the non-wetland milkweed species and interestingly, some of the adults may shift over to the Mullein plant, where they overwinter in the dead leaves; I have seen pollen being taken by the Great Golden Digger Wasp *Sphex ichneumoneus*.

Spiders; see Appendix D.

Human/Economic Use; a tea from the thick roots was reportedly used by Colonists to prepare an emetic and diuretic and to treat intestinal worms, asthma, and venereal disease; the Fox Indians also used this for intestinal worms; the young buds were used as food and the stem fibers for cloth.

Human Impacts on Wetlands

Human activity in or near wetlands can lead to their alteration or ultimate destruction. For example, filling or draining of a wetland leading to its conversion to agriculture leads to decreased water levels which has an obvious negative impact on these wetlands. Furthermore, fertilizer runoff to wetlands from these agricultural fields can lead to increased nutrients and ultimately eutrophication. Newly constructed impervious surfaces, such as parking lots and rooftops, can raise water levels in wetlands by increasing storm water runoff and in turn can permanently alter the type of wetland which can exist under these conditions. Increased disturbances to wetlands can result from the use of off-road vehicles which can compact soil and thereby affect infiltration, damage vegetation and thus habitat, and create noise which disturbs wildlife.

Swamp Pink *Arethusa bulbosa L.*

ORCHIDACEAE (Orchid Family)

General Description -
Native herb growing to 10 inches in height.

Stem; no stem.

Leaves; single, linear, basal leaf appearing after flowering.

Flower; usually a single pink flower with three erect sepals and a hood hanging over a spotted lip, appearing May-June.

Habitat; bogs.

WIS; OBL

Swamp Pink Interactions

 Community Interactions; this plant is similar in its role to that of Rose Pogonia, *Pogonia ophioglossoides.*

Human/Economic Use; a small delicate and fragrant orchid of great aesthetic value; reported as a masticatory (chewing) remedy for toothache.

Need To Know about its interactions with all animal groups as very little has been observed for this beautiful herb.

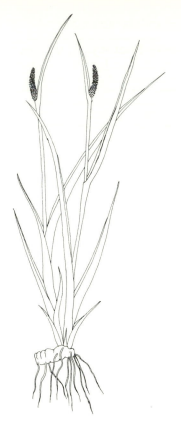

Sweet Flag *Acorus calamus* L.

ARACEAE (Arum Family)

General Description -
Native aromatic herb growing to 5 feet in height.

Stem; none above ground but with a rhizome imbedded in mud.

Leaves; fan out from the base where they are connected to rhizome; approximately 1 inch in diameter, robust, and with an off-center midvein.

Flower; in dense yellow-green spadix (spike-like) arising towards the middle of a 2-edged stem which resembles a leaf.

Habitat; fresh marshes, shallow water bordering ponds and slow moving streams.

WIS; OBL

Sweet Flag Interactions

Community Interaction; the fairly wide spreading root system serves to anchor wetland soils, thereby minimizing erosion effects; plant affords minimal cover and food for wildlife.

Mammals; Muskrat have been observed eating the rootstocks.

Birds; Wood Ducks might occasionally be seen eating the seeds.

Insects; Honey bees utilize the pollen and assist in pollination.

Human/Economic Use; plant has a global distribution which saw dried root preparation chewed to cure toothaches and aid in digestion; powdered roots were used as a dentrifice; roots contain oils used as insect repellent; calamus oil obtained from plant is a flavoring for gin and bitters; it is suspected that its active principle is acorin, a glycoside; a root decoction proved effective against *Staphylococcus auareus* and Shigella, a cause of dysentery in local waters; it is widely cultivated for its oils which are used in perfumes and flavoring for candies; root has been used by the Cherokee as an antidiarrheal, to treat colds, sore throats, and headaches.

Need To Know about its interactions with other plants, amphibians, reptiles, and spiders.

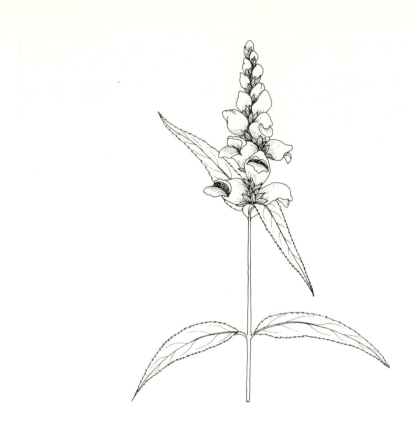

Turtlehead *Chelone glabra* L.

SCROPHULARIACEAE (Figwort Family)

General Description -
Native perennial herb growing to 3 1/2 feet in height.

Stem; erect, smooth.

Leaves; lanceolate, toothed, smooth, opposite, nearly stalkless, and with a prominent mid vein.

Flower; insect pollinated white spikes at branch ends, with petals fused into 2-lipped tubes, appearing August-September.

Habitat; wet meadows, and marshes, swamps, and stream edges.

WIS; OBL

Turtlehead Interactions

Community Interactions; growing quite tall, these plants can serve to stratify the herbal layer thereby creating additional habitat off the ground for wildlife.

Reptiles; it is possible that Box and Wood Turtles feed on the leaves, at times; during flooding the leaves may become available to Snapping and Painted Turtles.

Amphibians; the metamorphs of most aquatic and semiaquatic frogs and salamanders are likely to take refuge beneath dense stands of Turtleheads and associated plants; insects and other invertebrates attracted to the flowers and leaves are likely to serve as prey for the aforementioned.

Insects; as the larval food plant for the Baltimore Butterfly *Euphydryas phaeton,* you may observe or expect to observe it here; various bees take pollen from these flowers; this is also a larval food plant for a somewhat inconspicuous stem borer moth *Papaipema nepheleptina.*

Human/Economic Use; tea from the leaves or entire plant can be powdered and used as a laxative or to treat jaundice; plant extracts were known by the Cherokee to reduce skin inflammations.

Need To Know about interactions involving mammals, other plants, birds, and spiders.

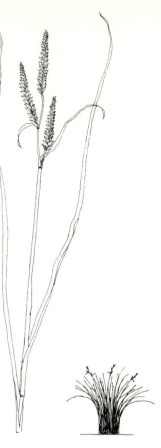

Tussock Sedge *Carex stricta* **Lam.**

CYPERACEAE (Sedge Family)

General Description -
Native perennial herb growing to 2-3 feet in height in very dense clusters.

Stem; commonly absent, but when present they grow above the leaf clump and are three-angled.

Leaves; grow in dense clumps, are thin, linear, stiff, with rough margins, keeled below, and tapering to a point.

Flower; small male spike at tip of stem above larger female spike, pollinated primarily by wind, occasionally gravity and even by insects such as flies which may be seen visiting the flowers which appear May-June; seeds are usually wind or water dispersed.

Habitat; fresh marsh, wet meadows, and shrub and tree swamps.

WIS; OBL

Tussock Sedge Interactions

Community Interactions; one of the most commonly used sedges for food by wildlife; not a strong competitor with cultivated crops in wet meadow areas; their creeping rhizomes play a role in anchoring soils and preventing erosion during flooding; their decomposition contributes substantially to soil building in wetlands; thick growth of this serves as good cover for wildlife.

Mammals; patient observations can be rewarded by a number of potential visitors including Muskrat, Whitetail Deer, Moose, Black Bear, Beaver, Gray Squirrel, Chipmunk, and the Common Mole which feed on leaves, roots, sprouts, and seeds.

Birds; several birds including the Red-winged Blackbird, Wilson's Warbler, the American Wigeon, Rails (King and Sora), Sedge Wren, and occasionally the Blue-winged Teal may breed, nest, and find protective cover in this sedge; the seeds are eaten by such birds as Wood Duck, Mallard and Black Ducks, the Sora Rail, Ring-necked Pheasant, Woodcock, Wild Turkey, Cardinal, and the Swamp Sparrow; in a wooded swamp, this along with sphagnum moss may serve as a nesting site for the Canada Warbler; the American Woodcock may nest on the ground between these tussocks when near an open field where they can go to feed.

Amphibians; dense stands of this are a favored habitat for the Pickerel Frogs and the Northern Leopard Frogs that can be found breeding among these sedges; Spring Peepers are often abundant in Tussock Sedge.

Reptiles; you may see Spotted Turtles sunning themselves on this or possibly a Bog Turtle consuming the seeds; although I've only observed it passing among the tussocks, it has been suggested that the Eastern Ribbon Snake may breed here as well; N. Water Snakes, Redbelly Snakes, and Garter Snakes sun and forage among these sedges.

Insects; ants are known to carry these seeds to their nests where they consume the elaiosomes or small hair-like appendages on the seed surface and then 'dump' the seeds in the colony refuse heap where they may germinate- in this way, ants are important in planting and dispersing the sedge; if one enjoys moths and butterflies, your observations may turn up quite a variety of species since this is the

(continued)

Tussock Sedge Interactions

Insects (continued); larval food plant for such butterflies as the Northern Eyed Brown, Appalachian Brown, Mulberry Wing, Black Dash, the Sedge or Dion Skipper, Two-Spotted Skipper, and occasionally for the somewhat rare Mitchell's Satyr which oviposits here; in addition, this is food for several moths including Putnam's Looper, Henry's Marsh, the Black-dotted Lithacodia, and for the sedge borer larval stage of a rather inconspicuous Owlet Moth, *Hyposoena inquinata*; also expected for dinner are the Leaf Beetles, Seed Bugs including *Oedancala* spp.; and careful inspection may turn up the Shore Bug *Salda provancheri* hiding within the clumps.

Human/Economic Use; has been primarily used as a straw in stables.

Need To Know about interactions involving other plants, fish, and spiders.

Wetland Value- Wildlife Habitat

Wildlife is disappearing from earth at an alarming rate because of human activity causing destruction of their habitat. It is clear that wetlands provide important wildlife habitat. It is also a fact that large amounts of vegetated wetlands are disappearing. Many of these vegetated wetland habitats are characterized by vertical stratification, which means that the plant life is divided into layers from top to bottom. The upper layer or woody overstory is made up of trees and is often referred to as the canopy. Beneath this layer there is often another woody layer of saplings and short trees called the subcanopy. The layer below the subcanopy consists of woody plants and is called the shrub zone. The lowest level is typically made up of tree and shrub seedlings and herbaceous plants and is known as the groundcover layer or zone. Wetlands differ one from another in the number of these vegetative layers. The important thing to realize is that each layer provides a different habitat. Some animals may dwell in the canopy, while others prefer shrubs or groundcover. This means that the more layers present in a wetland, the greater is its potential for supplying habitat to animal life. Each layer can provide a variety of functional values for wildlife, including areas for breeding, feeding, cover, overwintering, and migration. Another extremely important structural component of wetlands are their edges and ecotones. Edges are where a specific vegetative community abruptly ends and another one begins. An example might be where a wet meadow meets a shrub swamp and where there is a clear line of difference in the vegetation. What this means is that there is no mingling of wet meadow vegetation in the shrub swamp nor any shrub swamp plants in the wet meadow. An ecotone is where two wetland communities not only meet, but blend one into the other. In this case, the wet meadow vegetation would invade the fringes of the shrub swamp and in turn some of the shrubs would make their way out into the wet meadow. Both edges and ecotones are very busy places for wildlife which require more than one kind of vegetative community for their survival. An example is the American Woodcock which often selects tree swamps with dense groundcover for nesting within 40–50 yards of a wet meadow or cultivated field where it forages for insects and earthworms. Similar to verticle stratification, edges and ecotones provide wildlife with areas for breeding, feeding, cover, overwintering, and migration. The vast number of animals found in this field guide is an indication that vegetated wetlands provide very important wildlife habitat.

Umbrella Sedge *Cyperus strigosus* L.

CYPERACEAE (Sedge Family)

General Description -
Native grass-like herb growing to 2 feet in height.

Stem; several erect 3-sided stems arising from a common root.

Leaves; basal leaves are soft, flat, and narrow growing to 8 inches with two to seven shorter leaves clustered just beneath the inflorescence.

Flower; small wind pollinated flowers clustered in brown diverging spiklets at stem tip below which are a cluster of shorter leaves.

Habitat; fresh marshes, wet meadows, pond and lake borders.

WIS; FACW

Umbrella Sedge Interactions

 Community Interactions; this sedge if very similar to Wool-grass in its contributions to the community; it does have a creeping stolon which helps it establish dense stands which contribute to wildlife cover.

 Mammals; those which find Wool-grass useful can be expected to relate in similar fashion to the Umbrella Sedge.

 Birds; birds observed nesting in these include the Long-Billed Marsh Wren, Red-winged Blackbird, and the Swamp Sparrow; stands form ideal habitat for the American Bittern; Pintails have been observed eating the seeds while the Woodcock, Wild Turkey, Teals (Blue-/Green-winged), Coots, Mallards, and Red-winged Blackbirds eat seeds and stolons (creeping above ground stems).

 Insects; occasionally this is visited by the Little Wood Satyr Butterfly for which it may be a larval food plant; several moths including Henry's Marsh Moth, Putnam's Looper Moth, and the Stem-boring Glyphipterigid Moth use this for larval food.

 Spiders; very similar to Wool-grass in their relationship to spiders.

Human/Economic Use; the rhizomes are edible and the leaves and stems can be used as roof thatch, for baskets or for mat making.

Need To Know about interactions involving other plants, amphibians, and reptiles.

299

Water Smartweed *Polygonum punctatum* Elliott

POLYGONACEAE (Buckwheat Family)

General Description -
Native perennial herb vigorously spreading by rootstock or runners and growing to 18 inches in height.

Stem; erect to reclining and loosely spreading.

Leaves; deep green, narrowly lanceolate, growing to 6 inches, punctate (dots on surface) and with a bristled sheathing leaf base.

Flower; small white flowers in spike-like clusters at stem tips, appearing July-October.

Habitat; fresh marsh, wet meadows, quiet pond and stream edges.

WIS; OBL

Water Smartweed Interactions

Community Interactions; these are often one of the first invaders of wet farm land left fallow; the extensive growth often characteristic of this plant is from propagation by means of runners resulting in a tangled mass of stems several feet high, affording considerable wildlife cover; it also has a highly branching root system serving to stabilize soils; the seeds can pass through the digestive tracts of horses, cattle, and deer unharmed thereby assisting in plant dispersal; seeds are tolerant of flooding, and actually capable of germinating in water.

Mammals; leaves and stems occasionally eaten by Porcupine, Muskrat, and Raccoon; seeds are food for Chipmunks and White-footed Mice.

Birds; this is a very valuable food source, supplying seeds for a large number of birds including the Northern Pintail Duck, Red-wing Blackbird, Ring-necked Pheasant, Woodcock, Black Duck, Mallard, Wood Duck, Teals (Blue- and Green-Winged), Whistling Swan, Rails (Sora, Clapper, Virginia, and King), Swamp and Seaside Sparrows, and Cardinals; you may observe the Least Bittern utilizing this plant for food and as nesting material, and if vigililant, you may notice other birds nesting here as well.

Reptiles; Box Turtles can be expected to eat the seeds; Wood Turtles may feed on the foliage.

Amphibians; recently metamorphosed frogs and salamanders often feed in areas where this plant grows.

Insects; Red-head Flea Beetle *Systena frontalis* feeds on leaves and stems; the Waterlily Leaf Beetle *Galerucella nymphaeae* consumes the leaves; one may find a plant bug *Deraeocoris* spp., a predacious species, hunting for other insects on this plant; one can also expect to observe a Snout Beetle *Rhinoncus* spp. here; this is a larval food plant for the Bronze Copper Butterfly and several moths including the Black-Dotted Lithacodia, the Pink-Barred Lithacodia, the Chickweed Geometer and the Bent-Line Carpet.

Spiders; see Appendix D.

Human/Economic Use; the leaves contain high levels of calcium oxalate (7% or more) poisonous to humans and possibly fatal to live-stock; however, there are reports that the Chippewa used this as a cure for stomachaches.

Need To Know about interactions involving spiders.

Watercress *Rorippa nasturtium - aquaticum* (L.) Hayek

CRUCIFERAE (Mustard Family)

General Description -
Introduced from Europe, now a naturalized perennial prostrate herb.

Stem; creeping or floating, smooth, and fleshy with stem rooting freely.

Leaves; alternate, pinnate with 3-11 leaflets which are oblong to round, smooth, fleshy, and with wavy to entire margins.

Flower; small, with four white petals, stalked and borne in a terminal cluster emerging above the water.

Habitat; fresh marsh.

WIS; OBL

Watercress Interactions

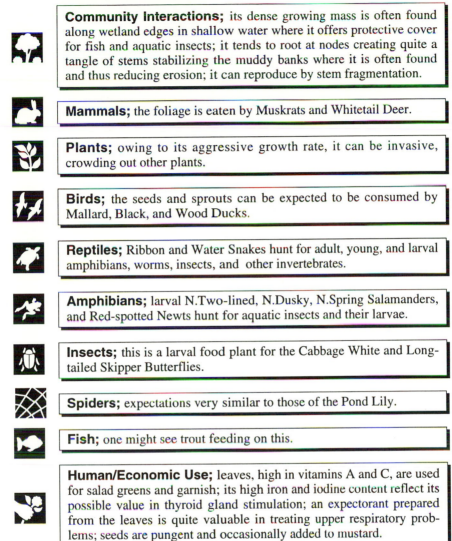

Community Interactions; its dense growing mass is often found along wetland edges in shallow water where it offers protective cover for fish and aquatic insects; it tends to root at nodes creating quite a tangle of stems stabilizing the muddy banks where it is often found and thus reducing erosion; it can reproduce by stem fragmentation.

Mammals; the foliage is eaten by Muskrats and Whitetail Deer.

Plants; owing to its aggressive growth rate, it can be invasive, crowding out other plants.

Birds; the seeds and sprouts can be expected to be consumed by Mallard, Black, and Wood Ducks.

Reptiles; Ribbon and Water Snakes hunt for adult, young, and larval amphibians, worms, insects, and other invertebrates.

Amphibians; larval N.Two-lined, N.Dusky, N.Spring Salamanders, and Red-spotted Newts hunt for aquatic insects and their larvae.

Insects; this is a larval food plant for the Cabbage White and Long-tailed Skipper Butterflies.

Spiders; expectations very similar to those of the Pond Lily.

Fish; one might see trout feeding on this.

Human/Economic Use; leaves, high in vitamins A and C, are used for salad greens and garnish; its high iron and iodine content reflect its possible value in thyroid gland stimulation; an expectorant prepared from the leaves is quite valuable in treating upper respiratory problems; seeds are pungent and occasionally added to mustard.

303

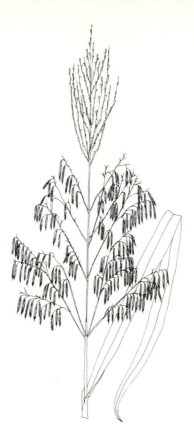

Wild Rice *Zizania aquatica* L.

GRAMINEAE (Grass Family)

General Description -
Native emergent grass-like herb growing to 8 feet in height.

Stem; erect, often growing in dense stands.

Leaves; underwater leaves are 3-4 feet long, thin with floating tips whereas aerial ones are 12-14 inches long, wide, flat, and with rough edges.

Flower; large flower head (1-2 feet long), with upper female flowers (grains) held erect and the lower male inflorescences drooping, both appearing August-September.

Habitat; generally standing in water at edges of marshes, ponds, and streams.

WIS; OBL

Wild Rice Interactions

Community Interaction; this plant is quite similar to Rice-cut-grass in its community roles; in addition, it is frequently planted in game management practice in order to provide food and shelter for wildlife.

Insects; a larval food plant for the Broad-winged Skipper butterfly.

Human/Economic Use; this plant is widely scattered by people who look to establish a food base for migratory waterfowl and other wildlife; in some areas it persist, while in others, it dies out quickly; this is an important food plant for Native Americans.

Need To Know about . . . see rice-cut grass.

Wool-grass *Scirpus cyperinus* (L.) Kunth

CYPERACEAE (sedge Family)

General Description -
Native perennial herb growing to 6 feet in height.

Stem; erect, robust, and triangular to round.

Leaves; from base of stem, the leaves grow up to 2 feet in length while those immediately below the flower are in clusters of 3-5 and may reach 5 inches and droop at the tips.

Flower; cluster of wind pollinated spiklets at ends of drooping stems.

Habitat; fresh marsh, wet meadow.

WIS; FACW+

Wool-grass Interactions

Community Interactions; propagating by rhizomes, dense scattered groupings of this rather tall sedge create edges where wildlife can retreat for cover, enjoy a seedy meal from its flowers, or simply perch; research has shown that this plant is resistant to fuel oil spills, persisting where other members of the community cannot.

Mammals; this is quite similar in its interactions with mammals to that of the Bulrush.

Birds; in addition to serving as a nesting site for the Red-winged Blackbird it provides nesting material for the Common Loon, and supplies seeds eaten by the American Coot; other interactions to be expected are those presented for the Bulrush.

Reptiles; no doubt Ribbon, Water, Garter, and other snakes hunt for food here.

Amphibians; semiaquatic frogs including Pickerel, Leopard, Cricket, Chorus, and Green Frogs often forage in and around Wool-grass stands.

Insects; two moths using this for larval food are the Ignorant Apamea and Lost Owlet; this is a larval food plant for another moth, the Owlet *Meropleon diversicolor*, whose larva is a semiaquatic borer; a Seed Bug *Oedancala dorsalis* has been observed in the flower heads presumably eating the seeds as its name suggests; larva of the Sedge or Dion Skipper butterfly feed on this plant; a very common damselfly, the American Ruby Spot *Hetaerina americana* can be seen resting on this.

Spiders; both the Six-spotted Orb Weaver *Araniella displicata* and the Shamrock Spider *Araneus trifolium* are found using this and other marsh plants for web support.

Human/Economic Use; as is the case for many rushes, this one has roots high in starch and reportedly were consumed by Native Americans much like a small potato or they were ground into flour or the pollen formed into edible cakes; the stems can be chewed to control bad breath.

Need To Know about interactions involving other plants.

307

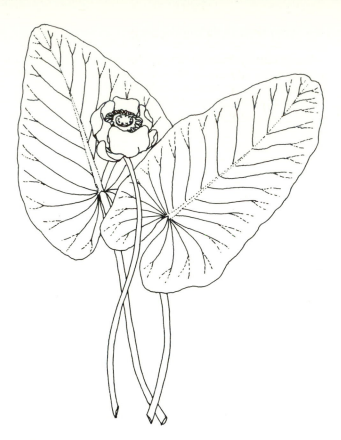

Yellow Pond Lily *Nuphar variegatum* Durand

NYMPHAEACEAE (Pond Lily Family)

General Description -
Native perennial herb with floating leaves and with flowers floating or held just above the water level.

Stem; thick underground rhizome which serve as a means of vegetative propagation of this plant.

Leaves; ovate, up to 1 foot long, floating with a split (sinus) at base near point of stalk attachment.

Flower; roundish insect pollinated flower with thick yellow petals often held just above the water surface by means of a long flower stalk (petiole) arising from the underwater rhizome.

Habitat; marshes, ponds, stream borders.

WIS; OBL

Yellow Pond Lily Interactions

Community Interactions; this is very similar to the Pond Lily *Nymphaea odorata* in its role in the community; this is often very abundant in the low or continuously flooded marsh; Spatter-dock crowds out more valuable wildlife serving plants because it better tolerates mud flats and reduced water levels; it also is quite resistant to water draw downs and fuel oil spills where in some cases they become more prominent following such accidents than before.

Mammals; the entire plant is consumed by Porcupine, Beaver, and Muskrat, whereas Whitetail Deer might be seen eating leaves and flowers.

Plants; in my observations, this is commonly found growing as a co-dominant with the Duckweed.

Birds; the seeds are frequently taken by the Wood Duck and Virginia Rail.

Reptiles; many turtles, including Eastern Painted, Western Painted, Eastern and Florida Softshells, occasionally Snapping, Musk, and Spotted turtles bask and forage around these leaves.

Amphibians; careful observation may yield the sighting of Mink Frog eggs attached to leaves and petioles; Green and Bull frogs often bask on the floating leaves.

Insects; this may serve as a larval food plant for several Pyralid Moths *Synclita obliteralis* and *Parapoynx obscuralis*, as they are occasionally observed on them; Whirligig Beetles *Gyrinus limbatus* can be seen swimming around the leaves and resting upon them; also attacked by the Waterlily Beetle *Donacia piscatrix* and the Waterlily Leaf Beetle *Galerucella nymphaeae.*

Spiders; very similar to the Pond Lily *Nymphaea odorata.*

Fish; plant affords shelter and shade as well as insects living on the lower surfaces which serve as a food source.

Human/Economic Use; rhizome is high in starch and can be eaten raw, cooked, or roasted with meat; American Natives ground the seeds and added into a soup to thicken the broth; the Algonquin used the rhizomes to create a poultice to apply to cuts and bruises.

Glossary

AMBIENT - of the air.

ANTHER - the pollen containing part of the stamen.

BARRIER BEACH- a protective stretch of sand existing between the open water and a resource area, such as a salt marsh.

BIOSYSTEMATIC - classification of living systems.

COMMUNITY - a group of more than one population in the same environment, such as cardinals and robins.

DECIDUOUS - seasonal shedding of leaves or other plant parts.

DETRITUS - dead organic matter; a food chain type that begins with bacteria decomposing detritus.

ECOTONE - a transitional zone between two different vegetative communities; thus, there is a blending of the communities at this point.

EDGE - area where two or more different vegetative communities meet.

EMERGENT - a plant rooted in the substrate below the water surface but has its stems and leaves growing above the water surface.

ESTUARINE- deep water, saline, tidal habitats including tidal (salt marsh) wetlands; also receive fresh water run off from inlands.

EUTROPHICATION- lake with high levels of nitrogen and phosphorous that leads to excessive plant growth.

FIDDLEHEAD - a young curled fern leaf (frond).

FRESH WATER- salinity 0.5% or less.

FROND - a fern leaf.

FRUIT - a mature ovary that serves to house seeds and is important as a food source to wildlife.

GREENHOUSE EFFECT - the accumulation of carbon dioxide in the atmosphere that traps heat and thereby contributes to global warming.

HABITAT - the home or environment of an organism.

HALINE- indicates level of salt (salinity).

HERBS - non-woody plants.

HYDROPHYTE - water-loving plant.

INTERTIDAL - an area along a coast that is alternately flooded and exposed to air through tidal action.

KEYSTONE - see the Introduction.

LARVA - the caterpillar stage of an insect.

LENTICEL - small openings in the bark that allow for gas exchange.

LIGULE - in grasses, an outgrowth from the upper and inner side of the leaf where it joins the sheath.

METAMORPHOSED - very young stage of an amphibian that resembles the adult in appearance.

NICHE - the "job" an organism does in the environment usually referring to its trophic (feeding) level; i.e., Is it a producer,consumer, herbivore, carnivore, or omnivore?

OMBROTROPHIC - obtaining water and nutrients through precipitation.

OVARY - swollen lower portion of the pistil containing ovules (seeds) and becomes the fruit.

OVULE - the portion of the pistil that becomes a seed.

PALUSTRINE- nontidal fresh water vegetated wetland including bogs, fresh marshes, wet meadows, shrub swamps, and tree swamps.

PATHOGENIC - disease inducing agent or causal factor.

PERSISTENT- an emergent plant, parts of which remain standing throughout the year to the next growing season.

PETALS - a flower part that is usually quite colorful and plays an important role in attracting pollinators.

PETIOLE - stalk of a leaf serving to attach it to a branch.

PHYTOPLANKTON- free-floating or motile single or multicellular microscopic fresh or salt water plants.

PISTIL - collective term for the female reproductive structure that is made up of the stigma, style, and ovary.

PITH - tissue at the center of a stem.

POIKILOTHERM - an organism whose body temperature follows that of the environment, commonly but incorrectly referred to as a "cold blooded" organism.

POLLINATION - the transfer of pollen from the anther to the stigma of the flower.

POPULATION - a group of organisms of the same species in the same environment, such as a group of robins.

PREDACIOUS - a living organism that captures and eats other living organisms.

RHIZOME - an underground stem.

SEED - the mature ovule made up of a seed coat, embryo, and a food supply.

SEPALS - the outermost flower structure that often serves as the bud covering (scales).

SESSILE - a plant part; e.g., a leaf, fruit, or flower that lacks a stalk for attachment and rests by its base directly on its supportive structure or branch.

SHRUB - a perennial woody plant having multiple stems and growing no more than 20 feet in height.

STAMENS - collective term for the male reproductive structure of a flower, that consists of the filament (stalk) and anther (pollen sac).

STIGMA - upper most portion of the pistil that receives the pollen.

STIPULE - small leaf-like appendages at the base of a true leaf.

STOLON - also known as a runner, it is a horizontal above ground stem.

STRATIFICATION - layers of vegetative growth, such as a shrub layer over the ground cover.

SUCKER - a shoot developed from a cut or uncut stem or root crown that is usually quite rapid in its growth.

THALLUS - a flat multicellular plant body usually photosynthetic and lacking true roots, leaves, and stems.

THERMOREGULATING - adjusting the body temperature, usually by absorbing the heat from the sun as is the case for most poikilotherms including insects, amphibians, and many reptiles.

TREE - perennial woody plant usually having a single stem and growing 20 feet or more in height.

TROPHIC LEVEL - feeding level (see niche).

WEED - term used to connote an undesirable intruder (plant) that competes with cultivated plants. However, many of these plants are natural members of the landscape and play vital roles in the ecological community.

Appendix A

COMPARISON OF WETLAND CLASSIFICATION SYSTEMS

There are many wetland classification systems in use throughout the United States. Because many different criteria are used, no comparison of wetland systems can be done precisely. The following table attempts to compare the systems used in this guide with that of the *"Classification of Wetlands and Deepwater Habitats of the United States"* by L.M. Cowardin, V. Carter, F.G. Golet, and E. T. LaRoe of the U. S. Fish and Wildlife Service (see reference section).

Comparison of Wetland Systems

REDINGTON SYSTEM ▼	USFWS System					
	SYSTEM	SUB SYSTEM	CLASS	SUB CLASS	WATER REGIME	CHEMIST RY
BOG	Palustrine	---	Moss/lichen	Moss	Saturated	Fresh (Acid)
FRESH MARSH	Palustrine	---	Emergent	Persistent	Semi to Permanently Flooded	Fresh
SALT MARSH	Estuarine	Intertidal	Emergent	Persistent	Regularly Flooded	Eusaline
WET MEADOW	Palustrine	---	Emergent	Non Persistent	Temporarily Flooded	Fresh
SHRUB SWAMP	Palustrine	---	Scrub/Shrub	Broad Leaved Deciduous	Nontidal to Permanently Flooded	Fresh
TREE SWAMP	Palustrine	---	Forested	Broad Leaved Deciduous	Nontidal to Permanently Flooded	Fresh

Appendix B

VALUES OF WETLANDS

Wetlands are usually considered to be bug infested areas which should be filled. Upon closer consideration, such assumptions are far from the truth. Wetlands have ecological and economic significance. It has been calculated that one acre of wetlands may be worth nearly $200,000 in benefits to a community. The following is a list of some of the values of wetlands:

1. Wetlands are sources of drinking water, either by discharging groundwater into lakes, streams, and reservoirs or by recharge (adding) of the water table.

2. Wetlands control pollution, acting as natural filters keeping drinking water clean. For example, some wetland plants can absorb toxic heavy metals, and the nitrogen and phosphorous which might otherwise cause algal blooms.

3. Wetlands protect property from flooding, erosion, and coastal storm damage.

4. Wetlands provide breeding, rearing, and feeding habitat for wildlife including nurseries for fish and shellfish. They also provide critical feeding and resting areas for migratory animals.

5. Wetlands are troves of unique and varied beauty, including both plant and animal life.

6. Coastal wetlands are among the world's highest producers of food energy.

7. Wetlands provide recreational value including photography, hiking, hunting, fishing, birding, and solitude to nourish the spirit.

Appendix C

List of plants and animals used in the Guide and LIFE LIST

Common Name	Scientific Name
AMPHIBIANS	
American Toad	*Bufo americanus*
Bullfrog	*Rana catesbeiana*
Carpenter Frog	*Rana virgatipes*
Eastern Spadefoot Toad	*Scaphiopus holbrooki*
Four-toed Salamander	*Hemidactylium scutatum*
Fowler's Toad	*Bufo woodhousei fowleri*
Green Frog	*Rana clamitans*
Gray Treefrog	*Hyla versicolor*
Jefferson/Blue-spotted complex	*Ambystoma jeffersonianum/laterale*
Marbled Salamander	*Ambystoma opacum*
Mink Frog	*Rana septentrionalis*
Mountain Dusky Salamander	*Desmognathus ochrophaeus*
Northern Cricket Frog	*Acris crepitans crepitans*
Northern Dusky Salamander	*Desmognathes fuscus fuscus*
Northern Leopard Frog	*Rana pipiens*
Northern Red Salamander	*Pseudotriton ruber ruber*
Northern Spring Salamander	*Gyrinophilus p. porphyriticus*
Northern Two-lined Salamander	*Eurycea bislineata bislineata*
Spring Peeper	*Pseudacris crucifer*
Pickeral Frog	*Rana palustris*
Pine Barrens Treefrog	*Hyla andersoni*
Red-spotted Newt	*Notophthalmus viridescens*
Redback Salamander	*Plethodon cinereus*
Spotted Salamander	*Ambystoma maculatum*
Upland Chorus Frog	*Pseudacris triseriata feriarum*
Wood Frog	*Rana sylvatica*
BIRDS	
Alder Flycatcher	*Empidonax alnorum*
American Goldfinch	*Carduelis tristis*
American Oystercatcher	*Haematopus palliatus*
American Woodcock	*Philohela minor*
American Robin	*Turdus migratorius*
American Coot	*Fulica americana*
American Bittern	*Botaurus lentiginosus*
American Wigeon	*Anas americana*
Baltimore Oriole	*Icterus galbula*

Common Name	Scientific Name
Barred Owl	*Strix varia*
BIRDS (continued)	
Black Skimmer	*Rynchops niger*
Black Duck, American	*Anas rubripes*
Black Tern	*Chlidonias nigra*
Black-billed Cuckoo	*Coccyzus erythropthalmus*
Black-crowned Night-Heron	*Nycticorax nycticorax*
Blackburnian Warbler	*Dendroica fusca*
Blacked-capped Chickadee	*Parus atricapillus*
Blue Jay	*Cyanocitta cristata*
Blue-winged Teal	*Anas discors*
Boat-tailed Grackle	*Quiscalus major*
Bobolink	*Dolichonyx oryzivorus*
Bobwhite, Northern	*Colinus virginianus*
Brown Thrasher	*Toxostoma rufum*
Bufflehead	*Bucephala albeola*
Canada Warbler	*Wilsonia canadensis*
Canada Goose	*Branta canadensis*
Canvasback	*Aythya valisineria*
Cardinal, Northern	*Cardinalis cardinalis*
Carolina Wren	*Thryothorus indovicianus*
Catbird, Gray	*Dumetella carolinensis*
Cattle Egret	*Bubulcus ibis*
Cedar Waxwing	*Bombycilla cedrorum*
Clapper Rail	*Rallus longirostris*
Common Moorehen	*Gallinula chloropus*
Common Goldeneye	*Bucephala clangula*
Common Grackle	*Quiscalus quiscula*
Common Loon	*Gavia immer*
Common Snipe	*Capella gallinago*
Common Tern	*Sterna hirundo*
Common Yellow-throat	*Geothylypis trichas*
Crow, Common	*Corvus brachyrhynchos*
Downy Woodpecker	*Picoides pubescens*
Eastern Bluebird	*Sialia sialis*
Eastern Kingbird	*Tyrannus tyrannus*
Evening Grosbeak	*Hesperiphona vespertina*
Field Sparrow	*Spizella pusilla*
Gadwall	*Anas strepera*
Glossy Ibis	*Plegadis falcinellus*
Golden-crowned Kinglet	*Regulus satrapa*
Great Black-backed Gull	*Larus argentatus*
Great Blue Heron	*Ardea herodias*
Great Egret	*Casmerodius albus*
Green-backed Heron	*Butorides striatus*
Green-winged Teal	*Anas crecca*
Hairy Woodpecker	*Picoides villosus*

Common Name	Scientific Name	Common Name	Scientific Name

BIRDS (continued)

Common Name	Scientific Name
Henslow's Sparrow	*Passerherbulus henslowii*
Hermit Thrush	*Catharus guttatus*
Herring Gull	*Larus argentatus*
Hoary Redpoll	*Carduelis hornemanni*
Hooded Warbler	*Wilsonia citrina*
King Rail	*Rallus elegans*
Laughing Gull	*Larus atricilla*
Least Bittern	*Ixobrychus exilis*
Lesser Scaup	*Aythya affinis*
Lincoln's Sparrow	*Melospiza lincolnii*
Mallard	*Anas platyrhynchos*
Marsh Wren	*Cistothorus palustris*
Mockingbird, Northern	*Mimus polyglottus*
Mourning Dove	*Zenaida macroura*
Mourning Warbler	*Oporornis philadelphia*
Mute Swan	*Cygnus olor*
Northern Harrier	*Circus cyaneus*
Northern Pintail	*Anas acuta*
Northern Saw-whet Owl	*Aegolius acadicus*
Northern Waterthrush	*Seiurus noveboracensis*
Palm Warbler	*Dendroica palmarum*
Parula Warbler	*Parula americana*
Phoebe, Eastern	*Sayornis phoebe*
Pied-billed Grebe	*Podilymbus podiceps*
Pine Siskin	*Carduelis pinus*
Prothonotary Warbler	*Protonotaria citrea*
Purple Finch	*Carpodacus purpureus*
Red Crossbill	*Loxia curvirostra*
Red-bellied Woodpecker	*Centurus carolinus*
Red-eyed Vireo	*Vireo olivaceus*
Red-headed Woodpecker	*Melanerpes erythrocephalus*
Red-shouldered Hawk	*Buteo lineatus*
Red-tailed Hawk	*Buteo jamaicensis*
Red-winged Blackbird	*Agelaius phoeniceus*
Ring-necked Pheasant	*Phasianus colchicus*
Rock Ptarmigan	*Lagopus mutus*
Rose-breasted Grosbeak	*Pheucticus ludovicianus*
Ruby-throated Hummingbird	*Archilochus colubris*
Ruffed Grouse	*Bonasa umbellus*
Sanderling	*Calidris alba*
Savannah Sparrow	*Passerculus sandwichensis*
Screech Owl, Eastern	*Otus asio*
Seaside Sparrow	*Ammospiza maritima*
Sedge Wren	*Cistothorus platensis*
Semipalmated Sandpiper	*Calidris pusilla*
Sharp-shinned Hawk	*Accipiter striatus*
Sharp-tailed Sparrow	*Ammospiza caudacuta*
Short-eared Owl	*Asio flammeus*
Shoveler, Northern	*Anas clypeata*
Snow Goose (Blue phase)	*Chen caerulescens*
Snowy Egret	*Egretta thula*
Song Sparrow	*Melospiza melodia*
Sora	*Porzana carolina*
Spruce Grouse	*Canachites canadensis*
Starling, European	*Sturnus vulgaris*
Swainson's Thrush	*Catharus ustulatus*
Swamp Sparrow	*Melospiza georgiana*
Tennessee Warbler	*Vermivora peregrina*

BIRDS (continued)

Common Name	Scientific Name
Tree Sparrow	*Spizella arborea*
Tree Swallow	*Iridoprocne bicolor*
Tricolored Heron	*Egretta tricolor*
Tufted Titmouse, Eastern	*Parus bicolor*
Veery	*Catharus fuscescens*
Virginia Rail	*Rallus limicola*
Whistling Swan	*Olor columbianus*
White-breasted Nuthatch	*Sitta carolinensis*
White-eyed Vireo	*Vireo griseus*
Wild Turkey	*Meleagris gallopavo*
Willet	*Catoptrophorus semipalmatus*
Willow Flycatcher	*Empidonax traillii*
Wilson's Warbler	*Wilsonia pusilla*
Wood Duck	*Aix sponsa*
Wood Thrush	*Hylocichla mustelina*
Yellow Warbler	*Dendroica petechia*
Yellow-bellied Sapsucker	*Sphyrapicus varius*
Yellow-bellied Flycatcher	*Empidonax flaviventris*
Yellow-billed Cuckoo	*Coccyzus americanus*
Yellow-shafted Flicker	*Colaptes auratus*
Yellow-throated Warbler	*Dendroica dominica*

BUTTERFLIES

Common Name	Scientific Name
Acadian Hairstreak	*Satyrium acadica*
American Copper	*Lycaena phlaeas*
Aphrodite	*Speyeria aphrodite*
Appalachian Brown	*Satyrodes appalachia*
Baltimore	*Euphydryas phaeton*
Black Dash	*Euphyes conspicua*
Black Swallowtail	*Papilio polyxenes*
Bog Elfin	*Incisalia lanoraieensis*
Bog Fritillary	*Proclossiana eunomia*
Bog Copper	*Epidemia epixanthe*
Broad-winged Skippper	*Poanes viator*
Bronze Copper	*Hyllolycaena hyllus*
Brown Elfin	*Incisalia augustinus*
Buckeye	*Junonia coenia*
Cabbage White	*Artogeia rapae*
Common Checkered Skipper	*Pyrgus communis*
Compton Tortoiseshell	*Nymphalis vau-album*
Dreamy Duskywing	*Erynnis icelus*
Eyed Brown	*Satyrodes eurydice*
Gray Hairstreak	*Strymon melinus*
Great Spangled Fritillary	*Speyeria cybele*
Great Gray Copper	*Gaeides xanthoides*
Harvester (Orange)	*Feniseca tarquinius*
Henry's	*ElfinIncisalia henrici*
Hessel's Hairstreak	*Mitoura hesseli*
Hickory Hairstreak	*Satyrium caryaevorus*
Hobomok Skipper	*Poanes hobomok*
Hop Merchant	*Polygonia comma*
Indian Skipper	*Hesperia sassacus*
Jutta Artic	*Oeneis jutta*
Juvenal's Duskywing	*Erynnis juvenalis*
Large Wood Nymph	*Cercyonis pegala*
Least Skipperling	*Ancyloxypha numitor*
Leonardus Skipper	*Hesperia leonardus*
Little Wood Satyr	*Megisto cymela*
Long Dash Skipper	*Polites mystic*

Common Name	Scientific Name	Common Name	Scientific Name

BUTTERFLIES (continued)

Common Name	Scientific Name
Long-tailed Skipper	*Urbanus proteus*
Meadow Fritillary	*Clossiana bellona*
Mitchell's Marsh Satyr	*Neonympha mitchellii*
Monarch	*Danaus plexippus*
Mourning Cloak	*Nymphalis antiopa*
Mulberry Wing	*Poanes massasoit*
Northern Broken Dash	*Wallengrenia egeremet*
Painted Lady	*Vanessa cardui*
Pepper-and-salt Skipper	*Amblyscirtes hegon*
Pink-edged Sulphur	*Colias interior*
Pipevive Swallowtail	*Battus philenor*
Prairie Ringlet	*Coenonympha inornata*
Queen	*Danaus gilippus*
Question Mark	*Polygonia interrogationis*
Red-spotted Purple	*Basilarchia astyanax*
Regal Fritillary	*Speyeria idalia*
Saffron Skipper	*Poanes aaroni*
Salt Marsh Skipper	*Panoquina panoquin*
Sedge Skipper	*Euphyes dion*
Silver-bordered Fritillary	*Clossiana selene*
Spicebush Swallowtail	*Pterourus troilus*
Spring Azure	*Celastrina ladon*
Striped Hairstreak	*Satyrium liparops*
Tawney-edged Skipper	*Polites themistocles*
Tiger Swallowtail	*Pterourus glaucus*
Titania's Fritillary	*Clossiana titania*
Two-spotted Skipper	*Euphyes bimacula*
Viceroy	*Basilarchia archippus*
White Admiral	*Basilarchia arthemis*
Yellowpatch Skipper	*Polites coras*
Zabulon Skipper	*Poanes zabulon*

FISH

Common Name	Scientific Name
Bluegill	*Lepomis macrochirus*
Cattfish (Brown Bullhead)	*Ictaluris nebulosus*
Common Carp	*Cyprinus carpio*
Golden Shiner	*Notemigonus crysoleucus*
Northern Pike	*Esox lucius*
Pumpkinseed	*Lepomis gibbosus*
Sheepshead Minnow	*Cyprinoden spp.*
Silversides	*Menidia beryllina*
Small-mouth Bass	*Micropterus dolomieui*
Sunfish	*Lepomis auritus*
Tilapia	*Tilapia mossambicus*
Trout, Brook	*Salvelinus fontinalis*

INSECTS (Other than Butterflies and Moths)

Common Name	Scientific Name
Alder Leaf Beetle	*Altica (bimarginata)* *
Ambush Bug	*Phymata americana*
American Ruby Spot Damselfly	*Hetaerina americana*
Ant	*Formica spp.*
Aphid	*Aphis spiraecola*
Assassin Bug	*Apiomerus spp.*
Backswimmer Bug	*Notonecta undulata*
Baldfaced Wasp	*Vespula maculata*
Bassett's Blackberry Gall Wasp	*Diastrophus bassettii*
Beech Borer	*Goes pulverulentus*
Big-headed Fly	*Tomosvaryella spp.*

INSECTS (continued)

Common Name	Scientific Name
Billbug	*Shenophorus (calendra)*
Birch Gall Mites	*(Eriophyes betulae)*
Black-wing Damselfly	*Calopteryx maculata*
Blackhorned Tree Cricket	*Oecanthus nigricornis*
Bluet Damselfly	*Enallagma civile*
Boneset Gall Fly	*Neolasioptera perfoliata*
Buffalo Tree Hopper	*Stictocephala bisonia*
Bumblebee	*Bombus fraternus*
Checkered Beetle	*Cymatodera spp.*
Click Beetle	*Ampedus rubricus*
Click Beetle	*Ampedus (pedalis)*
Click Beetle	*Ampedus (nigricollis)*
Click Beetle	*Ampedus (collaris)*
Cocklebur Weevil	*Rhodobaenus tredecim punctatus*
Common Walking Stick	*Diapheromera femorata*
Common Skimmer	*Celithemis eponina*
Cottonwood Leaf Beetle	*Chrysomela (scripta)*
Cottony Cushion	*Scalelcerya purchasi*
Crane Fly	*Tipula spp.*
Cynipid Gall Wasp	*Amphibolips confluenta*
Deer Fly	*Chrysops callidus*
Digger Bee	*Ptilothrix bombiformis*
Dogwood Twig Borer	*Obera tripunctata*
Dubious Checkered Flower	*Thanasimus dubius*
Eastern Larch Beetle	*Dendroctonus simplex*
Eastern Dobsonfly	*Corydalus cornutus*
Elderberry Longhorn Beetle	*Desmocerus palliatus*
Elm Bark Beetle (Native)	*Hylurgopinus rufipes*
Elm Bark Beetle (European)	*Scolytus multistriatus*
False Antlike Flower Beetle	*Macratia spp.*
False Darkling Beetle	*Anaspis rufa*
Flathead Borer	*Chrysobothris spp.*
Flatheaded Borer	*Chrysobothris (dentipes)*
Flea Beetle(Toothed)	*Chaetocnema denticulata*
Flea Weevil	*Rhynchaenus spp.*
Fly	*Dasyneura spp.*
Fork-tailed Bush Katydid	*Scudderia furcata*
Fruit Fly	*Eurosta spp.*
Gall Midge	*Lasioptera spp.*
Gall Mite	*Eriophyes amelanchieri*
Gall-wasp	*Callirhytis (palustris)*
Giant Water Bug	*Lethocerus americanus*
Gladiolus Thrip	*Thrips simplex*
Golden Saltmarsh Mosquito	*Aedes taeniorhynchus*
Golden-haired Flower	*Leptura (chrysocoma)*
Goldenrod or Pennsylvania Soldier Beetle	*Chauliognathes pennsylvanicus*
Grape Flea Beetle	*Altica chalybea*
Great Golden Digger Wasp	*Sphex ichneumoneus*
Green Ground Beetle	*Chlaenius sericeous*
Greenhead Fly	*Tabanus americanus*

* ( ) Tentative identification at species level.

Common Name	Scientific Name

INSECTS (continued)

Common Name	Scientific Name
Hemlock Borer Beetle	*Melanophila fulvoguttata*
Honey Bee	*Apis mellifera*
Horse Fly	*Tabanus atratus*
Hover Fly	*Volucella bomylans*
Icchneuman Wasp	*Rhyssa lineolata*
Imported Willow Leaf	
Beetle	*Plagiodera versicolor*
Japanese Beetle	*Popillia japonica*
Lace Bug	*Galeatus spp.*
Lace Bug	*Corythucha spp.*
Ladybird Beetle	*Hippodamia convergens*
Larch Sawfly	*Pristiphora erichsonii*
Large Milkweed Bug	*Oncopeltus fasciatus*
Leaf Beetle(Goldenrod)	*Trirhabda spp.*
Leaf-eating Beetle	*Trirhabda spp.*
Lesser Water Weevil	*Lissorhoptrus oryzophilus*
Longhorned Beetle	*Phymatodes dimidiatus*
Longhorned Beetle	*Obera (ruficollis)*
Longhorned Beetle	*Saperda (obliqua)*
Lurid Flathead Borer	*Dicera lurida*
Marsh Beetle	*Cyphon collaris*
Marsh Fly	*Tetanocera spp.*
Met.Wood-boring Beetle	*Anthaxia (quercata)*
Met.Wood-boring Beetle	*Dicera spp.*
Met.Wood-boring Beetle	*Dicera (divaricata)*
Mossy-rose Gall Wasp	*Diplolepis rosae*
Net-winged Beetle	*Calopteron reticulatum*
Oak Lace Bug	*Corythucha arcuata*
Oystershell Scale Insect	Diaspididae *(family)*
Pale Soft-winged Flower	*Attalus scinetus*
Periodical Cicada	*Magicicada spp.*
Petaled Willow Gall Gnat	*Rhabdophaga (brasscoides)*
Pine Webworm	*Acantholyda*
	erythrocephala
Pitcher-plant Mosquito	*Wyeomyia smithii*
Plant Bug	*Deraeocoris spp.*
Plant Bug	*Ilnacora (malina)*
Plant Bug	*Monalocoris americanus*
Plant Bug	*Adelphocoris spp.*
Plant Hopper	*Prokelisia (marginata)*
Poison Ivy Gall Mite	*Eriophyes rhois*
Pollen Feeding Beetle	*Asclera (ruficollis)*
Pomace Fly	*Drosophilidae*
Potato Leafhopper	*Empoasca fabae*
Red Milkweed Longhorn	*Tetraopes basalis*
Beetle	
Red-headed Flea Beetle	*Systena frontalis*
Rhubarb Curculio Weevil	*Lixis concavus*
Rove Beetle	*Anthobium hornii*
Saltmarsh Grasshopper	*Orchelimum spp.*
Sap-feeding Beetle	*Brachypterus (urticae)*
Sawfly	*Macrophya trisyllaba*
Seed Bug	*Antillocoris spp.*
Seed Bug	*Oedancala dorsalis*
Shore Bug	*Salda provancheri*
Small Water Strider	*Paravelia (stagnalis)*
Small Milkweed Bug	*Lygaeus kalmii*
Smut Beetle	*Phalacrus politus*
Snout Beetle	*Listronotus (caudatus)*
Snout Beetle	*Rhinoncus spp.*
Snout Beetle	*Mononychus vulpeculus*

INSECTS (continued)

Common Name	Scientific Name
Snout Beetle	*Tanysphyrus lemnae*
Snowy Tree Cricket	*Oecanthus fultoni*
Soldier Beetle	*Cantharis spp.*
Spined Stink Bug	*Podisus maculatus*
Spirea Pod Gall Midge	*Rhabdophaga (salicifolia)*
Spirea Cabbage Gall	*Contarina (spiraeina)*
Spittle Bug	*Philaenus spumarius*
Spruce Cone Axis Midge	*Dasineura (rachiphage)*
Spruce Cone Maggot	*Lasiomma (anthraacinum)*
Spruce Coneworm	*Dioryctria reniculelloides*
Spruce Gall Louse	*Adelges abietis*
Squash Bug	*Anasa tristis*
Squash Bug	*Anasa spp.*
Stag Beetle (Pinch Bug)	*Pseudolucanus capreolus*
Stalk-eyed Fly (rare)	*Sphyracephala brevicornis*
Swamp Milkweed Leaf	
Beetle	*Labidomera clivicolis*
Treehopper	*Stitocephala diceros*
Tumbling Flower Beetle	Mordella marginata
Tumbling Flower Beetle	*Mordella atrata*
Two-winged	
Gall-forming Midge	*Cecidomyia spp.*
Two-winged	
Gall-forming Midge	*Cecidomyia pudibunda*
Vampire Leafhopper	*Draeculacephala spp.*
Velvet Water Bug	*Merragata hebroides*
Velvety Shore Bug	*Ochterus americanus*
Water Strider	*Gerris remigis*
Water Scavenger Beetle	*Paracymus spp.*
Water Scavenger Beetle	*Hydrobius fuscipes*
Waterlily Leaf Beetle	*Galerucella nymphaeae*
Waterlily Beetle	*Donacia piscatrix*
Whirligig Beetle	*Gyrinus limbatus*
Willow Cone Gall Fly	*Rhabdophaga strobiloides*
Willow Longhorn Beetle	*Xylotrechus insignis*
Willow-beaked	
Gall Midge	*Mayetiola rigidae*
Woolly Larch Aphid	*Adelges strobilobius*
Wooly Alder Aphid	*Prociphilus tessellatus*
Wooly Aphid	*Prociphilus spp.*
Yellow Plant Bug	*Horcias dislocatus*

MAMMALS

Beaver	*Castor canadensis*
Black Bear	*Ursus americanus*
Common Mole	*Scalopus aquaticus*
Deer Mouse	*Peromyscus maniculatus*
Eastern Chipmunk	*Tamias striatus*
Eastern Cottontail	*Sylvilagus floridanus*
Eastern Harvest Mouse	*Reithrodontomys humulis*
Eastern Gray Squirrel	*Sciurus carolinensis*
Gray Fox	*Urocyon cinereoargenteus*
Keen's Bat (Myotis)	*Myotis keeni*
Marsh Rice Rat	*Oryzomys palustris*
Marten	*Martes americana*
Masked Shrew	*Sorex cinereus*
Meadow Vole (Field Mouse)	*Microtus pennsylvanicus*
Meadow Jumping Mouse	*Zapus hudsonius*
Mink	*Mustela vison*
Moose	*Alces alces*

Common Name	Scientific Name	Common Name	Scientific Name

MAMMALS (continued)

Muskrat	*Ondatra zibethicus*		
New England Cottontail	*Sylvilagus transitionalis*		
Northern Red-backed Vole	*Clethrionomys rutilus*		
Northern Water Shrew	*Sorex palustris*		
Opossum	*Didelphis virginiana*		
Otter	*Lutra canadensis*		
Porcupine	*Erethizon dorsatum*		
Raccoon	*Procyon lotor*		
Red Fox	*Vulpes vulpes*		
Red Squirrel	*Tamiasciurus hudsonicus*		
Short-tailed Shrew	*Blarina brevicauda*		
Silver-haired Bat	*Lasionycteris noctivagans*		
Snowshoe Hare	*Lepus americanus*		
Southern Red-backed Vole	*Clethrionomys gapperi*		
Southern Bog Lemming	*Synaptomys cooperi*		
Star-nosed Mole	*Condylura cristata*		
Striped Skunk	*Mephitis mephitis*		
White-footed Mouse	*Peromyscus leucopus*		
Whitetailed Deer	*Odocoileus virginianus*		
Woodchuck(Groundhog)	*Marmota monax*		
Woodland Jumping Mouse	*Napaeozapus insignis*		

MOTHS

American Dagger	*Acronicta americana*		
Andromeda Underwing	*Catocala andromedea*		
Apple Sphinx	*Sphinx gordius*		
Ash Tip Borer	*Papaipema furcata*		
Ash Sphinx	*Manduca jasminearum*		
Azalea Sphinx	*Darapsa pholus*		
Beautiful Wood-nymph	*Eudryas grata*		
Beautiful Eutelia	*Eutelia pulcherrima*		
Bella	*Utetheisa bella*		
Bent-line Carpet	*Orthonama centrostrigaria*		
Bicolored	*Eilema bicolor*		
Big Poplar Sphinx	*Pachysphinx modesta*		
Black-dotted Lithacodia	*Lithacodia synochitis*		
Blinded Sphinx	*Paonis excaecatus*		
Borer	*Papaipema lysimachiae*		
Borer (stem and root)	*Papaipema sulphurata*		
Borer	*Eucosma spp.*		
Brown-spotted Zale	*Zale helata*		
Burdock Borer	*Papaipema cataphracta*		
Casebearer	*Coleophora atromarginata*		
Cattail Borer	*Bellura obliqua*		
Cecropia	*Hyalophora cecropia*		
Chain-dotted Geometer	*Cingilia catenaria*		
Chickweed Geometer	*Haematopis grataria*		
Clymene	*Haploa clymene*		
Common Eupithecia	*Eupithecia miserulata*		
Common Hyppa	*Hyppa xylinoides*		
Common Tan Wave	*Pleuroprucha insulsaria*		
Connubial Underwing	*Catocala connubialis*		
Cranberry Spanworm	*Ematurga amitaria*		
Curve-lined Angle	*Semiothisa continuata*		
Dark-spotted Palthis	*Palthis angulalis*		
Darling Underwing	*Catocala cara*		
Definite Tussock	*Orgyia definita*		
Delightful Bird-dropping	*Acontia delecta*		
Dock Borer	*Papaipema nitela*		
Dogwood Probole	*Probole nyssaria*		

MOTHS (continued)

Dogwood Borer	*Synanthedon scitula*
Dot-lined White	*Artace cribraria*
Dotted Graylet	*Hyperstrotia pervertens*
Double-lined Doryodes	*Doryodes bistrialis*
Double-toothed Prominent	*Nerice bidentata*
Doubleday's Baileya	*Baileya doubledayi*
Drab Brown Wave	*Lobocleta ossularia*
Eastern Panthea	*Panthea furcilla*
Elder Shoot Borer	*Achatodes zeae*
Elm Sphinx	*Ceratomia amyntor*
Elm Spanworm	*Ennomos subsignaria*
Epermeniid	*Epermenia cicutaella*
Eupatorium Borer	*Carmenta bassiformis*
Eyed Paectes	*Paectes oculatrix*
False Crocus Geometer	*Xanthotype urticaria*
Filbertworm Moth	*Melissopus latiferreanus*
Fine-lined Sallow	*Catabena lineolata*
Flannel	*Lagoa crispata*
Forest Tent Caterpillar	*Malacosoma disstria*
Frank's Sphinx	*Sphinx franckii*
Golden Looper Moth	*Argyrogramma verruca*
Goldenrod Gall	*Gnorimoschema gallaesolidaginis*
Graceful Underwing	*Catocala gracilis*
Gray Spruce Looper	*Caripeta divisata*
Great Ash Sphinx	*Sphinx chersis*
Grote's Sallow	*Copivaleria grotei*
Gypsy	*Lymantria dispar*
Hemlock Angle	*Semiothisa fissinotata*
Henry's Marsh	*Simyra henrici*
Hog Sphinx	*Darapsa myron*
Hollow-spotted Angle	*Semiothisa gnophosaria*
Hydrangia Sphinx	*Darapsa versicolor*
Ignorant Apamea	*Apamea indocilis*
Imperial	*Eacles imperialis*
Io	*Automeris io*
Iris Borer	*Macronoctua onusta*
Jacose Sallow	*Feralia jocosa*
Lappet	*Phyllodesma americana*
Larch Casebearer	*Coleophora laricella*
Large Purplish Gray	*Anacamptodes vellivolata*
Large Looper	*Autographa ampla*
Large Tolype	*Tolype velleda*
LeafminerMoth	*Coptodisca kalmiella*
Light Marathyssa	*Marathyssa basalis*
Lobellia Dagger Moth	*Acronicta lobeliae*
Looper	*Syngrapha microgamma*
Lost Owlet	*Ledaea perditalis*
Luna	*Actias luna*
Major Datana	*Datana Major*
Many-lined Wainscot	*Leucania multilinea*
Maple Looper	*Parallelia bistriaris*
Maple Spanworm	*Ennomos magnaria*
Meal Moth	*Pyralis farinalis*
Milkweed Tussock	*Euchaetes egle*
Morning-glory Prominent	*Schizura ipomoeae*
Mottled Gray Carpet	*Cladara limitaria*
Mustard Sallow	*Pyreferra hesperidago*
Nameless Pinion	*Lithophane innominata*
New England Buck	*Hemileuca lucina*
Noctuid	*Bagisara rectifascia*

Common Name	Scientific Name
MOTHS (continued)	
Northern Variable	DartAnomogyna badicollis
Oblong Sedge Borer	Archanara oblonga
Obtuse Euchlaena	Euchlaena obtusaria
Old Maid	Catocala coelebs
Once-married Underwing	Catocala unijuga
One-spotted Variant	Hypagyrtis unipunctata
Osmunda Borer	Papaipema speciosissima
Owlet	Hypocoena inquinata
Owlet (Borer)	Meropleon diversicolor
Owlet	Hemipachnobia subporphyrea monochromatea
Owlet	Spartiniphaga inops
Pale-marked Angle	Semiothisa signaria
Pearly Wood-nymph	Eudryas unio
Pickerelweed Borer	Bellura densa
Pine Sphinx	Lapara bombycoides
Pink-barred Lithacodia	Lithacodia carneola
Pink-shaded Fern Moth	Callopistria mollissima
Pitcher Plant Borer	Papaipema appassionata
Polyphemus	Antheraea polyphemus
Porcelain Gray	Protoboarmia porcelaria
Praeclara Underwing	Catocala praeclara
Promethea	Callosamia promethea
Purple Arches	Polia purpurissata
Putnam's Looper	Plusia putnami
Pyralid	Condylolomia participialis
Pyralid	Munroessa icciusalis
Pyralid	Parapoynx obscuralis
Pyralid	Synclita obliteralis
Pyralid	Munroessa gyralis
Red Groundling	Perigea xanthioides
Red-fronted Emerald	Nemoria rubrifrontaria
Renounced Hydriomena	Hydriomena renunciata
Retarded Dagger	Acronicta retardata
Rose Hooktip	Oreta rosea
Rubbed Dart	Euxoa detersa
Ruby Tiger	Phragmatobia fuliginosa
Rusty Tussock	Orgyia antiqua
Scalloped Sack-bearer	Lacosoma chiridota
Sensitive Fern Borer	Papaipema inquaesita
Sharp-lined Yellow	Sicya macularia
Shield Bearer	Antispila nysaefoliella
Shy Cosmet	Limnaecia phragmitella
Silver-spotted Fern Moth	Callopistria cordata
Silver-spotted Ghost	Sthenopis argenteomaculatus
Sleeping Baileya	Baileya dormitans
Slug Caterpillar	Apoda y-inversum
Small-eyed Sphinx	Paonias myops
Sordid Bromolocha	Bomolocha sordidula
Sordid Underwing	Catocala sordida
Spear-marked Black	Rheumaptera hastata
Spicebush Silkmoth	Callosamia promethea
Spiny Oakworm	Anisota stigma
Spotted Apatelodes	Apatelodes torrefacta
Spotted Grass Moth	Rivula propinqualis
Spotted Fireworm	Choristoneura parallela
Spruce Budworm	Choristoneura fumiferana
Stem Borer	Papaipema nepheleptina
Stem-borer Moth	Papaipema marginidens
Stem-boring Glyphipterigid	Diploschizia impigritella
Subflava Sedge Borer	Archanara subflava

Common Name	Scientific Name
MOTHS (continued)	
Tephra Tussock	Dasychira tephra
The Half-Yellow	Tarachidia semiflava
Three-lined Flower	Schinia trifascia
Toothed Brown Carpet	Xanthorhoe lacustrata
Tortricid Moth	Eucosma spp.
Tortricid Moth	Olethreutes spp.
Twin-spotted Sphinx	Smerinthus jamaicensis
Unadorned Carpet	Hydrelia inornata
Variegated Cutworm	Peridroma saucia
Verbena	Crambodes talidiformis
Waved Sphinx	Ceratomia undulosa
White Slant-line	Tetracis cachexiata
White Triangle Tortrix	Clepsis persicana
White-banded Toothed	Epirrhoe alternata
White-marked Tussock	Orgyia leucostigma
White-striped Black	Trichodezia albovittata
White-tailed Diver (Borer)	Bellura gortynoides
Woolly Bear Tiger	Pyrrharctia isabella
Yellow Bear Tiger	Spilosoma virginica
Yellow-haired Dagger	Acronicta impleta

REPTILES

Common Name	Scientific Name
Atlantic Green Turtle	Chelonia mydas mydas
Atlantic Leatherback Turtle	Dermochelys coriacea coriacea
Atlantic Loggerhead Turtle	Caretta caretta caretta
Black Racer	Coluber constrictor
Blandings Turtle	Emydoidea blandingi
Bog Turtle	Clemmys muhlenbergi
Chicken Turtle	Deirochelys reticularia
Common Garter Snake	Thamnophis sirtalis
Diamondback Terrapin	Malaclemys terrapin terrapin
Eastern Box Turtle	Terrapene carolina
Eastern Hognose Snake	Heterodon platyrhinos
Eastern Milk Snake	Lampropeltis triangulum triangulum
Eastern Softshell Turtle	Trionyx spiniferus spiniferus
Painted Turtle	Chrysemys picta
Eastern Ribbon Snake	Thamnophis s. sauritus
Five-lined Skink	Eumeces fasciatus
Florida Softshell Turtle	Trionyx ferox
Massasauga	Sistrurus c. catenatus
Midland Painted Turtle	Chrysemys picta marginata
Northern Copperhead	Agkistrodon contortix
Northern Brown Snake	Storeria dekayi dekayi
Northern Ribbon Snake	Thamnophis sauritus septentrionalis
Northern Ringneck Snake	Diadophis punctatus edwardsi
Northern Water Snake	Nerodia sipedon
Plymouth Redbelly Turtle	Pseudemys rubriventris bangsi
Red-bellied Water Snake	Natrix erythrogaster erythrogaster
Red-eared Turtle	Chrysemys scripta elegans
Redbelly Snake	Storeria occipitomaculata

Common Name	Scientific Name	Common Name	Scientific Name

REPTILES (continued)

Common Name	Scientific Name
Smooth Green Snake	*Opheodrys vernalis*
Snapping Turtle, Common	*Chelydra serpentina*
Spotted Turtle	*Clemmys guttata*
Stinkpot Turtle	*Sternotherus odoratus*
Timber Rattlesnake	*Crotalus horridus*
Western Painted Turtle	Chrysemys *picta belli*
Wood Turtle	*Clemmys insculpta*

SPIDERS

Common Name	Scientific Name
Branch-tip	*Dictyna sublata*
Brownish Gray Fishing	*Dolomedes tenebrosus*
Comb-footed Spider	*Theridion murarium*
Comb-footed Spider	*Theridula emertoni*
Crab Spider/Goldenrod	*Misumena vatia*
Crab Spider	*Oxyptila conspurcata*
Crab Spider	*Misumena formosipes*
Crab Spider	*Philodromus washita*
Fishing Spider	*Dolomedes sexpunctatus*
Fishing Spider	*Dolomedes scriptus*
Fishing Spider	*Dolomedes striatus*
Goldenrod/Crab	*Misumena vatia*
Grass Spider	*Hahnia cinerea*
Grass Spider	*Neoantistea agilis*
Line Weaving Spider	*Stemonyphantes blauveltae*
Line-weaving Spider	*Linyphia clathrata*
Long-jawed Orb Weaver	*Tetragnatha laboriosa*
Long-jawed Orb Weaver	*Tetragnatha straminea*
Long-jawed Orb Weaver	*Tetragnatha versicolor*
Long-jawed Orb Weaver	*Tetragnatha elongata*
Nursery-web Spider	*Pisaurina spp.*
Nursery-web Spider	*Pelopatis undulata*
Orange Spider	*Dysdera crocata*
Orb Weaver	*Uloborus americana*
Orb Weaver	*Argiope (riparia)*
Ray Spider	*Theridiosoma radiosa*
Shamrock Spider	*Araneus trifolium*
Six-spotted Orb Weaver	*Araniella displicata*
Six-spotted Fishing Spider	*Dolomedes triton*
Thick-jawed Orb Weaver	*Pachygnatha autumnalis*
Thick-jawed Orb Weaver	*Pachygnatha tristriata*
Thick-jawed Orb Weaver	*Pachygnatha xanthostomata*
Thin-legged Wolf Spider	*Pardosa (mackenziana)*
Thin-legged Wolf Spider	*Pardosa saxatilis*
Thin-legged Wolf Spider	*Pardosa milvina*
Triangle	*Hyptiotes cavatus*
True Spider	*Dictyna spp.*
Two-clawed Hunting Spider	*Clubiona spp.*
Two-spotted Spider Mite	*Tetranychus urticae*
Wolf Spider	*Lycosa (pseudannulata)*
Wolf Spider	*Trabea aurantiaca*
Wolf Spider	*Pirata maculatus*
Wolf Spider	*Pirata insularis*
Wolf Spider	*Pirata minutus*
Wolf Spider	*Pirata montanus*

Plants, Keystone Species

HERBS

Common Name	Scientific Name
Arrowhead	*Sagittaria latifolia*
Bladderwort	*Utricularia vulgaris*
Blue Flag	*Iris versicolor*
Blue Vervain	*Verbena hastata*
Boneset	*Eupatorium perfoliatum*
Bulrush	*Scirpus atrovirens*
Bur-reed	*Sparganium americanum*
Cardinal Flower	*Lobelia cardinalis*
Cinnamon Fern	*Osmunda cinnamomea*
Cleavers Bedstraw	*Galium palustre*
Common Cattail	*Typha latifolia*
Common Glasswort	*Salicornia europaea*
Common Reed Grass	*Phragmites australis*
Cotton-grass	*Eriophorum virginicum*
Curled Dock	*Rumex crispus*
Duckweed	*Lemna sp.*
Fowl-meadow Grass	*Poa palustris*
Goldthread	*Coptis trifolia var. groenlandica*
Grass-leaved Goldenrod	*Euthamia graminifolia*
Indian Poke	*Veratrum viride*
Jack-in-the-pulpit	*Arisaema triphyllum*
Jewelweed	*Impatiens capensis*
Joe-Pye-weed	*Eupatorium maculatum*
Marsh Fern	*Dryopteris thelypteris*
Marsh Marigold	*Caltha palustris*
Mint	*Mentha arvensis*
Narrow-leaved Cattail	*Typha angustifolia*
Northern White Violet	*Viola macloskeyi var. pallens*
Panic-grass	*Panicum rigidulum*
Pickerelweed	*Pontederia cordata*
Pitcher Plant	*Sarracenia purpurea*
Pond orWaterlily Lily	*Nymphaea odorata*
Purple Loosestrife	*Lythrum salicaria*
Reed-Canary Grass	*Phalaris arundinacea*
Rice-Cutgrass	*Leersia oryzoides*
Rose Mallow	*Hibiscus moscheutos*
Rose Pogonia	*Pogonia ophioglossoides*
Salt Marsh Bulrush	*Scirpus robustus*
Saltmarsh Cordgrass	*Spartina alterniflora*
Saltmeadow Cordgrasss	*Spartina patens*
Sea Lavender	*Limonium carolinianum*
Seaside Goldenrod	*Solidago sempervirens*
Sensitive Fern	*Onoclea sensibilis*
Skunk Cabbage	*Symplocarpus foetidus*
Soft Rush	*Juncus effusus*
Sphagnum Moss	*Sphagnum palustre and S. rubrum*
Spotted Cowbane or Water-hemlock	*Cicuta maculata*
Stick-tight	*Bidens connata*
Sundew	*Drosera rotundifolia*
Swamp Candles	*Lysimachia terrestris*
Swamp Milkweed	*Asclepias incarnata*
Swamp Pink	*Arethusa bulbosa*
Sweet Flag	*Acorus calamus*

Common Name	Scientific Name	Common Name	Scientific Name

HERBS (continued)

Common Name	Scientific Name
Turtlehead	*Chelone glabra*
Tussock Sedge	*Carex stricta*
Umbrella Sedge	*Cyperus strigosus*
Water Smartweed	*Polygonum punctatum*
Watercress	*Rorippa nasturtium-aquaticum*
Wild Rice	*Zizania aquatica*
Wool-grass	*Scirpus cyperinus*
Yellow Pond Lily or Spatterdock	*Nuphar variegatum*

SHRUBS

Common Name	Scientific Name
Alder Buckthorn	*Rhamnus frangula*
American Cranberry	*Vaccinium macrocarpon*
Bog Laurel	*Kalmia polifolia*
Bog Rosemary	*Andromeda glaucophylla*
Buttonbush	*Cephalanthus occidentalis*
Common Elderberry	*Sambucus canadensis*
Highbush Blueberry	*Vaccinium corymbosum*
Labrador Tea	*Ledum groenlandicum*
Leatherleaf	*Chamaedaphne calyculata*
Maleberry	*Lyonia ligustrina*
Marsh Elder	*Iva frutescens*
Meadowsweet	*Spirea alba var. latifolia*
Northern Arrowwood	*Viburnum dentatum var. lucidum*
Poison Ivy	*Toxicodendron radicans*
Poison Sumac	*Toxicodendron vernix*
Pussy Willow	*Salix discolor*

SHRUBS (continued)

Common Name	Scientific Name
Rugosa Rose	*Rose rugosa*
Shadbush	*Amelanchier canadensis*
Sheep Laurel	*Kalmia angustifolia*
Silky Dogwood	*Cornus amomum*
Speckled Alder	*Alnus incana var. americana*
Spicebush	*Lindera benzoin*
Swamp Azalea	*Rhododendron viscosum*
Swamp Loosestrife	*Decodon verticillatus*
Swamp Rose	*Rosa palustris*
Sweet Gale	*Myrica gale*
Sweet Pepperbush	*Clethra alnifolia*
Trailing Swamp Blackberry	*Rubus hispidus*
Winterberry	*Ilex verticillata*

TREES

Common Name	Scientific Name
American Elm	*Ulmus americana L.*
Atlantic White Cedar	*Chamaecyparis thyoides*
Black Spruce	*Picea mariana*
Green Ash	*Fraxinus pennsylvanica*
Hemlock	*Tsuga canadensis*
Ironwood	*Carpinus caroliniana*
Larch or Tamarack	*Larix laricina*
Pin Oak	*Quercus palustris*
Red Maple	*Acer rubrum .*
Swamp White Oak	*Quercus bicolor*
Tupelo	*Nyssa sylvatica*
Yellow Birch	*Betula lutea*

Appendix D

SPIDERS

Spiders are a paradox to most of us. The perceived notion is that they are scary, evil, poisonous and of little or no value to the world. To the contrary, most spiders remain secluded or out of the way of humans, few are seriously poisonous enough to pose a threat to humans, and they are of great benefit in snagging unwanted insects. Whenever one of these little creatures moves into my house, I never kill it but rather leave it alone to do insect clean up work. In this guide they are placed in association with plants with which I am familiar, where others have seen them, or where they might be expected to be observed. Spiders are carnivores and are generally wide ranging within their habitat and have only a casual relationship with most plants. What this generally means is that a spider of the meadow, for instance, will associate with many different plants of this community rather than being dependent upon one specific species. While it is true that some spiders may be associated more often than not with a particular habitat, this is not to mean that they will not be found in a different habitat. For example, if you find the Six-spotted Orb Weaver *Araniella dispicata* on Wool-grass *Scirpus cyperinus* in the fresh marsh, it is quite possible you could find this same spider on buttonbush in this community or in a shrub swamp. The observer's chance of encountering them is improved because of this "generalist" nature of plant-spider interaction. This relationship is usually one related to structure, whereby the spider uses the plant for support to build its web or to sit upon as it stalks its prey.

As our understanding of biological interactions increases, perhaps we will discover that there are more species specific relationships between plants and spiders.

Although spiders are often difficult even for experts (Arachnologists) to identify, I have included some of the more familiar ones in the following lists. These are spiders I may have seen or have expected to see and ones which you can easily locate in "How to Know the Spiders" by B.J. Kaston (3rd Ed.), Wm. C. Brown or in "Spiders and their Kin" by H. W. Levi, New York, 1968.

In this section, I have placed some of the spiders into artificial groupings reflecting where they are most commonly seen and where you might expect to find them. I have also included additional comments with many of the spiders listed in this section which may help with their location and identification.

The Spiders

1. THOSE FOUND ALONG MARGINS OF STREAMS & PONDS, ON WATER, OR DIVING

Wolf Spiders

Pirata minutus
P. montanus
P. insularis
P. maculatus
Lycosa (pseudannulata)

Fishing Spiders

Dolomedes scriptu
D. tenebrosus
D. sexpunctatus

Nursery-web Spider

Pelopatis undulata

Pisaurina spp., nearly always found near water and can be seen running across water surface for great distances.

2. ON TREES, SHRUBS, HERBS NEAR OR IN WETLANDS

Fishing Spiders - See Wolf Spiders above

Thick-jawed Orb Weavers

Pachygnatha autumnalis
P. tristriata
P. xanthostomata

Long-jawed Orb Weavers (often found on grass-like vegetation)

Tetragnatha elongata- may see egg sacs attached to branches and covered with greenish threads.

T. laborios
T. straminea
T. versicolor

Ray Spider

Theridiosoma radiosa (see Silky Dogwood shrub)

Thin-Legged Wolf Spider

Pardosa milvina
P. saxatilis
P. (mackenziana)

Garden Spider (Black and Yellow Garden Spider)

Argiope aurantia - one of the most common spiders in the U.S. which builds its nest in wet meadows, although it can be found almost anywhere.

"True" Spider

Dictyna spp., a snare building spider

Comb-Footed Spider

Theridula emertoni (often on trees and shrubs)

Line Weaving Spider

Stemonyphantes blauveltae - found in marshes, under mass where it builds a snare trap.

Grass Spider

Hahnia cinerea - must look carefully for its small and delicate web near ground in wetlands, preferring wetlands where there is a mossy or grassy ground cover for web attachment.

Wolf Spider

Trabea aurantiaca - can be found in shrubswamps and deciduous forested wetlands hiding in or scampering about on the ground cover looking for prey.

Crab Spider

Oxyptila conspurcata

3. ON FLOWERS (ambush prey)

Crab Spider

Misumena vatia (Goldenrod or Flower Spider) - produces no web; wanders over flowers where it may change its color to match the background.

M. formosipes-similar to the above

Comb-Footed Spider

Theridion murarium - has been found on dried flowers.

4. OFTEN ASSOCIATED WITH SALT MARSHES

Line Weaving Spider

Linyphia clathrata

Grass Spider

Neoantistea agilis - found building very thin webs low on vegetation.

Two-Clawed Hunting Spider

Clubiona spp.

Selected Useful References

1. Covell, C.V., Jr. 1984. *A field Guide to the Moths of Eastern North America.* Boston: Houghton Mifflin.

2. Gleason, H.A. and A. Cronquist.1991. *Manual of Vascular Plants of N.E. United States and Adjacent Canada.* 2nd Edition. NYC: New York Botanical Garden.

3. Bull, J. and J. Farrand, Jr.1987. *The Audubon Society Field Guide to North American Birds-Eastern Region.* New York: A.A. Knopf.

4. Cowardin, L.M., V. Carter, F.C. Golet, and E.T. LaRoe.1979. *Classification of Wetlands and Deepwater Habitats of the United States.* Washington, D.C.: U.S. Government Printing Office.

5. Reed, P.B., Jr.1988. *National List of Plant Species that Occur in Wetlands.* Washington, D.C.: U.S. Government Printing Office.

6. Arnett, R.H., Jr.1985. *American Insects—a Handbook of the Insects of America and N. Mexico.* NYC: Van Nostrand Reinhold Co.

7. Borror, D.J. and R.E. White.1970. *A Field Guide to Insects.* Boston: Houghton Mifflin.

8. Burt, W.H. and R.P. Grossenheider.1976. *A Field Guide to the Mammals of North America North of Mexico.* Boston: Houghton Mifflin.

9. Kaston, B.J.1978. *How to Know the Spiders.* 3rd Edition. Dubuque:Wm.C. Brown.

10. Tyning, Thomas F.1990. *A Guide to Amphibians and Reptiles.* Boston:Little, Brown and Co.

11. Klots, A.B.1979. *A Field Guide to the Butterflies.* Boston:Houghton Mifflin.

12. Cobb, B.1963. *A Field Guide to the Ferns.* Boston:Houghton Mifflin.

13. Pyle, R.M.1981. *The Audubon Society Field Guide to North American Butterflies.* New York:A.A. Knopf.

14. Conant, R. 1975. *A Field Guide to Reptiles and Amphibians*. Boston: Houghton Mifflin.

15.White, R.E.1983. *A Field Guide to the Beetles*. Boston:Houghton Mifflin.

16. Tiner, R.W.1987. *A Field Guide to Coastal Wetland Plants of the N.E, United States*. Amherst: The University of Massachusetts Press.

17. Magee, D.W.1981. *Freshwater Water Wetlands, A Guide to Common Indicator Plants of the Northeast*. Amherst: The University of Massachusetts Press.

18. Peterson, R.T. and M. McKenny.1968. *A Field guide to Wildflowers of Northeastern and Northcentral North America*. Boston: Houghton Mifflin.

19. Petrides, G.A.1958. *A Field Guide to Trees and Shrubs*. Boston: Houghton Mifflin.

20. Little, E.L.1983. *The Audubon Society Field Guide to North American Trees*. New York:A.A. Knopf.

21. DeGraaf, R.M. and D.D. Rudis.1987. *New England Wildlife:Habitat, Natural History, and Distribution*. Broomall, PA: Gen.Tech. Rep. NE-108, U.S. Department of Agriculture, Forest Service, Northeastern Forest Experiment Station.

22. Whitaker, J.O., Jr.1988. *The Audubon Society Field Guide to North American Mammals*. New York:A.A. Knopf.

23. Newcomb, L.1977. *Newcomb's Wildflower Guide*. Boston: Little, Brown.

24. Harrison, H.H.1975. *A Field Guide to Birds' Nests in the United States East of the Mississippi River*. Boston: Houghton Mifflin

25. Hinds, H.R. and W.A. Hathaway.1968. *Wildflowers of Cape Cod*. Chatham: Chatham Press.

26. Martin, A.C., H.S. Zim, and A.L. Nelson.1961. *American Wildlife and Plants*. New York: Dover.

Observer's Name: _____

Field Data Form: **A. Cranberry**

Observer's Address _____

Scientific Name of Plant _____

Common Name of Animal _____

Scientific Name of Animal _____

Date Collected / Observed _____

Where collected/observed; describe geographical location so you could find the place again by recording the following;

State _____ County _____ City/Town _____

Road _____

Landmark/Compass bearings _____

Describe habitat found in; such as a bog, marsh, swamp; use habitat catagories found in this field guide. _____

_____

Interaction; describe what you observed going on between the plant and animal such as;

Breeding site _____

Food Source _____

Cover _____

Other _____

_____

Field Data Form: **A. White Cedar**

Observer's Address _____

Scientific Name of Plant _____

Common Name of Animal _____

Scientific Name of Animal _____

Date Collected / Observed _____

Where collected/observed; describe geographical location so you could find the place again by recording the following;

State _____ County _____ City/Town _____

Road _____

Landmark/Compass bearings _____

Describe habitat found in; such as a bog, marsh, swamp; use habitat catagories found in this field guide. _____

_____

Interaction; describe what you observed going on between the plant and animal such as;

Breeding site _____

Food Source _____

Cover _____

Other _____

_____

Observer's Name: _____

Field Data Form: ## Alder Buckthorn

Observer's Address _____

Scientific Name of Plant _____

Common Name of Animal _____

Scientific Name of Animal _____

Date Collected /Observed _____

Where collected/observed; describe geographical location so you could find the place again by recording the following;

State _____ County _____ City/Town _____

Road _____

Landmark/Compass bearings _____

Describe habitat found in; such as a bog, marsh, swamp; use habitat catagories found in this field guide. _____

_____

Interaction; describe what you observed going on between the plant and animal such as;

Breeding site _____

Food Source _____

Cover _____

Other _____

_____

Field Data Form: ## American Elm

Observer's Address _____

Scientific Name of Plant _____

Common Name of Animal _____

Scientific Name of Animal _____

Date Collected /Observed _____

Where collected/observed; describe geographical location so you could find the place again by recording the following;

State _____ County _____ City/Town _____

Road _____

Landmark/Compass bearings _____

Describe habitat found in; such as a bog, marsh, swamp; use habitat catagories found in this field guide. _____

Interaction; describe what you observed going on between the plant and animal such as;

Breeding site _____

Food Source _____

Cover _____

Other _____

_____

Observer's Name: _____

Field Data Form: Arrowhead

Observer's Address _____

Scientific Name of Plant _____

Common Name of Animal _____

Scientific Name of Animal _____

Date Collected /Observed _____

Where collected/observed; describe geographical location so you could find the place again by recording the following;

State _____ County _____ City/Town _____

Road _____

Landmark/Compass bearings _____

Describe habitat found in; such as a bog, marsh, swamp; use habitat catagories found in this field guide. _____

_____

Interaction; describe what you observed going on between the plant and animal such as;

Breeding site _____

Food Source _____

Cover _____

Other _____

_____

Field Data Form: Black Spruce

Observer's Address _____

Scientific Name of Plant _____

Common Name of Animal _____

Scientific Name of Animal _____

Date Collected /Observed _____

Where collected/observed; describe geographical location so you could find the place again by recording the following;

State _____ County _____ City/Town _____

Road _____

Landmark/Compass bearings _____

Describe habitat found in; such as a bog, marsh, swamp; use habitat catagories found in this field guide. _____

_____

Interaction; describe what you observed going on between the plant and animal such as;

Breeding site _____

Food Source _____

Cover _____

Other _____

_____

Observer's Name: _____

Field Data Form: **Blue Flag**

Observer's Address _____

Scientific Name of Plant _____

Common Name of Animal _____

Scientific Name of Animal _____

Date Collected /Observed _____

Where collected/observed; describe geographical location so you could find the place again by recording the following;

State _____ County _____ City/Town _____

Road _____

Landmark/Compass bearings _____

Describe habitat found in; such as a bog, marsh, swamp; use habitat catagories found in this field guide. _____

_____

Interaction; describe what you observed going on between the plant and animal such as;

Breeding site _____

Food Source _____

Cover _____

Other _____

_____

Field Data Form: **Blue Vervain**

Observer's Address _____

Scientific Name of Plant _____

Common Name of Animal _____

Scientific Name of Animal _____

Date Collected /Observed _____

Where collected/observed; describe geographical location so you could find the place again by recording the following;

State _____ County _____ City/Town _____

Road _____

Landmark/Compass bearings _____

Describe habitat found in; such as a bog, marsh, swamp; use habitat catagories found in this field guide. _____

_____

Interaction; describe what you observed going on between the plant and animal such as;

Breeding site _____

Food Source _____

Cover _____

Other _____

_____

Observer's Name: _____

Field Data Form: Bog Laurel

Observer's Address _____

Scientific Name of Plant _____

Common Name of Animal _____

Scientific Name of Animal _____

Date Collected /Observed _____

Where collected/observed; describe geographical location so you could find the place again by recording the following;

State _____ County _____ City/Town _____

Road _____

Landmark/Compass bearings _____

Describe habitat found in; such as a bog, marsh, swamp; use habitat catagories found in this field guide. _____

_____

Interaction; describe what you observed going on between the plant and animal such as;

Breeding site _____

Food Source _____

Cover _____

Other _____

_____

Field Data Form: Bog Rosemary

Observer's Address _____

Scientific Name of Plant _____

Common Name of Animal _____

Scientific Name of Animal _____

Date Collected /Observed _____

Where collected/observed; describe geographical location so you could find the place again by recording the following;

State _____ County _____ City/Town _____

Road _____

Landmark/Compass bearings _____

Describe habitat found in; such as a bog, marsh, swamp; use habitat catagories found in this field guide. _____

_____

Interaction; describe what you observed going on between the plant and animal such as;

Breeding site _____

Food Source _____

Cover _____

Other _____

_____

337

Observer's Name: _____

Field Data Form: **Boneset**

Observer's Address _____
Scientific Name of Plant _____
Common Name of Animal _____
Scientific Name of Animal _____
Date Collected/Observed _____

Where collected/observed; describe geographical location so you could find the place again by recording the following;

State _____ County _____ City/Town _____
Road _____
Landmark/Compass bearings _____

Describe habitat found in; such as a bog, marsh, swamp; use habitat catagories found in this field guide. _____
_____

Interaction; describe what you observed going on between the plant and animal such as;
Breeding site _____
Food Source _____
Cover _____
Other _____
_____

Field Data Form: **Bulrush**

Observer's Address _____
Scientific Name of Plant _____
Common Name of Animal _____
Scientific Name of Animal _____
Date Collected/Observed _____

Where collected/observed; describe geographical location so you could find the place again by recording the following;

State _____ County _____ City/Town _____
Road _____
Landmark/Compass bearings _____

Describe habitat found in; such as a bog, marsh, swamp; use habitat catagories found in this field guide. _____
_____

Interaction; describe what you observed going on between the plant and animal such as;
Breeding site _____
Food Source _____
Cover _____
Other _____
_____

Observer's Name: _____

Field Data Form: # Bur-reed

Observer's Address _____

Scientific Name of Plant _____

Common Name of Animal _____

Scientific Name of Animal _____

Date Collected/Observed _____

Where collected/observed; describe geographical location so you could find the place again by recording the following;

State _____ County _____ City/Town _____

Road _____

Landmark/Compass bearings _____

Describe habitat found in; such as a bog, marsh, swamp; use habitat catagories found in this field guide. _____

_____

Interaction; describe what you observed going on between the plant and animal such as;

Breeding site _____

Food Source _____

Cover _____

Other _____

_____

Field Data Form: # Buttonbush

Observer's Address _____

Scientific Name of Plant _____

Common Name of Animal _____

Scientific Name of Animal _____

Date Collected/Observed _____

Where collected/observed; describe geographical location so you could find the place again by recording the following;

State _____ County _____ City/Town _____

Road _____

Landmark/Compass bearings _____

Describe habitat found in; such as a bog, marsh, swamp; use habitat catagories found in this field guide. _____

_____

Interaction; describe what you observed going on between the plant and animal such as;

Breeding site _____

Food Source _____

Cover _____

Other _____

_____

Observer's Name: _____

Field Data Form: ## C. Reed Grass

Observer's Address _____
Scientific Name of Plant _____
Common Name of Animal _____
Scientific Name of Animal _____
Date Collected /Observed _____

Where collected/observed; describe geographical location so you could find the place again by recording the following;

State _____ County _____ City/Town _____
Road _____
Landmark/Compass bearings _____

Describe habitat found in; such as a bog, marsh, swamp; use habitat catagories found in this field guide. _____
_____

Interaction; describe what you observed going on between the plant and animal such as;
Breeding site _____
Food Source _____
Cover _____
Other _____
_____

Field Data Form: ## Cardinal Flower

Observer's Address _____
Scientific Name of Plant _____
Common Name of Animal _____
Scientific Name of Animal _____
Date Collected /Observed _____

Where collected/observed; describe geographical location so you could find the place again by recording the following;

State _____ County _____ City/Town _____
Road _____
Landmark/Compass bearings _____

Describe habitat found in; such as a bog, marsh, swamp; use habitat catagories found in this field guide. _____
_____

Interaction; describe what you observed going on between the plant and animal such as;
Breeding site _____
Food Source _____
Cover _____
Other _____
_____

Observer's Name: _____

Field Data Form: **Cinnamon Fern**

Observer's Address _____
Scientific Name of Plant _____
Common Name of Animal _____
Scientific Name of Animal _____
Date Collected/Observed _____

Where collected/observed; describe geographical location so you could find the place again by recording the following;

State _____ County _____ City/Town _____
Road _____
Landmark/Compass bearings _____

Describe habitat found in; such as a bog, marsh, swamp; use habitat catagories found in this field guide. _____
_____

Interaction; describe what you observed going on between the plant and animal such as;
Breeding site _____
Food Source _____
Cover _____
Other _____
_____

Field Data Form: **Cleavers Bedstraw**

Observer's Address _____
Scientific Name of Plant _____
Common Name of Animal _____
Scientific Name of Animal _____
Date Collected/Observed _____

Where collected/observed; describe geographical location so you could find the place again by recording the following;

State _____ County _____ City/Town _____
Road _____
Landmark/Compass bearings _____

Describe habitat found in; such as a bog, marsh, swamp; use habitat catagories found in this field guide. _____
_____

Interaction; describe what you observed going on between the plant and animal such as;
Breeding site _____
Food Source _____
Cover _____
Other _____
_____

Observer's Name: _____

Field Data Form: # Common Bladderwort

Observer's Address _____
Scientific Name of Plant _____
Common Name of Animal _____
Scientific Name of Animal _____
Date Collected/Observed _____

Where collected/observed; describe geographical location so you could find the place again by recording the following;

State _____ County _____ City/Town _____
Road _____
Landmark/Compass bearings _____

Describe habitat found in; such as a bog, marsh, swamp; use habitat catagories found in this field guide. _____
_____

Interaction; describe what you observed going on between the plant and animal such as;

Breeding site _____
Food Source _____
Cover _____
Other _____
_____

Field Data Form: # Common Cattail

Observer's Address _____
Scientific Name of Plant _____
Common Name of Animal _____
Scientific Name of Animal _____
Date Collected/Observed _____

Where collected/observed; describe geographical location so you could find the place again by recording the following;

State _____ County _____ City/Town _____
Road _____
Landmark/Compass bearings _____

Describe habitat found in; such as a bog, marsh, swamp; use habitat catagories found in this field guide. _____
_____

Interaction; describe what you observed going on between the plant and animal such as;

Breeding site _____
Food Source _____
Cover _____
Other _____
_____

Observer's Name: _____

Field Data Form: # Common Elderberry

Observer's Address _____

Scientific Name of Plant _____

Common Name of Animal _____

Scientific Name of Animal _____

Date Collected/Observed _____

Where collected/observed; describe geographical location so you could find the place again by recording the following;

State _____ County _____ City/Town _____

Road _____

Landmark/Compass bearings _____

Describe habitat found in; such as a bog, marsh, swamp; use habitat catagories found in this field guide. _____

_____

Interaction; describe what you observed going on between the plant and animal such as;

Breeding site _____

Food Source _____

Cover _____

Other _____

_____

Field Data Form: # Common Glasswort

Observer's Address _____

Scientific Name of Plant _____

Common Name of Animal _____

Scientific Name of Animal _____

Date Collected/Observed _____

Where collected/observed; describe geographical location so you could find the place again by recording the following;

State _____ County _____ City/Town _____

Road _____

Landmark/Compass bearings _____

Describe habitat found in; such as a bog, marsh, swamp; use habitat catagories found in this field guide. _____

_____

Interaction; describe what you observed going on between the plant and animal such as;

Breeding site _____

Food Source _____

Cover _____

Other _____

_____

Field Data Form: **Cotton-grass**

Observer's Address _____

Scientific Name of Plant _____

Common Name of Animal _____

Scientific Name of Animal _____

Date Collected /Observed _____

Where collected/observed; describe geographical location so you could find the place again by recording the following;

State _____ County _____ City/Town _____

Road _____

Landmark/Compass bearings _____

Describe habitat found in; such as a bog, marsh, swamp; use habitat catagories found in this field guide. _____

_____

Interaction; describe what you observed going on between the plant and animal such as;

Breeding site _____

Food Source _____

Cover _____

Other _____

_____

Field Data Form: **Curled Dock**

Observer's Address _____

Scientific Name of Plant _ _____

Common Name of Animal _____

Scientific Name of Animal _____

Date Collected /Observed _____

Where collected/observed; describe geographical location so you could find the place again by recording the following;

State _____ County _____ City/Town _____

Road _____

Landmark/Compass bearings _____

Describe habitat found in; such as a bog, marsh, swamp; use habitat catagories found in this field guide. _____

_____

Interaction; describe what you observed going on between the plant and animal such as;

Breeding site _____

Food Source _____

Cover _____

Other _____

_____

Observer's Name: _____

Field Data Form: Duckweed

Observer's Address _____

Scientific Name of Plant _____

Common Name of Animal _____

Scientific Name of Animal _____

Date Collected /Observed _____

Where collected/observed; describe geographical location so you could find the place again by recording the following;

State _____ County _____ City/Town _____

Road _____

Landmark/Compass bearings _____

Describe habitat found in; such as a bog, marsh, swamp; use habitat catagories found in this field guide. _____

_____

Interaction; describe what you observed going on between the plant and animal such as;

Breeding site _____

Food Source _____

Cover _____

Other _____

_____

Field Data Form: Fowl-meadow Grass

Observer's Address _____

Scientific Name of Plant _____

Common Name of Animal _____

Scientific Name of Animal _____

Date Collected /Observed _____

Where collected/observed; describe geographical location so you could find the place again by recording the following;

State _____ County _____ City/Town _____

Road _____

Landmark/Compass bearings _____

Describe habitat found in; such as a bog, marsh, swamp; use habitat catagories found in this field guide. _____

_____

Interaction; describe what you observed going on between the plant and animal such as;

Breeding site _____

Food Source _____

Cover _____

Other _____

_____

Observer's Name: _____

Field Data Form: # Goldthread

Observer's Address _____

Scientific Name of Plant _____

Common Name of Animal _____

Scientific Name of Animal _____

Date Collected /Observed _____

Where collected/observed; describe geographical location so you could find the place again by recording the following;

State _____ County _____ City/Town _____
Road _____
Landmark/Compass bearings _____

Describe habitat found in; such as a bog, marsh, swamp; use habitat catagories found in this field guide. _____
_____

Interaction; describe what you observed going on between the plant and animal such as;
Breeding site _____
Food Source _____
Cover _____
Other _____
_____

Field Data Form: # Grass-leaved Goldenrod

Observer's Address _____

Scientific Name of Plant _ _____

Common Name of Animal _____

Scientific Name of Animal _____

Date Collected /Observed _____

Where collected/observed; describe geographical location so you could find the place again by recording the following;

State _____ County _____ City/Town _____
Road _____
Landmark/Compass bearings _____

Describe habitat found in; such as a bog, marsh, swamp; use habitat catagories found in this field guide. _____
_____

Interaction; describe what you observed going on between the plant and animal such as;
Breeding site _____
Food Source _____
Cover _____
Other _____
_____

346

Observer's Name: _____

Field Data Form: # Green Ash

Observer's Address	_____
Scientific Name of Plant	_____
Common Name of Animal	_____
Scientific Name of Animal	_____
Date Collected/Observed	_____

Where collected/observed; describe geographical location so you could find the place again by recording the following;

State _____ County _____ City/Town _____
Road _____
Landmark/Compass bearings _____

Describe habitat found in; such as a bog, marsh, swamp; use habitat catagories found in this field guide. _____
_____

Interaction; describe what you observed going on between the plant and animal such as;
Breeding site _____
Food Source _____
Cover _____
Other _____
_____

Field Data Form: # Hemlock

Observer's Address	_____
Scientific Name of Plant	_____
Common Name of Animal	_____
Scientific Name of Animal	_____
Date Collected/Observed	_____

Where collected/observed; describe geographical location so you could find the place again by recording the following;

State _____ County _____ City/Town _____
Road _____
Landmark/Compass bearings _____

Describe habitat found in; such as a bog, marsh, swamp; use habitat catagories found in this field guide. _____
_____

Interaction; describe what you observed going on between the plant and animal such as;
Breeding site _____
Food Source _____
Cover _____
Other _____
_____

347

Observer's Name: _____

Field Data Form: **Highbush Blueberry**

Observer's Address _____

Scientific Name of Plant _____

Common Name of Animal _____

Scientific Name of Animal _____

Date Collected/Observed _____

Where collected/observed; describe geographical location so you could find the place again by recording the following;

State _____ County _____ City/Town _____
Road _____
Landmark/Compass bearings _____

Describe habitat found in; such as a bog, marsh, swamp; use habitat catagories found in this field guide. _____
_____

Interaction; describe what you observed going on between the plant and animal such as;

Breeding site _____
Food Source _____
Cover _____
Other _____
_____

Field Data Form: **Indian Poke**

Observer's Address _____

Scientific Name of Plant _____

Common Name of Animal _____

Scientific Name of Animal _____

Date Collected/Observed _____

Where collected/observed; describe geographical location so you could find the place again by recording the following;

State _____ County _____ City/Town _____
Road _____
Landmark/Compass bearings _____

Describe habitat found in; such as a bog, marsh, swamp; use habitat catagories found in this field guide. _____
_____

Interaction; describe what you observed going on between the plant and animal such as;

Breeding site _____
Food Source _____
Cover _____
Other _____
_____

Observer's Name: _____

Field Data Form: Ironwood

Observer's Address _____

Scientific Name of Plant _____

Common Name of Animal _____

Scientific Name of Animal _____

Date Collected /Observed _____

Where collected/observed; describe geographical location so you could find the place again by recording the following;

State _____ County _____ City/Town _____

Road _____

Landmark/Compass bearings _____

Describe habitat found in; such as a bog, marsh, swamp; use habitat catagories found in this field guide. _____

_____

Interaction; describe what you observed going on between the plant and animal such as;

Breeding site _____

Food Source _____

Cover _____

Other _____

_____

Field Data Form: Jack-in-the-pulpit

Observer's Address _____

Scientific Name of Plant _____

Common Name of Animal _____

Scientific Name of Animal _____

Date Collected /Observed _____

Where collected/observed; describe geographical location so you could find the place again by recording the following;

State _____ County _____ City/Town _____

Road _____

Landmark/Compass bearings _____

Describe habitat found in; such as a bog, marsh, swamp; use habitat catagories found in this field guide. _____

_____

Interaction; describe what you observed going on between the plant and animal such as;

Breeding site _____

Food Source _____

Cover _____

Other _____

_____

Observer's Name: _____

Field Data Form: Jewelweed

Observer's Address _____

Scientific Name of Plant _____

Common Name of Animal _____

Scientific Name of Animal _____

Date Collected /Observed _____

Where collected/observed; describe geographical location so you could find the place again by recording the following;

State _____ County _____ City/Town _____

Road _____

Landmark/Compass bearings _____

Describe habitat found in; such as a bog, marsh, swamp; use habitat catagories found in this field guide. _____

_____

Interaction; describe what you observed going on between the plant and animal such as;

Breeding site _____

Food Source _____

Cover _____

Other _____

_____

Field Data Form: Joe-Pye-weed

Observer's Address _____

Scientific Name of Plant _____

Common Name of Animal _____

Scientific Name of Animal _____

Date Collected /Observed _____

Where collected/observed; describe geographical location so you could find the place again by recording the following;

State _____ County _____ City/Town _____

Road _____

Landmark/Compass bearings _____

Describe habitat found in; such as a bog, marsh, swamp; use habitat catagories found in this field guide. _____

_____

Interaction; describe what you observed going on between the plant and animal such as;

Breeding site _____

Food Source _____

Cover _____

Other _____

_____

350

Observer's Name: _____

Field Data Form: Labrador Tea

Observer's Address _____
Scientific Name of Plant _____
Common Name of Animal _____
Scientific Name of Animal _____
Date Collected /Observed _____

Where collected/observed; describe geographical location so you could find the place again by recording the following;

State _____ County _____ City/Town _____
Road _____
Landmark/Compass bearings _____

Describe habitat found in; such as a bog, marsh, swamp; use habitat catagories found in this field guide. _____
_____

Interaction; describe what you observed going on between the plant and animal such as;
Breeding site _____
Food Source _____
Cover _____
Other _____
_____

Field Data Form: Larch

Observer's Address _____
Scientific Name of Plant _____
Common Name of Animal _____
Scientific Name of Animal _____
Date Collected /Observed _____

Where collected/observed; describe geographical location so you could find the place again by recording the following;

State _____ County _____ City/Town _____
Road _____
Landmark/Compass bearings _____

Describe habitat found in; such as a bog, marsh, swamp; use habitat catagories found in this field guide. _____
_____

Interaction; describe what you observed going on between the plant and animal such as;
Breeding site _____
Food Source _____
Cover _____
Other _____
_____

Observer's Name: _____

Field Data Form: **Leatherleaf**

Observer's Address _____

Scientific Name of Plant _____

Common Name of Animal _____

Scientific Name of Animal _____

Date Collected/Observed _____

Where collected/observed; describe geographical location so you could find the place again by recording the following;

State _____ County _____ City/Town _____

Road _____

Landmark/Compass bearings _____

Describe habitat found in; such as a bog, marsh, swamp; use habitat catagories found in this field guide. _____

_____

Interaction; describe what you observed going on between the plant and animal such as;

Breeding site _____

Food Source _____

Cover _____

Other _____

_____

Field Data Form: **Maleberry**

Observer's Address _____

Scientific Name of Plant _____

Common Name of Animal _____

Scientific Name of Animal _____

Date Collected/Observed _____

Where collected/observed; describe geographical location so you could find the place again by recording the following;

State _____ County _____ City/Town _____

Road _____

Landmark/Compass bearings _____

Describe habitat found in; such as a bog, marsh, swamp; use habitat catagories found in this field guide. _____

_____

Interaction; describe what you observed going on between the plant and animal such as;

Breeding site _____

Food Source _____

Cover _____

Other _____

_____

Observer's Name: _____

Field Data Form: **Marsh Elder**

Observer's Address _____

Scientific Name of Plant _____

Common Name of Animal _____

Scientific Name of Animal _____

Date Collected/Observed _____

Where collected/observed; describe geographical location so you could find the place again by recording the following;

State _____ County _____ City/Town _____

Road _____

Landmark/Compass bearings _____

Describe habitat found in; such as a bog, marsh, swamp; use habitat catagories found in this field guide. _____

_____

Interaction; describe what you observed going on between the plant and animal such as;

Breeding site _____

Food Source _____

Cover _____

Other _____

_____

Field Data Form: **Marsh Fern**

Observer's Address _____

Scientific Name of Plant _____

Common Name of Animal _____

Scientific Name of Animal _____

Date Collected/Observed _____

Where collected/observed; describe geographical location so you could find the place again by recording the following;

State _____ County _____ City/Town _____

Road _____

Landmark/Compass bearings _____

Describe habitat found in; such as a bog, marsh, swamp; use habitat catagories found in this field guide. _____

_____

Interaction; describe what you observed going on between the plant and animal such as;

Breeding site _____

Food Source _____

Cover _____

Other _____

_____

Observer's Name: _____

Field Data Form: **Marsh Marigold**

Observer's Address _____

Scientific Name of Plant _____

Common Name of Animal _____

Scientific Name of Animal _____

Date Collected/Observed _____

Where collected/observed; describe geographical location so you could find the place again by recording the following;

State _____ County _____ City/Town _____

Road _____

Landmark/Compass bearings _____

Describe habitat found in; such as a bog, marsh, swamp; use habitat catagories found in this field guide. _____

_____

Interaction; describe what you observed going on between the plant and animal such as;

Breeding site _____

Food Source _____

Cover _____

Other _____

_____

Field Data Form: **Meadow-sweet**

Observer's Address _____

Scientific Name of Plant _____

Common Name of Animal _____

Scientific Name of Animal _____

Date Collected/Observed _____

Where collected/observed; describe geographical location so you could find the place again by recording the following;

State _____ County _____ City/Town _____

Road _____

Landmark/Compass bearings _____

Describe habitat found in; such as a bog, marsh, swamp; use habitat catagories found in this field guide. _____

_____

Interaction; describe what you observed going on between the plant and animal such as;

Breeding site _____

Food Source _____

Cover _____

Other _____

_____

Observer's Name: _____

Field Data Form: Mint

Observer's Address _____

Scientific Name of Plant _____

Common Name of Animal _____

Scientific Name of Animal _____

Date Collected/Observed _____

Where collected/observed; describe geographical location so you could find the place again by recording the following;

State _____ County _____ City/Town _____

Road _____

Landmark/Compass bearings _____

Describe habitat found in; such as a bog, marsh, swamp; use habitat catagories found in this field guide. _____

_____

Interaction; describe what you observed going on between the plant and animal such as;

Breeding site _____

Food Source _____

Cover _____

Other _____

_____

Field Data Form: N. Arrowwood

Observer's Address _____

Scientific Name of Plant _____

Common Name of Animal _____

Scientific Name of Animal _____

Date Collected/Observed _____

Where collected/observed; describe geographical location so you could find the place again by recording the following;

State _____ County _____ City/Town _____

Road _____

Landmark/Compass bearings _____

Describe habitat found in; such as a bog, marsh, swamp; use habitat catagories found in this field guide. _____

_____

Interaction; describe what you observed going on between the plant and animal such as;

Breeding site _____

Food Source _____

Cover _____

Other _____

_____

355

Observer's Name: _____

Field Data Form: # N. White Violet

Observer's Address _____

Scientific Name of Plant _____

Common Name of Animal _____

Scientific Name of Animal _____

Date Collected /Observed _____

Where collected/observed; describe geographical location so you could find the place again by recording the following;

State _____ County _____ City/Town _____

Road _____

Landmark/Compass bearings _____

Describe habitat found in; such as a bog, marsh, swamp; use habitat catagories found in this field guide. _____

_____

Interaction; describe what you observed going on between the plant and animal such as;

Breeding site _____

Food Source _____

Cover _____

Other _____

_____

Field Data Form: # Narrow-leaved Cattail

Observer's Address _____

Scientific Name of Plant _____

Common Name of Animal _____

Scientific Name of Animal _____

Date Collected /Observed _____

Where collected/observed; describe geographical location so you could find the place again by recording the following;

State _____ County _____ City/Town _____

Road _____

Landmark/Compass bearings _____

Describe habitat found in; such as a bog, marsh, swamp; use habitat catagories found in this field guide. _____

_____

Interaction; describe what you observed going on between the plant and animal such as;

Breeding site _____

Food Source _____

Cover _____

Other _____

_____

356

Observer's Name: _____

Field Data Form: **Panic-grass**

Observer's Address _____
Scientific Name of Plant _____
Common Name of Animal _____
Scientific Name of Animal _____
Date Collected /Observed _____

Where collected/observed; describe geographical location so you could find the place again by recording the following;

State _____ County _____ City/Town _____
Road _____
Landmark/Compass bearings _____

Describe habitat found in; such as a bog, marsh, swamp; use habitat catagories found in this field guide. _____
_____

Interaction; describe what you observed going on between the plant and animal such as;
Breeding site _____
Food Source _____
Cover _____
Other _____
_____

Field Data Form: **Pickerelweed**

Observer's Address _____
Scientific Name of Plant _____
Common Name of Animal _____
Scientific Name of Animal _____
Date Collected /Observed _____

Where collected/observed; describe geographical location so you could find the place again by recording the following;

State _____ County _____ City/Town _____
Road _____
Landmark/Compass bearings _____

Describe habitat found in; such as a bog, marsh, swamp; use habitat catagories found in this field guide. _____
_____

Interaction; describe what you observed going on between the plant and animal such as;
Breeding site _____
Food Source _____
Cover _____
Other _____
_____

Observer's Name: _____

Field Data Form: Pin Oak

Observer's Address _____

Scientific Name of Plant _____

Common Name of Animal _____

Scientific Name of Animal _____

Date Collected/Observed _____

Where collected/observed; describe geographical location so you could find the place again by recording the following;

State _____ County _____ City/Town _____

Road _____

Landmark/Compass bearings _____

Describe habitat found in; such as a bog, marsh, swamp; use habitat catagories found in this field guide. _____

_____

Interaction; describe what you observed going on between the plant and animal such as;

Breeding site _____

Food Source _____

Cover _____

Other _____

_____

Field Data Form: Pitcher Plant

Observer's Address _____

Scientific Name of Plant _____

Common Name of Animal _____

Scientific Name of Animal _____

Date Collected/Observed _____

Where collected/observed; describe geographical location so you could find the place again by recording the following;

State _____ County _____ City/Town _____

Road _____

Landmark/Compass bearings _____

Describe habitat found in; such as a bog, marsh, swamp; use habitat catagories found in this field guide. _____

_____

Interaction; describe what you observed going on between the plant and animal such as;

Breeding site _____

Food Source _____

Cover _____

Other _____

_____

Observer's Name: _____

Field Data Form: Poison Ivy

Observer's Address _____

Scientific Name of Plant _____

Common Name of Animal _____

Scientific Name of Animal _____

Date Collected/Observed _____

Where collected/observed; describe geographical location so you could find the place again by recording the following;

State _____ County _____ City/Town _____

Road _____

Landmark/Compass bearings _____

Describe habitat found in; such as a bog, marsh, swamp; use habitat catagories found in this field guide. _____

_____

Interaction; describe what you observed going on between the plant and animal such as;

Breeding site _____

Food Source _____

Cover _____

Other _____

_____

Field Data Form: Poison Sumac

Observer's Address _____

Scientific Name of Plant _____

Common Name of Animal _____

Scientific Name of Animal _____

Date Collected/Observed _____

Where collected/observed; describe geographical location so you could find the place again by recording the following;

State _____ County _____ City/Town _____

Road _____

Landmark/Compass bearings _____

Describe habitat found in; such as a bog, marsh, swamp; use habitat catagories found in this field guide. _____

_____

Interaction; describe what you observed going on between the plant and animal such as;

Breeding site _____

Food Source _____

Cover _____

Other _____

_____

Observer's Name: _____

Field Data Form: **Pond or Waterlily**

Observer's Address _____

Scientific Name of Plant _____

Common Name of Animal _____

Scientific Name of Animal _____

Date Collected /Observed _____

Where collected/observed; describe geographical location so you could find the place again by recording the following;

State _____ County _____ City/Town _____

Road _____

Landmark/Compass bearings _____

Describe habitat found in; such as a bog, marsh, swamp; use habitat catagories found in this field guide. _____

_____

Interaction; describe what you observed going on between the plant and animal such as;

Breeding site _____

Food Source _____

Cover _____

Other _____

_____

Field Data Form: **Purple Loosestrife**

Observer's Address _____

Scientific Name of Plant _____

Common Name of Animal _____

Scientific Name of Animal _____

Date Collected /Observed _____

Where collected/observed; describe geographical location so you could find the place again by recording the following;

State _____ County _____ City/Town _____

Road _____

Landmark/Compass bearings _____

Describe habitat found in; such as a bog, marsh, swamp; use habitat catagories found in this field guide. _____

_____

Interaction; describe what you observed going on between the plant and animal such as;

Breeding site _____

Food Source _____

Cover _____

Other _____

_____

Observer's Name: _____

Field Data Form: Pussy Willow

Observer's Address _____
Scientific Name of Plant _____
Common Name of Animal _____
Scientific Name of Animal _____
Date Collected /Observed _____

Where collected/observed; describe geographical location so you could find the place again by recording the following;

State _____ County _____ City/Town _____
Road _____
Landmark/Compass bearings _____

Describe habitat found in; such as a bog, marsh, swamp; use habitat catagories found in this field guide. _____
_____

Interaction; describe what you observed going on between the plant and animal such as;
Breeding site _____
Food Source _____
Cover _____
Other _____
_____

Field Data Form: Red Maple

Observer's Address _____
Scientific Name of Plant _____
Common Name of Animal _____
Scientific Name of Animal _____
Date Collected /Observed _____

Where collected/observed; describe geographical location so you could find the place again by recording the following;

State _____ County _____ City/Town _____
Road _____
Landmark/Compass bearings _____

Describe habitat found in; such as a bog, marsh, swamp; use habitat catagories found in this field guide. _____
_____

Interaction; describe what you observed going on between the plant and animal such as;
Breeding site _____
Food Source _____
Cover _____
Other _____
_____

361

Observer's Name: _____

Field Data Form: **Reed-Canary**

Observer's Address _____

Scientific Name of Plant _____

Common Name of Animal _____

Scientific Name of Animal _____

Date Collected/Observed _____

Where collected/observed; describe geographical location so you could find the place again by recording the following;

State _____ County _____ City/Town _____

Road _____

Landmark/Compass bearings _____

Describe habitat found in; such as a bog, marsh, swamp; use habitat catagories found in this field guide. _____

_____

Interaction; describe what you observed going on between the plant and animal such as;

Breeding site _____

Food Source _____

Cover _____

Other _____

_____

Field Data Form: **Rice-Cutgrass**

Observer's Address _____

Scientific Name of Plant _____

Common Name of Animal _____

Scientific Name of Animal _____

Date Collected/Observed _____

Where collected/observed; describe geographical location so you could find the place again by recording the following;

State _____ County _____ City/Town _____

Road _____

Landmark/Compass bearings _____

Describe habitat found in; such as a bog, marsh, swamp; use habitat catagories found in this field guide. _____

_____

Interaction; describe what you observed going on between the plant and animal such as;

Breeding site _____

Food Source _____

Cover _____

Other _____

_____

Observer's Name: _____

Field Data Form: # Rose Mallow

Observer's Address _____
Scientific Name of Plant _____
Common Name of Animal _____
Scientific Name of Animal _____
Date Collected /Observed _____

Where collected/observed; describe geographical location so you could find the place again by recording the following;

State _____ County _____ City/Town _____
Road _____
Landmark/Compass bearings _____

Describe habitat found in; such as a bog, marsh, swamp; use habitat catagories found in this field guide. _____
_____

Interaction; describe what you observed going on between the plant and animal such as;
Breeding site _____
Food Source _____
Cover _____
Other _____
_____

Field Data Form: # Rose Pogonia

Observer's Address _____
Scientific Name of Plant _____
Common Name of Animal _____
Scientific Name of Animal _____
Date Collected /Observed _____

Where collected/observed; describe geographical location so you could find the place again by recording the following;

State _____ County _____ City/Town _____
Road _____
Landmark/Compass bearings _____

Describe habitat found in; such as a bog, marsh, swamp; use habitat catagories found in this field guide. _____
_____

Interaction; describe what you observed going on between the plant and animal such as;
Breeding site _____
Food Source _____
Cover _____
Other _____
_____

Observer's Name: _____

Field Data Form: Rugosa Rose

Observer's Address _____
Scientific Name of Plant _____
Common Name of Animal _____
Scientific Name of Animal _____
Date Collected/Observed _____

Where collected/observed; describe geographical location so you could find the place again by recording the following;

State _____ County _____ City/Town _____
Road _____
Landmark/Compass bearings _____

Describe habitat found in; such as a bog, marsh, swamp; use habitat catagories found in this field guide. _____
_____

Interaction; describe what you observed going on between the plant and animal such as;
Breeding site _____
Food Source _____
Cover _____
Other _____
_____

Field Data Form: Salt Marsh Bulrush

Observer's Address _____
Scientific Name of Plant _____
Common Name of Animal _____
Scientific Name of Animal _____
Date Collected/Observed _____

Where collected/observed; describe geographical location so you could find the place again by recording the following;

State _____ County _____ City/Town _____
Road _____
Landmark/Compass bearings _____

Describe habitat found in; such as a bog, marsh, swamp; use habitat catagories found in this field guide. _____
_____

Interaction; describe what you observed going on between the plant and animal such as;
Breeding site _____
Food Source _____
Cover _____
Other _____
_____

Observer's Name: _____

Field Data Form: # Saltmarsh Cordgrass

Observer's Address _____

Scientific Name of Plant _____

Common Name of Animal _____

Scientific Name of Animal _____

Date Collected/Observed _____

Where collected/observed; describe geographical location so you could find the place again by recording the following;

State _____ County _____ City/Town _____

Road _____

Landmark/Compass bearings _____

Describe habitat found in; such as a bog, marsh, swamp; use habitat catagories found in this field guide. _____

_____

Interaction; describe what you observed going on between the plant and animal such as;

Breeding site _____

Food Source _____

Cover _____

Other _____

_____

Field Data Form: # Saltmeadow Cordgrass

Observer's Address _____

Scientific Name of Plant _____

Common Name of Animal _____

Scientific Name of Animal _____

Date Collected/Observed _____

Where collected/observed; describe geographical location so you could find the place again by recording the following;

State _____ County _____ City/Town _____

Road _____

Landmark/Compass bearings _____

Describe habitat found in; such as a bog, marsh, swamp; use habitat catagories found in this field guide. _____

_____

Interaction; describe what you observed going on between the plant and animal such as;

Breeding site _____

Food Source _____

Cover _____

Other _____

_____

365

Field Data Form: **Sea Lavender**

Observer's Address _____

Scientific Name of Plant _____

Common Name of Animal _____

Scientific Name of Animal _____

Date Collected/Observed _____

Where collected/observed; describe geographical location so you could find the place again by recording the following;

State _____ County _____ City/Town _____

Road _____

Landmark/Compass bearings _____

Describe habitat found in; such as a bog, marsh, swamp; use habitat catagories found in this field guide. _____

_____

Interaction; describe what you observed going on between the plant and animal such as;

Breeding site _____

Food Source _____

Cover _____

Other _____

_____

Field Data Form: **Seaside Goldenrod**

Observer's Address _____

Scientific Name of Plant _____

Common Name of Animal _____

Scientific Name of Animal _____

Date Collected/Observed _____

Where collected/observed; describe geographical location so you could find the place again by recording the following;

State _____ County _____ City/Town _____

Road _____

Landmark/Compass bearings _____

Describe habitat found in; such as a bog, marsh, swamp; use habitat catagories found in this field guide. _____

_____

Interaction; describe what you observed going on between the plant and animal such as;

Breeding site _____

Food Source _____

Cover _____

Other _____

_____

Observer's Name: _____

Field Data Form: **Sensitive Fern**

Observer's Address _____

Scientific Name of Plant _____

Common Name of Animal _____

Scientific Name of Animal _____

Date Collected /Observed _____

Where collected/observed; describe geographical location so you could find the place again by recording the following;

State _____ County _____ City/Town _____

Road _____

Landmark/Compass bearings _____

Describe habitat found in; such as a bog, marsh, swamp; use habitat catagories found in this field guide. _____

_____

Interaction; describe what you observed going on between the plant and animal such as;

Breeding site _____

Food Source _____

Cover _____

Other _____

_____

Field Data Form: **Shadbush**

Observer's Address _____

Scientific Name of Plant _____

Common Name of Animal _____

Scientific Name of Animal _____

Date Collected /Observed _____

Where collected/observed; describe geographical location so you could find the place again by recording the following;

State _____ County _____ City/Town _____

Road _____

Landmark/Compass bearings _____

Describe habitat found in; such as a bog, marsh, swamp; use habitat catagories found in this field guide. _____

_____

Interaction; describe what you observed going on between the plant and animal such as;

Breeding site _____

Food Source _____

Cover _____

Other _____

_____

367

Observer's Name: _____

Field Data Form: Sheep Laurel

Observer's Address _____

Scientific Name of Plant _____

Common Name of Animal _____

Scientific Name of Animal _____

Date Collected /Observed _____

Where collected/observed; describe geographical location so you could find the place again by recording the following;

State _____ County _____ City/Town _____

Road _____

Landmark/Compass bearings _____

Describe habitat found in; such as a bog, marsh, swamp; use habitat catagories found in this field guide. _____

_____

Interaction; describe what you observed going on between the plant and animal such as;

Breeding site _____

Food Source _____

Cover _____

Other _____

_____

Field Data Form: Silky Dogwood

Observer's Address _____

Scientific Name of Plant _____

Common Name of Animal _____

Scientific Name of Animal _____

Date Collected /Observed _____

Where collected/observed; describe geographical location so you could find the place again by recording the following;

State _____ County _____ City/Town _____

Road _____

Landmark/Compass bearings _____

Describe habitat found in; such as a bog, marsh, swamp; use habitat catagories found in this field guide. _____

_____

Interaction; describe what you observed going on between the plant and animal such as;

Breeding site _____

Food Source _____

Cover _____

Other _____

_____

Observer's Name: _____

Field Data Form: Skunk Cabbage

Observer's Address _____
Scientific Name of Plant _____
Common Name of Animal _____
Scientific Name of Animal _____
Date Collected /Observed _____

Where collected/observed; describe geographical location so you could find the place again by recording the following;

State _____ County _____ City/Town _____
Road _____
Landmark/Compass bearings _____

Describe habitat found in; such as a bog, marsh, swamp; use habitat catagories found in this field guide. _____

Interaction; describe what you observed going on between the plant and animal such as;
Breeding site _____
Food Source _____
Cover _____
Other _____

Field Data Form: Soft Rush

Observer's Address _____
Scientific Name of Plant _____
Common Name of Animal _____
Scientific Name of Animal _____
Date Collected /Observed _____

Where collected/observed; describe geographical location so you could find the place again by recording the following;

State _____ County _____ City/Town _____
Road _____
Landmark/Compass bearings _____

Describe habitat found in; such as a bog, marsh, swamp; use habitat catagories found in this field guide. _____

Interaction; describe what you observed going on between the plant and animal such as;
Breeding site _____
Food Source _____
Cover _____
Other _____

369

Observer's Name: _____

Field Data Form: Speckled Alder

Observer's Address _____
Scientific Name of Plant _____
Common Name of Animal _____
Scientific Name of Animal _____
Date Collected/Observed _____

Where collected/observed; describe geographical location so you could find the place again by recording the following;

State _____ County _____ City/Town _____
Road _____
Landmark/Compass bearings _____

Describe habitat found in; such as a bog, marsh, swamp; use habitat catagories found in this field guide. _____
_____

Interaction; describe what you observed going on between the plant and animal such as;
Breeding site _____
Food Source _____
Cover _____
Other _____
_____

Field Data Form: Sphagnum Moss

Observer's Address _____
Scientific Name of Plant _____
Common Name of Animal _____
Scientific Name of Animal _____
Date Collected/Observed _____

Where collected/observed; describe geographical location so you could find the place again by recording the following;

State _____ County _____ City/Town _____
Road _____
Landmark/Compass bearings _____

Describe habitat found in; such as a bog, marsh, swamp; use habitat catagories found in this field guide. _____
_____

Interaction; describe what you observed going on between the plant and animal such as;
Breeding site _____
Food Source _____
Cover _____
Other _____
_____

370

Observer's Name: _____

Field Data Form: # Spicebush

Observer's Address _____

Scientific Name of Plant _____

Common Name of Animal _____

Scientific Name of Animal _____

Date Collected/Observed _____

Where collected/observed; describe geographical location so you could find the place again by recording the following;

State _____ County _____ City/Town _____

Road _____

Landmark/Compass bearings _____

Describe habitat found in; such as a bog, marsh, swamp; use habitat catagories found in this field guide. _____

_____

Interaction; describe what you observed going on between the plant and animal such as;

Breeding site _____

Food Source _____

Cover _____

Other _____

_____

Field Data Form: # Spotted Cowbane

Observer's Address _____

Scientific Name of Plant _____

Common Name of Animal _____

Scientific Name of Animal _____

Date Collected/Observed _____

Where collected/observed; describe geographical location so you could find the place again by recording the following;

State _____ County _____ City/Town _____

Road _____

Landmark/Compass bearings _____

Describe habitat found in; such as a bog, marsh, swamp; use habitat catagories found in this field guide. _____

_____

Interaction; describe what you observed going on between the plant and animal such as;

Breeding site _____

Food Source _____

Cover _____

Other _____

_____

Observer's Name: _____

Field Data Form: **Stick-tight**

Observer's Address _____

Scientific Name of Plant _____

Common Name of Animal _____

Scientific Name of Animal _____

Date Collected /Observed _____

Where collected/observed; describe geographical location so you could find the place again by recording the following;

State _____ County _____ City/Town _____

Road _____

Landmark/Compass bearings _____

Describe habitat found in; such as a bog, marsh, swamp; use habitat catagories found in this field guide. _____

_____

Interaction; describe what you observed going on between the plant and animal such as;

Breeding site _____

Food Source _____

Cover _____

Other _____

_____

Field Data Form: **Sundew**

Observer's Address _____

Scientific Name of Plant _____

Common Name of Animal _____

Scientific Name of Animal _____

Date Collected /Observed _____

Where collected/observed; describe geographical location so you could find the place again by recording the following;

State _____ County _____ City/Town _____

Road _____

Landmark/Compass bearings _____

Describe habitat found in; such as a bog, marsh, swamp; use habitat catagories found in this field guide. _____

_____

Interaction; describe what you observed going on between the plant and animal such as;

Breeding site _____

Food Source _____

Cover _____

Other _____

_____

Observer's Name: _____

Field Data Form: **Swamp Azalea**

Observer's Address _____

Scientific Name of Plant _____

Common Name of Animal _____

Scientific Name of Animal _____

Date Collected/Observed _____

Where collected/observed; describe geographical location so you could find the place again by recording the following;

State _____ County _____ City/Town _____

Road _____

Landmark/Compass bearings _____

Describe habitat found in; such as a bog, marsh, swamp; use habitat catagories found in this field guide. _____

_____

Interaction; describe what you observed going on between the plant and animal such as;

Breeding site _____

Food Source _____

Cover _____

Other _____

_____

Field Data Form: **Swamp Blackberry**

Observer's Address _____

Scientific Name of Plant _____

Common Name of Animal _____

Scientific Name of Animal _____

Date Collected/Observed _____

Where collected/observed; describe geographical location so you could find the place again by recording the following;

State _____ County _____ City/Town _____

Road _____

Landmark/Compass bearings _____

Describe habitat found in; such as a bog, marsh, swamp; use habitat catagories found in this field guide. _____

_____

Interaction; describe what you observed going on between the plant and animal such as;

Breeding site _____

Food Source _____

Cover _____

Other _____

_____

373

Observer's Name: _____

Field Data Form: Swamp Candles

Observer's Address _____
Scientific Name of Plant _____
Common Name of Animal _____
Scientific Name of Animal _____
Date Collected/Observed _____

Where collected/observed; describe geographical location so you could find the place again by recording the following;

State _____ County _____ City/Town _____
Road _____
Landmark/Compass bearings _____

Describe habitat found in; such as a bog, marsh, swamp; use habitat catagories found in this field guide. _____
_____

Interaction; describe what you observed going on between the plant and animal such as;
Breeding site _____
Food Source _____
Cover _____
Other _____
_____

Field Data Form: Swamp Loosestrife

Observer's Address _____
Scientific Name of Plant _____
Common Name of Animal _____
Scientific Name of Animal _____
Date Collected/Observed _____

Where collected/observed; describe geographical location so you could find the place again by recording the following;

State _____ County _____ City/Town _____
Road _____
Landmark/Compass bearings _____

Describe habitat found in; such as a bog, marsh, swamp; use habitat catagories found in this field guide. _____
_____

Interaction; describe what you observed going on between the plant and animal such as;
Breeding site _____
Food Source _____
Cover _____
Other _____
_____

374

Observer's Name: _____

Field Data Form: Swamp Milkweed

Observer's Address _____

Scientific Name of Plant _____

Common Name of Animal _____

Scientific Name of Animal _____

Date Collected /Observed _____

Where collected/observed; describe geographical location so you could find the place again by recording the following;

State _____ County _____ City/Town _____

Road _____

Landmark/Compass bearings _____

Describe habitat found in; such as a bog, marsh, swamp; use habitat catagories found in this field guide. _____

_____

Interaction; describe what you observed going on between the plant and animal such as;

Breeding site _____

Food Source _____

Cover _____

Other _____

_____

Field Data Form: Swamp Pink

Observer's Address _____

Scientific Name of Plant _____

Common Name of Animal _____

Scientific Name of Animal _____

Date Collected /Observed _____

Where collected/observed; describe geographical location so you could find the place again by recording the following;

State _____ County _____ City/Town _____

Road _____

Landmark/Compass bearings _____

Describe habitat found in; such as a bog, marsh, swamp; use habitat catagories found in this field guide. _____

_____

Interaction; describe what you observed going on between the plant and animal such as;

Breeding site _____

Food Source _____

Cover _____

Other _____

_____

Observer's Name: _____

Field Data Form: Swamp Rose

Observer's Address _____

Scientific Name of Plant _____

Common Name of Animal _____

Scientific Name of Animal _____

Date Collected /Observed _____

Where collected/observed; describe geographical location so you could find the place again by recording the following;

State _____ County _____ City/Town _____
Road _____
Landmark/Compass bearings _____

Describe habitat found in; such as a bog, marsh, swamp; use habitat catagories found in this field guide. _____
_____

Interaction; describe what you observed going on between the plant and animal such as;
Breeding site _____
Food Source _____
Cover _____
Other _____
_____

Field Data Form: Swamp White Oak

Observer's Address _____

Scientific Name of Plant _____

Common Name of Animal _____

Scientific Name of Animal _____

Date Collected /Observed _____

Where collected/observed; describe geographical location so you could find the place again by recording the following;

State _____ County _____ City/Town _____
Road _____
Landmark/Compass bearings _____

Describe habitat found in; such as a bog, marsh, swamp; use habitat catagories found in this field guide. _____
_____

Interaction; describe what you observed going on between the plant and animal such as;
Breeding site _____
Food Source _____
Cover _____
Other _____
_____

Observer's Name: _____

Field Data Form: Sweet Flag

Observer's Address _____
Scientific Name of Plant _____
Common Name of Animal _____
Scientific Name of Animal _____
Date Collected/Observed _____

Where collected/observed; describe geographical location so you could find the place again by recording the following;

State _____ County _____ City/Town _____
Road _____
Landmark/Compass bearings _____

Describe habitat found in; such as a bog, marsh, swamp; use habitat catagories found in this field guide. _____

_____

Interaction; describe what you observed going on between the plant and animal such as;

Breeding site _____
Food Source _____
Cover _____
Other _____

_____

Field Data Form: Sweet Gale

Observer's Address _____
Scientific Name of Plant _____
Common Name of Animal _____
Scientific Name of Animal _____
Date Collected/Observed _____

Where collected/observed; describe geographical location so you could find the place again by recording the following;

State _____ County _____ City/Town _____
Road _____
Landmark/Compass bearings _____

Describe habitat found in; such as a bog, marsh, swamp; use habitat catagories found in this field guide. _____

_____

Interaction; describe what you observed going on between the plant and animal such as;

Breeding site _____
Food Source _____
Cover _____
Other _____

_____

Observer's Name: _____

Field Data Form: Sweet Pepperbush

Observer's Address _____
Scientific Name of Plant _____
Common Name of Animal _____
Scientific Name of Animal _____
Date Collected /Observed _____

Where collected/observed; describe geographical location so you could find the place again by recording the following;

State _____ County _____ City/Town _____
Road _____
Landmark/Compass bearings _____

Describe habitat found in; such as a bog, marsh, swamp; use habitat catagories found in this field guide. _____
_____

Interaction; describe what you observed going on between the plant and animal such as;
Breeding site _____
Food Source _____
Cover _____
Other _____
_____

Field Data Form: Tupelo

Observer's Address _____
Scientific Name of Plant _____
Common Name of Animal _____
Scientific Name of Animal _____
Date Collected /Observed _____

Where collected/observed; describe geographical location so you could find the place again by recording the following;

State _____ County _____ City/Town _____
Road _____
Landmark/Compass bearings _____

Describe habitat found in; such as a bog, marsh, swamp; use habitat catagories found in this field guide. _____
_____

Interaction; describe what you observed going on between the plant and animal such as;
Breeding site _____
Food Source _____
Cover _____
Other _____
_____

Observer's Name: _____

Field Data Form: **Turtlehead**

Observer's Address	_____
Scientific Name of Plant	_____
Common Name of Animal	_____
Scientific Name of Animal	_____
Date Collected /Observed	_____

Where collected/observed; describe geographical location so you could find the place again by recording the following;

State _____ County _____ City/Town _____
Road _____
Landmark/Compass bearings _____

Describe habitat found in; such as a bog, marsh, swamp; use habitat catagories found in this field guide. _____

_____

Interaction; describe what you observed going on between the plant and animal such as;

Breeding site _____
Food Source _____
Cover _____
Other _____

_____

Field Data Form: **Tussock Sedge**

Observer's Address	_____
Scientific Name of Plant	_____
Common Name of Animal	_____
Scientific Name of Animal	_____
Date Collected /Observed	_____

Where collected/observed; describe geographical location so you could find the place again by recording the following;

State _____ County _____ City/Town _____
Road _____
Landmark/Compass bearings _____

Describe habitat found in; such as a bog, marsh, swamp; use habitat catagories found in this field guide. _____

_____

Interaction; describe what you observed going on between the plant and animal such as;

Breeding site _____
Food Source _____
Cover _____
Other _____

_____

Observer's Name: _____

Field Data Form: Umbrella Sedge

Observer's Address _____

Scientific Name of Plant _____

Common Name of Animal _____

Scientific Name of Animal _____

Date Collected /Observed _____

Where collected/observed; describe geographical location so you could find the place again by recording the following;

State _____ County _____ City/Town _____

Road _____

Landmark/Compass bearings _____

Describe habitat found in; such as a bog, marsh, swamp; use habitat catagories found in this field guide. _____

_____

Interaction; describe what you observed going on between the plant and animal such as;

Breeding site _____

Food Source _____

Cover _____

Other _____

_____

Field Data Form: Water Smartweed

Observer's Address _____

Scientific Name of Plant _____

Common Name of Animal _____

Scientific Name of Animal _____

Date Collected /Observed _____

Where collected/observed; describe geographical location so you could find the place again by recording the following;

State _____ County _____ City/Town _____

Road _____

Landmark/Compass bearings _____

Describe habitat found in; such as a bog, marsh, swamp; use habitat catagories found in this field guide. _____

_____

Interaction; describe what you observed going on between the plant and animal such as;

Breeding site _____

Food Source _____

Cover _____

Other _____

_____

Observer's Name: _____

Field Data Form: Watercress

Observer's Address _____

Scientific Name of Plant _____

Common Name of Animal _____

Scientific Name of Animal _____

Date Collected/Observed _____

Where collected/observed; describe geographical location so you could find the place again by recording the following;

State _____ County _____ City/Town _____

Road _____

Landmark/Compass bearings _____

Describe habitat found in; such as a bog, marsh, swamp; use habitat catagories found in this field guide. _____

_____

Interaction; describe what you observed going on between the plant and animal such as;

Breeding site _____

Food Source _____

Cover _____

Other _____

_____

Field Data Form: Wild Rice

Observer's Address _____

Scientific Name of Plant _____

Common Name of Animal _____

Scientific Name of Animal _____

Date Collected/Observed _____

Where collected/observed; describe geographical location so you could find the place again by recording the following;

State _____ County _____ City/Town _____

Road _____

Landmark/Compass bearings _____

Describe habitat found in; such as a bog, marsh, swamp; use habitat catagories found in this field guide. _____

_____

Interaction; describe what you observed going on between the plant and animal such as;

Breeding site _____

Food Source _____

Cover _____

Other _____

_____

Observer's Name: _____

Field Data Form: **Winterberry**

Observer's Address _____

Scientific Name of Plant _____

Common Name of Animal _____

Scientific Name of Animal _____

Date Collected /Observed _____

Where collected/observed; describe geographical location so you could find the place again by recording the following;

State _____ County _____ City/Town _____

Road _____

Landmark/Compass bearings _____

Describe habitat found in; such as a bog, marsh, swamp; use habitat catagories found in this field guide. _____

_____

Interaction; describe what you observed going on between the plant and animal such as;

Breeding site _____

Food Source _____

Cover _____

Other _____

_____

Field Data Form: **Wool-grass**

Observer's Address _____

Scientific Name of Plant _____

Common Name of Animal _____

Scientific Name of Animal _____

Date Collected /Observed _____

Where collected/observed; describe geographical location so you could find the place again by recording the following;

State _____ County _____ City/Town _____

Road _____

Landmark/Compass bearings _____

Describe habitat found in; such as a bog, marsh, swamp; use habitat catagories found in this field guide. _____

_____

Interaction; describe what you observed going on between the plant and animal such as;

Breeding site _____

Food Source _____

Cover _____

Other _____

_____

Observer's Name: _____

Field Data Form: **Yellow Birch**

Observer's Address _____

Scientific Name of Plant _____

Common Name of Animal _____

Scientific Name of Animal _____

Date Collected /Observed _____

Where collected/observed; describe geographical location so you could find the place again by recording the following;

State _____ County _____ City/Town _____

Road _____

Landmark/Compass bearings _____

Describe habitat found in; such as a bog, marsh, swamp; use habitat catagories found in this field guide. _____

_____

Interaction; describe what you observed going on between the plant and animal such as;

Breeding site _____

Food Source _____

Cover _____

Other _____

_____

Field Data Form: **Yellow Pond Lily**

Observer's Address _____

Scientific Name of Plant _____

Common Name of Animal _____

Scientific Name of Animal _____

Date Collected /Observed _____

Where collected/observed; describe geographical location so you could find the place again by recording the following;

State _____ County _____ City/Town _____

Road _____

Landmark/Compass bearings _____

Describe habitat found in; such as a bog, marsh, swamp; use habitat catagories found in this field guide. _____

_____

Interaction; describe what you observed going on between the plant and animal such as;

Breeding site _____

Food Source _____

Cover _____

Other _____

_____

Index

* ( ) Refers to page for plant location in part II.

386